NOW YOU KNOW

NOW YOU KNOW

BIG
BOOK OF
ANSWERS

Doug Lennox

THE DUNDURN GROUP
TORONTO

Editor: Andrea Waters
Design: Alison Carr
Printer: Trancontinental

Library and Archives Canada Cataloguing in Publication

Lennox, Doug
    Now you know big book of answers / Doug Lennox.

ISBN 978-1-55002-741-9

    1. Questions and answers. 2. Curiosities and wonders.
I. Title.

AG195.L45 2007   031.02   C2007-903004-1

1   2   3   4   5   11   10   09   08   07

 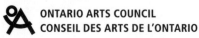

ONTARIO ARTS COUNCIL
CONSEIL DES ARTS DE L'ONTARIO

We acknowledge the support of **The Canada Council for the Arts** and the **Ontario Arts Council** for our publishing program. We also acknowledge the Wnancial support of the Government of Canada through the Book Publishing Industry Development Program and **The Association for the Export of Canadian Books**, and the Government of Ontario through the **Ontario Book Publishers Tax Credit** program, and the **Ontario Media Development Corporation**.

Care has been taken to trace the ownership of copyright material used in this book. The author and the publisher welcome any information enabling them to rectify any references or credits in subsequent editions.

J. Kirk Howard, President

Printed and bound in Canada.
Printed on recycled paper.

www.dundurn.com

Illustrations on pages 15, 20, 29, 40, 46, 62, 73, 88, 102, 114, 140, 161, 162, 177, 187, 201, 203, 238, 251, 310, 318, 327, 349, 385, 389 by Catriona Wight.
Illustrations on pages 119, 278, 295, 308, 324 by Julia Bell.

Dundurn Press	Gazelle Book Services Limited	Dundurn Press
3 Church Street, Suite 500	White Cross Mills	2250 Military Road
Toronto, Ontario, Canada	High Town, Lancaster, England	Tonawanda, NY
M5E 1M2	LA1 4XS	U.S.A. 14150

This book is dedicated to my sister Marie
and the memory of Tony Derro.

Nothing worth possessing can ever be quite possessed.
D.L.

contents

acknowledgements

Some mentors can be younger than you.
My example is: Jean-Marie Heimrath.

preface

My interest in why we say and do things comes from my fascination and research into human history as entertainment for earlier projects. My interest in statistics runs parallel with this, because the observation of both these subjects, as diverse as they are, always seems to initiate the same kind of surprise — which must indicate that we are functioning without a clear understanding of what we are saying or doing. It was Mark Twain who said, "There are lies, damn lies, and then there are statistics." The lies, however, are not within the statistics but rather within their application by those seeking to advance their own causes, and so it is with language.

We often hear expressions and words used in dramatic ways that, when examined closely, lose their logic. For example, some people say "street smarts" are an advantage in business, which is absurd. "Street smarts" (1972) means a basic cunning that is only useful on the street; to believe otherwise is delusional. "Business smarts" may have the same survivalist intent as "street smarts," but they require far more sophistication.

All languages reveal the history of those who speak them, and none more so than English. As the "global language," English is spoken as a first or second language by a third of the world's population, approximately 1.9 billion people. Only Chinese and Hindi, through the sheer numbers of their populations, have more speakers. (If all the people in China began walking past a single point, the line would never end.)

During and after the Second World War, because they share the same language, the American and British governments took active measures to ensure that through conquest and occupation, their language would become the predominant means of communication on the planet. Their opponents were the Germans and the French. Spanish had diminished as a contender after Spain lost its empire. Today English is the official language of the United Nations and the European Union and by treaty is the international language for air traffic control and maritime communications. It is the principal language of the Internet, business, sports, and science. Knowing the proper use of the language is empowerment.

The English language is a fascinating conglomeration of words and expressions, from those begun by the invaders (Romans, Angles, Jutes, Saxons, Celts, and Vikings) who conquered and assimilated the native population of early Britain to the backwoods creations of North Americans (both enslaved and free) whose isolation and close proximity to the Native peoples gave the language a unique new richness. Other living everyday expressions and phrases were brought back from adventures, military and otherwise, from distant lands and the high seas to be assimilated into the English-speaking world's common language.

For three hundred years after the 1066 conquest by William the Conqueror, French was the official language in Britain, with common English existing as a lower language of the people, and to this day French makes up 28.3 percent of the language we all speak and call English.

Although all entries in this book have been thoroughly researched, it is not an academic study. It is an entertaining and concise collection of the origins of our everyday language, customs, and rituals as well as some intriguing statistics and odds and ends to encourage a fun read. A way of passing time while picking up knowledge through what some might call trivia. It explores the DNA of our society and reveals how the things we say and do every day tie us to one rich heritage … Enjoy!

Doug Lennox
www.douglennox.com

common
superstitions

Why is a horseshoe thought to bring good luck?

A horseshoe's charm comes from the legend of Saint Dunstan, who, because of his talent as a blacksmith, was asked by the Devil to shoe his cloven hoof. Saint Dunstan agreed, but in carrying out the task he caused the Devil such pain that he was able to make him promise never to enter a house that has a horseshoe hanging above the doorway. Thus, from the Middle Ages on, the horseshoe has been considered good luck.

Why does breaking a wishbone ensure good luck?

Twenty-four hundred years ago, because roosters heralded the sunrise and hens squawked before laying an egg, the Etruscans thought they were soothsayers. Because the sacred fowl's collarbone resembled a human groin, it was believed to have special powers and was called a wishbone. The Romans introduced the custom of two people pulling on the wishbone to see whom luck favoured. The winner was said to have gotten "a lucky break."

Why is the ladybug a sign of good luck?

Called either "ladybird" or "ladybug," the little red beetle with the black spots is the well-known and beloved subject of a nursery rhyme. It is called a "lady" after the Virgin Mary because it emerges around March 25, the time of the Feast of the Annunciation, which is also known as Lady Day. Called the Mary bug in German, the ladybug brings good luck to a garden by eating unwanted pests.

Why is it bad luck to walk under a ladder?

This superstition comes from the fact that many early cultures considered a triangle to be a sacred symbol of life. For Christians, a triangle represents the Holy Trinity. A ladder against a wall forms a triangle with the ground, and so to walk beneath it would be to disrupt a sanctified space and risk divine wrath. Early Christians considered the ladder resting against a wall to represent crucifixion, and therefore evil. For this reason condemned criminals were forced to walk under the gallows ladder — the entranceway to eternal darkness. The executioner always walked around it to position the noose.

Why is Friday the thirteenth considered to be bad luck?

The number thirteen represents Judas, the thirteenth to arrive at the Last Supper. Friday by itself is unlucky because it was the day of Christ's crucifixion. Years ago, the British set out to disprove these superstitions. They named a new vessel HMS *Friday*, laid her keel on a Friday, and then sent her to sea on a Friday that fell on the thirteenth. The plan backfired: neither ship nor crew was ever heard from again. Then, of course, there's *Apollo 13*...

Did the near tragedy of Apollo 13 cause the NASA scientists to become superstitious?

Apollo 13 was launched on the eleventh of the fourth month in the seventieth year of that century. One plus one plus four plus seven plus zero totals thirteen. Liftoff was at 1313 central military time, and the explosion took place on the thirteenth day of April. NASA claims no superstition — but has never again used the number thirteen on a manned space flight.

Do people really fear Friday the thirteenth?

On Friday, October 13, 1307, the Grand Master and sixty of the Knights Templar were arrested, tortured, and then murdered by King Philip IV of France. Each year, thousands who fear the date fall ill or are injured in accidents. In North America, over $900 million is lost in business on Friday the thirteenth because some workers and consumers are afraid to leave the house. Over any given four-hundred-year cycle the thirteenth day of the month occurs 4,800 times. The distribution of thirteenth day of the month is as follows:

- Monday, 685 or 14.27 percent
- Tuesday, 685 or 14.27 percent
- Wednesday, 687 or 14.31 percent
- Thursday, 684 or 14.25 percent
- Friday, 688 or 14.34 percent
- Saturday, 684 or 14.25 percent
- Sunday, 687 or 14.31 percent

This means the thirteenth day of the month is only slightly more likely to occur on a Friday!

Where else, other than on a Friday, is the number thirteen considered unlucky?

Friday the thirteenth is considered unlucky, but the superstition also applies to apartments, 80 percent of which don't have a thirteenth floor. Airplanes have no thirteenth aisle, and hospitals and hotels have no room number thirteen. The most bizarre superstition is called the Devil's luck, for those with thirteen letters in their names, including Jack the Ripper, Charles Manson, Jeffrey Dahmer, Theodore Bundy, Albert De Salvo — and Douglas Lennox.

How did spilling salt become bad luck?

As man's first food seasoning, and later a food preservative and a medicine, salt has been a precious commodity for ten thousand years, so spilling it was costly as well as bad luck. This superstition was enhanced by Leonardo da Vinci's painting of the Last Supper, within which Judas has spilled the table salt as a foreboding of tragedy. Because good spirits sat on the right shoulder and evil on the left, tossing spilled salt over the left shoulder became an antidote.

Why do we cross our fingers for good luck?

Crossing our fingers for luck predates Christianity and originally involved two people. In the pagan ritual, a close friend placed his or her index finger over the index finger of the person making the wish in order to help trap the wish at the centre of a perfect cross, which is where benevolent spirits lived. To ensure the wish stayed in place and on the wisher's mind, it was often tied to the finger with string, a practice that eventually evolved into a memory aid.

What is the curse on the Hope diamond?

The Hope diamond is a steel blue, forty-four-and-a-half-carat, walnut-sized diamond that is supposedly cursed, since it was stolen from the statue of a Hindu god in 1642. Since then, its owners, including Marie Antoinette, have all had brushes with madness and violent death. It's named after a British banking family who were financially ruined. It's now at the Smithsonian Institute and is owned by the government of the United States of America.

Why is lighting three on a match considered bad luck?

Lighting three cigarettes in a row with one match was common practice among smokers until the advent of lighters and was especially practical to outdoorsmen or soldiers who needed to ration their matches. "Three on a match" became bad luck during the Boer War (1899–1902) when Commonwealth soldiers discovered the hard way that an enemy sniper would train his sights on a match when it was struck and then focus and fire by the time the third man lit his cigarette.

Why do we say "Bless you" after a sneeze?

The ancient Greeks believed a blessing might prevent evil from entering your body during its unguarded state while you sneeze. Our tradition comes from the black plague of 1665, when sneezing was believed to be one of the first symptoms of the disease. Infection meant certain death, and so the symptom was greeted with the prayer "God bless you," which through time has been shortened to "Bless you!"

Why does knocking on wood protect us from harm?

When children play tag and hold a tree for safety, they are acting out a four-thousand-year-old custom of the North American Natives who believed that because the oak was most frequently struck by lightning, it was the home of the sky god. The Greeks came to this same conclusion two thousand years later and because both cultures believed that bragging or boasting offended that god, they knocked on the tree either to divert him from their bragging or to seek forgiveness.

What is the origin of the Tooth Fairy?

The ritual of placing a baby tooth under the pillow to be replaced overnight with money from the Tooth Fairy is a compilation of several European customs. In Venice an old witch did the job, while in France the Virgin Mary traded money and sometimes candy for children's teeth. Other cultures buried the tooth, or threw it at the sun for favours from the gods. The Fairy was of course an Irish innovation and took hold in North America during the middle of the nineteenth century.

Why do some people believe black cats are bad luck?

If you believe that a black cat crossing your path is bad luck, you believe in witchcraft. Legend has it that in the 1560s in England, a father and son threw stones at a cat that had startled them on a moonless night. The wounded cat ran into the nearby home of a suspected witch. The next day the old woman was seen in public limping and bruised, and a superstition was born which caused the burning alive of innocent women in the seventeenth century.

Why is a rabbit's foot a symbol of good luck?

If you realize that primitive societies couldn't tell the difference between a rabbit and a hare, then you'll understand the ancient logic as to why the rabbit's foot is a symbol of good luck. Hares are born with their eyes open, giving them knowledge of prenatal life. Rabbits burrow underground and share secrets with the underworld. Finally, both animals' incredible fertility could be shared by carrying the rabbit's foot as a phallus of good luck.

Why does breaking a mirror bring seven years of bad luck?

Before glass was introduced in 1300, manufactured mirrors were simply polished metal. Around 6 B.C., in much the same manner one would now use as a crystal ball, the Greeks began practising fortune-telling from a subject's reflected image in a bowl of water. If the bowl with the image fell and broke during a reading, it meant disaster. The Romans limited the curse to seven years because they believed that's how long it took for human life to renew itself.

Why do we say during a bad day that you "got up on the wrong side of the bed"?

For centuries, to be left-handed was considered evil. In drawings, the Ancient Egyptians depict all the good armies as being right-handed, while their enemies are lefties. Until only recently left-handed children were forced to learn to use their right hands in school. The word *ambidextrous* means two right hands. "Getting up on the wrong side of the bed" means your left foot touched the floor first, signalling to the Devil that you were open to dark influences.

Why is it bad luck to open an umbrella indoors?

The umbrella is an ancient African innovation and was intended as a portable shade against the sun. After entering Europe through Spain in the twelfth century it became more valuable as a protection from the rain. The superstition of bad luck if opened indoors came from the African belief that to open an umbrella in the shade was an insult to the sun god and would cause him to bring down his wrath on the offender.

Why do people throw coins into a fountain?

There are thousands of fountains around the world inviting passersby to toss in coins for good luck, but they have all been inspired by the romance of the legend behind Rome's famous Trevi Fountain (Fontana di Trevi). Built over a thirty-year period in the mid-eighteenth century, the Trevi became the focus of a legend that said throwing a coin over one's shoulder and into the fountain meant one would visit Rome again. Pitching two coins ensured that the thrower would fall in love with someone from Rome, while tossing three coins signified the thrower would marry that someone.

Rome has 289 fountains. The Trevi Fountain was built from money raised by taxes on wine. It is located in Piazza di Trevi, which was erected to commemorate the completion of the Aqua Vergine in 19 B.C.

rock and roll trivia

What was the original meaning of "rock and roll"?

American slaves communicated secret codes past their white masters with music, and in 1951, when Alan Freed coined the phrase "rock and roll," he was doing the same thing. In blues and jazz, the words mean "having great sex" ("Good Rockin' Tonight," 1948, and "My Man Rocks Me With One Steady Roll," 1922). These coded lyrics were unfamiliar to the white broadcasters and gave Freed a way to cross the colour barrier and introduce white kids to rhythm and blues, where they soon learned how to "Rock Around the Clock."

Who first said, "Elvis has left the building"?

Today, "Elvis has left the building" is a catchphrase meaning "that's all she wrote" or "that's all there is." It was first spoken on December 15, 1956, by Horace Logan, the producer of a show called *Louisiana Hayride*. Elvis Presley had drawn a crowd of ten thousand kids to the Fairgrounds in Shreveport, Louisana. He was on the brink of superstardom, and after his forty-five-minute show, when the audience stormed the stage and exits,

Quickies

Did you know ...

- that Nickelback got its name from the bass player's experience as a Starbucks employee? He spent endless frustrating days telling customers, "Here's your nickel back."
- that Red Hot Chili Peppers started out as Tony Flow and the Miraculous Majestic Masters of Mayhem? The name was changed after Anthony Kiedis saw a psychedelic bush with the band's new name on it. He may have subconsciously known that legendary piano player Jelly Roll Morton's 1920s band was called The Red Hot Peppers.
- that Pink Floyd was known as Megadeth before the band adopted the names of Georgia blues artists Pink Anderson and Floyd Council?
- that ABBA is an acronym from the first letters of the group's Christian names: Agnethe, Bjorn, Benny and Anni-Frid?
- that B.B. King was born Riley B. King? When he became popular on the Sonny Boy Williamson radio show during the early 1950s he came up with the stage name Beal Street Blues Boy before shortening it to Blues Boy King, which led to another and final abbreviation, B.B. King. He named his guitar Lucille early in his career. After a kerosene lamp was knocked over during a fight between two men over a woman in a club where he was playing, a fire broke out, during which rescuing his guitar nearly cost him his life. Lucille was the name of the woman the men were fighting over.
- that Foo Fighters were named from an expression used by U.S. fighter pilots to describe UFOs in the shape of fireballs over Germany during the Second World War? "Foo" is an Americanization of the French word for fire, *feu*.
- that Black Sabbath was known as Earth until they were inspired by a 1963 horror movie starring Boris Karloff? The film was titled *Black Sabbath*. The movie gave the band not only a new name but also the title of its first original song.

Logan took the microphone and pleaded: "Please, young people … Elvis has left the building. He has gotten in his car and driven away…. Please take your seats." From that point on, "Ladies and gentlemen, Elvis has left the building" became the closing announcement for each of the King's concerts. The last time was at Elvis's final performance on June 26, 1977, after he had closed with "Can't Help Falling in Love," the last song he would ever sing in public.

military innovations
and traditions

What are the origins of the merry-go-round?

When medieval noblemen were looking for a sport to replace their brutal jousting tournaments, they turned to a training exercise of catching rings with their lances from horseback, known in Spanish as *carossela*, meaning "little war." *Carossela* gave us *carousel*. In time, live horses were replaced with hanging revolving seats, which in turn gave way to painted wooden horses, and from this evolved the merry-go-round.

Why is the bugle call at day's end and at military funerals called "Taps"?

In the seventeenth century, the British borrowed a Dutch army custom of sounding a drum and bugle to signal soldiers that it was time to stop socializing and return to their barracks for the night. The Dutch called it *taptoe*, meaning, "shut off the taps," and the abbreviated "taps" became a signal for tavern owners to turn off the spigots on their beer and wine casks. After lights out, Taps signals that the soldiers are safely home, which is why it's played at funerals.

Why is there a saddled, riderless horse in a military funeral procession?

The riderless horse in a military funeral was an ancient custom practised by the Romans. A soldier and his horse trained to fight as one unit in battle, making it almost impossible for the animal to have another master. If a soldier retired, so did his horse. For the same reason, if the soldier died in combat, the horse followed his coffin to the cemetery to be put down and buried with his companion. The two would ride together into the afterlife. The empty boots in the stirrups is a later tradition and signifies that no one else can ride that horse. Today it's simply a ceremony, and the animal isn't harmed.

Why do they fire a rifle volley of three shots over the grave of a fallen soldier?

Military funerals are filled with traditions, but none as ancient as firing a volley over the deceased. During the Napoleonic Wars, hostilities were ceased to clear the dead from the battlefield. When finished, the detail would fire three shots into the air as a signal that they were ready to resume the fight.

The tradition mirrors the ancient tribal practice of throwing spears into the air to ward off evil spirits hovering over the fallen.

The *caisson* was the wagon used to carry the dead soldiers from the battlefield.

Why are funeral flags flown at half-staff?

In the sixteenth century, ships would lower their flag halfway as a sign of submission during battle, and it was said they were flying at "half-mast." On reaching port, the flag remained half-lowered in honour of those who had sacrificed their lives. In the seventeenth century the ritual moved to land, where it was said the flags were at "half-staff" as a sign of respect for any individual who had died after serving his country beyond the call of duty.

Why do we say it's a "siege" when an army surrounds a fort or town?

The word *siege* conjures up visions of intense combat, with one force attacking a surrounded enemy with total and absolute ferocity. So it's interesting to note that *siege* means "sit." This origin is illustrated in the Arthurian legends, where the "siege perilous" was a vacant seat at the Round Table. The seat was supposed to be fatal to any except the knight destined to find the Holy Grail. Since the thirteenth century, the military sense of *siege* has meant an army sitting down around a fortress to wait for those inside to surrender.

Siege came to English through Old French as *sege*, meaning "seat" or "throne," and originated with *sedere*, the Latin word for "sit." *Siege* is also related to *sedentary*.

Why is a lightning-quick military attack called a "raid"?

A sudden raid is usually over quickly, with the attackers strategically withdrawing as soon as their mission is completed. It's always a surprise attack. Consider that the words *road* and *rode* both come from *ride*, as in horseback riding, and then consider that lightning-quick surprise attacks resulted from horsemen charging down a road. *Rade*, "a riding, journey," is the Old English and Scottish word for *raid*. When a hostile incursion came galloping down the road, the cry of "Rade!" went up, which easily became "Raid!" when retold in literature.

Why do we say someone has "dodged a bullet" after a close call?

You can't get much closer to danger than dodging a bullet. At close range nobody dodges a bullet, or so it would seem. The expression derives from soldiers in the First World War who talked about artillery shells that could be avoided because they arced through the air slowly enough to be seen. The odds of getting out of the way of rifle fire improved as the distance increased, because if you saw the muzzle flash, you had a second or two to move before the bullet got to you. Light travels faster than a bullet!

Why do we tell someone who with a bad attitude to "shape up or ship out"?

During the Second World War, if an American soldier's behaviour or deportment wasn't as disciplined as it should be, he was told by his sergeant to "shape up or ship out," meaning improve or be shipped overseas to a combat zone — "either get it together or start packin."

How close do you have to be before seeing the "whites of their eyes"?

"Don't shoot till you see the whites of their eyes" has echoed through history as an order for soldiers to hold their fire and their nerve until the last minute. At the Battle of Bunker Hill in June 1775 during the American Revolution, a U.S. colonel named William Prescott said it to his men. Before then, Prince Charles of Prussia issued the order at the Battle of Jägerndorf in 1757, and Frederick the Great (1712–1786) said it at the Battle of Prague the same year. At the Plains of Abraham in Quebec in 1759, General James Wolfe (1727–1759) told his men not to fire until they saw the whites of their eyes, which meant hold until the enemy was fifteen or twenty paces away, a distance of thirty to forty feet.

What do the words *hunky-dory* and *honcho* have in common?

If everything is great then it's hunky-dory, while a honcho is a big shot, and both words come from Japan. During the First World War, American sailors on leave discovered a Yokohama street named Huncho-dori that provided all the facilities for carnal pleasure. They brought home the name and the good feeling as *hunky-dory*. *Honcho* came out of the Second World War and is Japanese for "squad leader."

Why are the stalwart defenders of a status quo referred to as "the Old Guard"?

"The Old Guard" suggests an outdated group defending something whose time has passed, but the expression began in glory at the battle of Waterloo. Known for their fierce loyalty to Napoleon, the Imperial Guard was composed of the Young Guard, the Middle Guard, and the Old Guard. It was the Old Guard from this group who mounted the final brave but hopeless French charge at the Battle of Waterloo.

When did the United States draw up
modern-day plans for the invasion of Canada?

In 1974 it became public that in 1930 the United States had drawn up a strategic plan that included a successful invasion of Canada. The scheme was called "Plan — Red." It involved attacks on Montreal and Quebec, Winnipeg's railway centre, Ontario's nickel mines and power generators, and the Great Lakes. Naval blockades were to be set up on the Atlantic and Pacific coasts, and Halifax was to be captured and occupied. This proposal was one of several contingencies that could be used if the United States went to war with Britain, Japan, Germany, or Mexico.

The "Red" in the plan's title actually refers to Britain (Canada, as part of the British Commonwealth, was usually scarlet on maps) and was part of a global strategy for war with that nation. Plots for war with Japan were coded "Orange," war with Germany was "Black," and Mexico was "Green." A "White" plan was drawn up for a domestic insurrection, and a "Purple" proposal existed for war with a Central American country.

The idea that war was possible with Britain may have stemmed from a treaty between Britain and Japan that ended in 1924. The treaty prompted the United States to come up with a "Red-Orange" strategy that considered the threat of a British-Japanese alliance.

Of course, contingency plans are necessary, and as history from the time of the First and Second World Wars records, the Americans were very reluctant to go to war with anyone.

When did Canada plan to invade the United States?

It seems more than mildly absurd, but during the 1920s, while serving as the director of Canadian Military Operations and Intelligence, a man named James Sutherland Brown drew up "Defense Scheme Number One." He had heard that the Americans had drafted a similar plan for Canada's invasion, and as a descendant of United Empire Loyalists and because the United States had made several sorties into Canada during the nineteenth century, he didn't trust his southern neighbours. The proposal would have mobilized Canadian forces to capture and establish bases in Seattle and Minneapolis, stalling the U.S. Army long enough for the British to come to Canada's rescue.

Quickies

Did you know...
- approximately one out of every ten people ever born is alive today?
- there are 1,006.7 men for every 1,000 women in the world?
- there are 6 million more North American women than men?
- the average North American makes 2,571.8 phone calls per year?

wedding traditions

What is the origin of the engagement ring?

The diamond engagement ring was introduced by the Venetians, who discovered the diamond's value in the sixteenth century, but betrothal gifts hadn't included rings until A.D.860, when Pope Nicholas I decreed that a ring of value must be given as a statement of nuptial intent and that if the man called off the wedding, the jilted bride kept the ring. If the woman ended the engagement, she was to return the ring and be sent to a nunnery.

What is the origin of the wedding ring?

A school of thought persists that the first wedding rings were used by barbarians to tether the bride to her captor's home. This may or may not be true, but we do know that around 2800 B.C., because the Egyptians considered a circle to signify eternity, rings were used in marriage ceremonies. The Romans often added a miniature key welded to one side of the bride's ring to signify that she now owned half of her husband's wealth.

Why do bridegrooms have a best man?

In ancient times, most marriages were arranged, and so the groom wasn't always the bride's first choice. The man she favoured would often swear to carry her off before or during the wedding. To avoid this, the groom stood on the bride's right to keep his sword arm free and would enlist a warrior companion to fight off the rival if he showed up. This companion was, in fact, the "best man."

Why do brides wear "something old, something new, something borrowed, and something blue" to their weddings?

According to wedding tradition, the bride wears something old to remind the couple of the happiness of the courting period. She wears something new to represent the hopeful success of the couple's new life together, something borrowed to symbolize the support of friends, and something blue because it's the colour of fidelity. If a bride wears a single girlfriend's garter, it will improve that girl's prospects of marriage. The final line of the rhyme, "a silver sixpence in her shoe," which is rarely used today, symbolizes financial security.

Why is June the most popular month for weddings?

The ancient Greeks and Romans both suggested marriage during a full moon because of its positive influence on fertility. The Romans favoured June, a month they named after Juno, the goddess of marriage, because if the bride conceived right away, she wouldn't be too pregnant to help with the harvest. She also would probably have recovered from giving birth in time to help in the fields with the next year's harvest.

Why do brides wear wedding veils?

Although veils for women are today associated with Muslims, their origin goes back at least three thousand years before Mohammed was even born. Outside of the Middle East, this symbol of modesty had all but disappeared by 400 B.C., when the Romans introduced sheer translucent veils into the wedding ceremony to remind the woman that she was entering a new life of submission to her husband. Veils predate the wedding dress by several centuries.

Why is it bad luck for the groom to see his bride before the ceremony on their wedding day?

It's bad luck for the groom to see the bride within twenty-four hours of the wedding ceremony for the same reason that brides wear veils. When marriages were arranged by two families, the groom wasn't allowed to see or even meet his bride until he lifted her veil *after* they were married. This way, he couldn't refuse to marry her if he didn't like her looks. The twenty-four-hour ban descends from that ritual.

How did wedding cakes become so elaborate?

Most wedding rituals are to encourage fertility, and so it is with the wedding cake, which began with the Romans breaking small cakes of wheat and barley over the bride's head. During the reign of Charles II, the three-tier cake with white icing we use today was introduced. The cake takes its shape from the spire of Saint Bride's Church in London. The couple cuts the first piece together as a gesture of their shared future, whatever it might bring.

How did throwing confetti become a wedding custom?

Because the main purpose of marriage was to produce children, ancient peoples showered the new bride with fertility symbols such as wheat grain. The Romans baked this wheat into small cakes for the couple, to be eaten in a tradition known as *conferriatio*, or "eating together." The guests then threw handfuls of a mixture of honeyed nuts and dried fruits called *confetto* at the bride, which we copy by throwing confetti.

Why does a groom carry his bride over the threshold?

The custom of carrying a bride over the threshold comes from the kidnapping practices of the Germanic Goths around A.D. 200. Generally, these men only married women from within their own communities, but when the supply ran short, they would raid neighbouring villages and seize young girls to carry home as their wives. From this practice of abduction sprang the now symbolic act of carrying the bride over the threshold.

Why is marriage called "wedlock"?

Wedd is an Anglo-Saxon word meaning "to gamble," and there is no greater gamble than marriage. In the days when brides were bartered by their fathers, and a deal was reached with a prospective groom through an exchange of either property or cash, a young woman would have been bought and sold for breeding purposes to be finalized in a wedlock ritual called a wedding. This marriage led to *matrimony*, which in Latin means "the state of motherhood."

Why is a husband-to-be called a "groom"?

Bride comes from the Old English word *bryd*, while the word *guma* simply meant "a young man." The two together, *brydguma*, referred to a suitor looking for a wife. This compound changed in the sixteenth century when *groom* evolved within folk language to take over from *guma* as a description of a young man, boy, or lad who was commonly hired to work the stables and groom horses, among other chores, but who was still seeking a wife.

Why do we say that a married couple has "tied the knot"?

In Western culture, "tying the knot" suggests the pledge of inseparable unity made by a married couple. The expression comes from ancient India, when during the wedding ceremony the Hindu groom would put a brightly coloured ribbon around the bride's neck. During the time it took to tie the ribbon into a knot, the bride's father could demand a better price for his daughter, but once the knot was completed the bride became the groom's forever.

Why are wedding-related items referred to as "bridal"?

The expressions "bridal feast," "bridal bed," and "bridal cake," among other bridal references, all date back to around 1200, when a wedding was a rather boisterous and bawdy affair. The word *bridal* comes from "bride-ale," which was the special beer brewed for the wedding and then sold to the guests to raise money for the newlyweds. Because of the bride-ale, weddings were quite rowdy until around the seventeenth century, when the church managed to get a grip on the whole thing.

Why does the groom crush a glass with his foot at a Jewish wedding?

Near the end of a Jewish wedding ceremony, after the vows have been made, wine is poured into a new glass over which a blessing is recited by the rabbi. After the couple drinks from the glass, it is placed on the ground and crushed by the groom's foot. This symbolizes the destruction of the Holy Temple in Israel and reminds guests that love is fragile. Those gathered shout "mazel tov," and the couple kisses.

Why do we call the first weeks of marriage a "honeymoon"?

The custom of a honeymoon began over four thousand years ago in Babylon, when for a full lunar month after the wedding, the bride's father would supply his son-in-law with all the honey-beer he could drink. It was called the "honey month." The word *honeymoon* didn't enter our language until 1546, and because few people could afford a vacation, a honeymoon didn't mean a trip away from home until the middle of the nineteenth century.

Why do women cry at weddings?

Men might cry at weddings, but they have been socially conditioned that as protectors and warriors signs of weakness such as tears invite an attack. There is no such thing as "happy" crying. Psychologists suggest that when people cry at happy endings, they are reacting to the moment when the critical outcome was in doubt. A woman crying at a wedding is most likely expressing subconscious disappointment in the outcome of her own romantic dreams.

Quickies

Did you know...

- that a ton of ore must be mined to find enough gold for one wedding ring?
- today the average marriage lasts 9.3 years?
- couples who marry in January, February, and March tend to have the highest divorce rates?
- two out of three couples stay together through ten years of marriage? Less than half make it through twenty-five years together.

**everyday
expressions**

Why is someone lost if he "doesn't have a clue"?

The original spelling of *clue* was C-L-E-W, and its forgotten meaning is a "ball of yarn or string." A clew of string was unravelled as a guide out after entering an unfamiliar maze or a cave. If you became lost, all you had to do was follow the string back to the point of origin. In the modern cliché, if someone "doesn't have a clue," he is in the dark with no idea how to get out of his dilemma.

How did the expression "barefaced lie" originate?

A "barefaced lie" is one that is obvious and told straight out without flinching by someone who is either very stupid or very brave. The phrase is interchangeable with a "bald-faced lie," in reference to the sixteenth century when most men wore beards, sideburns, and moustaches. Only the rebellious ones who shaved their faces bare were considered bold enough to tell an obvious lie.

Why when suggesting an exhaustive search do we say, "Leave no stone unturned"?

The advice to "leave no stone unturned" comes from Greek mythology, wherein the Oracle of Delphi, through her communication with the gods, had acquired great wisdom. Euripides wrote that when the oracle was consulted about how to find a defeated general's hidden treasure, she advised that the only way was "to leave no stone unturned." The expression and the advice have been with us ever since.

Why do we say that something happened so quickly that it was over "before you could say Jack Robinson"?

Jack Robinson was a London social climber during the early eighteenth century. He made it his business to appear at as many gatherings as possible, where he would often present his card and have his name announced, then leave for the next function before meeting his hosts. This scandalous behaviour made its way into a popular song, and eventually "Before you could say Jack Robinson" meant any act of extreme haste.

Why do we say, "Put a sock in it" when we want someone to shut up?

The admonition "Put a sock in it," meaning "keep quiet," comes from the time of the earliest wind-up phonographs in which the sound emerged from a horn. These early acoustic record players didn't have electronic controls or any muting device to raise or lower the volume, so the only way to soften its sound was to stuff something into the horn. A sock was the perfect size, and so to lower the volume they would "put a sock in it."

When something valuable is destroyed while eliminating waste, why do we say they've "thrown the baby out with the bathwater"?

During the time when the entire family, beginning with the eldest, used the same bathwater, you had to be careful that a child wasn't still inside when it came time to throw out the dirty water. But the phrase was introduced in 1909 by George Bernard Shaw, who wrote, "Like all reactionaries, he usually empties the baby out with the bathwater."

Why do we call someone too smart for his or her own good a "smart aleck"?

The expression "smart aleck" for someone too cocky dates back to the 1840s, when New

York scam artist Aleck Hoag paid off police to look the other way while he had his wife pose as a prostitute to attract men before breaking in on them, revealing that he was the woman's husband, and demanding money from the frightened man. When Aleck Hoag stopped paying the police, they arrested the couple and coined "smart aleck" as meaning too clever for your own good.

Where did the expression
"Don't count your chickens before they hatch" originate?

"Don't count your chickens" is a commonly used saying, similar to New York Yankees catcher Yogi Berra's warning that "it ain't over till it's over." First written in the sixth century B.C., it is a quotation from one of Aesop's fables, called "The Milkmaid and Her Pail." It means that you shouldn't get ahead of yourself, because life is full of uncertainties. Aesop began life as a slave but was freed because of his wit and wisdom. "Don't count your chickens before they hatch" was first recorded in English in the late sixteenth century.

Why do we say, "When in Rome, do as the Romans do"?

If you wish to gain esteem and avoid grief, then it's wise to respect the customs of the majority within any culture you may find yourself. When St. Ambrose was sent on a mission to Rome by St. Augustine, he was concerned about which holy day to observe since the Romans fasted on a different day than was his custom. St. Augustine's wise advice is still with us: "When in Rome, do as the Romans do."

What is the origin of the expression "It's raining cats and dogs"?

The general legend about "raining cats and dogs" relates to the thatched roofs of the Middle Ages and would have you believe that when it rained, all sorts of creatures, including cats and dogs, slipped and fell in such abundance that it gave rise to the expression — but it is wrong! The truth is that the saying predates even the Dark Ages and goes back to a time when people believed that ghosts and goblins were around every corner. Cats and dogs had magical, mystical powers. Sailors believed that cats brought on storms and that witches rode those storms with their cats. To the early Norsemen, dogs and wolves symbolized the wind, and the Viking storm god Odin was always shown surrounded by dogs. So during a violent rainstorm, an angry Odin's dogs were set loose, and the cats, symbolizing the rain, caused people to say, "It's raining cats and dogs."

The word *cat* is derived from the ancient Greek word *catadupe* and means "waterfall." In Latin *cata doxas* means "contrary to experience" or "an unusual fall of rain."

Who coined the phrase "a New York minute"?

The push for urgency in our day-to-day existence is often expressed as a "New York minute" because that's how long it takes an impatient New Yorker to let you know you're a problem. It was discovered in 1967 as a response to a survey for a Dictionary of American English. One question asked was to fill in the blank after, "I'll be ready in …" to which a Jasper, Texas, policeman wrote "a New York minute."

Where did the expression "neck of the woods" come from?

Today, "this neck of the woods" would mean this specific neighbourhood. The phrase comes from the very beginning of European settlement in North America. It's from the Anglo adaptation of the Algonquin word *naiak*, meaning a narrow strip or corner of wooded land, usually protruding into water. *Naiak* was interpreted by white settlers as *neck*, and became "neck of the woods."

Why do the English use "by George" as an oath of surprise?

"By George" is always used as an exclamation, usually of surprise but often of determination. It's a reference to St George, the patron saint of England. "By George" began as a battle cry during the sixteenth century and a variation is used as such in Shakespeare's Henry V when the king shouts: "for Harry, England, and St. George"

A vision of St. George, who died in A.D. 303, inspired the first Crusade. His legendary slaying of the dragon was written during the thirteenth century, and his feast day, April 23, was first made a holiday in 1222.

Why do we say that someone speaking their mind is "blowing off steam"?

If someone is "blowing off steam" they are saying things in anger that have been previously suppressed by formality and circumstance. They are revealing their true feelings before they explode and cause even more damage. When boilers or engines containing water are heated the water turns to steam, which operates devices such as radiator systems or steam locomotives. The steam can build up considerable pressure, which, if not controlled, will cause an explosion. A system of valves is in place to prevent an explosion by releasing or "blowing off" steam.

What does it mean to "get your dander up"?

If you've "got your dander up" you're very upset. It means someone has caused you to burst into a sudden rage. The expression is from the Dutch *op donderen*. *Donder* is the Dutch word for thunder, so having someone get your dander up means they have caused you to lose your temper as violently and noisily as the arrival of a summer thunderstorm.

Why do we say, "Take a powder" when we want someone to leave?

"Take a powder" is a tough way of telling someone to get lost or get out of here and began as a rude dismissal of women. It was popularized in the gangster movies of the 1930s; when a tough guy was having a private conversation that he didn't want a woman to overhear, he would use the phrase that the girls used when they excused themselves to use the washroom or refresh their makeup. They'd say they were "taking a powder."

When adding a bonus why do we say, "I'll give you that to boot"?

If you're thinking of buying something, the salesman might offer to throw in an incentive, something "to boot." It's an add-on. This use of *boot* is from the very old Anglo-Saxon word *bot*, which survives in our modern language only in the phrase "to boot." Its use and meaning was generally replaced by *better* or *best* as in, "I'll throw this in as something extra to make it better for you."

When choices are meagre why do we say we're "scraping the bottom of the barrel"?

When all candidates are unqualified and the only choice we have isn't good enough, our only option is to "scrape the bottom of the barrel." This means the good wine has all been used and all that's left are the dregs. The phrase was introduced by Cicero (106–43 B.C.) as a reference to sediment left in an empty wine barrel, which he used to describe the lowest members of Roman society. Cicero also said: "If you aspire to the highest place, it is no disgrace to stop at the second, or even the third place."

Why is someone in a hopeless situation said to be "over a barrel"?

It you're "over a barrel" you're in big trouble. The expression became popular after it was used euphemistically by Raymond Chandler in his 1939 novel, *The Big Sleep*. During the nineteenth century difficult prisoners were stripped then strapped over a barrel and flogged. This form of corporal punishment was sometimes used to strap difficult schoolchildren.

I'd like to be a school-marm,
And with the school-marms stand,
With a bad boy over a barrel
And with a spanker in my hand
— Brick Pomeroy, *Nonsense*, 1869

Why do we use the expression "Close, but no cigar"?

"Close, but no cigar" is an expression we should be hearing less of as time goes on, as smokers are driven further to the fringes of society. The phrase originated at the end of the nineteenth century, when it was customary to give out cigars as prizes at carnivals. As these games of chance and skill were usually fixed in the carny's favour, you were most likely to come close but to win a cigar. The phrase has come to mean "nice try" in sports, business, and life in general.

Why might we say a father and son are "cut from the same cloth"?

If a son or daughter has characteristics similar to their father or mother, we say they are "cut from the same cloth." The expression originates with tailors, who try to make a suit by using only cloth from one dye batch in order to make sure colouring is consistent throughout. To make a second suit from that same batch or bolt would make it identical to the first. Telling someone they're "cut from the same cloth" can be good or bad depending upon how you regard the person with whom you're making the comparison

What's the origin of the expression "My bad"?

The slang expression "My bad" popped up in the 1970s as an acknowledgement of personal responsibility for making a mistake. The first written reference is in C. Wielgus and A. Wolff's 1986 book, *"Back-in-your-face": A Guide to Pick-up Basketball*. The phrase became popularized through the 1995 film *Clueless*, starring Alicia Silverstone.

Why do we say, "Every dog has his day"?

In ancient times, just as today in third-world societies, dogs lived miserable lives with little or no human care, which led to the hard-times expressions "It's a dog's life," "sick as a dog," and "dog-tired." As for the proverb "Every dog has his day," it was first recorded as an epilogue after the famed Greek playwright Euripides was killed by a pack of dogs in 405 B.C.

Why do we say, "A little knowledge is a dangerous thing"?

"A little knowledge is a dangerous thing" most often comes to mind while listening to a loud-mouthed narrow-minded radio or television talk show host. It simply means that anyone with a modicum of knowledge and limited intelligence who believes they are more aware than in fact they truly are can harmfully influence the understanding of a great many others. The phrase comes from the 1709 "Essay on Criticism" by Alexander Pope (1688–1744): "A little learning is a dangerous thing; drink deep, or taste not the Pierian spring: there shallow draughts intoxicate the brain, and drinking largely sobers us again."

Pieria was a region of ancient Macedonia, which included Mount Pierus where Orpheus and the muses were worshipped. The muses, of course, were the inspiration of creative thought.

Why is being meek or inoffensive called taking the "middle of the road"?

Someone who stays in the middle of the road is avoiding controversy or confrontation. Radio stations who brand themselves middle-of-the-road are trying not to offend anyone. In medieval times highwaymen ambushed travellers from the bushes on either side of the road so by walking the centre or middle of the road a person had a few extra seconds to prepare to defend themselves from an attack. They could also reveal to potential bandits that they were unarmed and had nothing worth stealing.

What is the origin of "A bird in the hand is worth two in the bush"?

This proverb means that it's wise to hold onto a small advantage rather than take a chance on losing everything while greedily grasping for more. The expression is ancient and has come down through the centuries in many forms. Although it is found in Latin texts from the thirteenth century, the earliest English version is from Wycliffe's translation of the Bible in 1382, in which Ecclesiastes IX read: "A living dog is better than a dead lion." In 1539, the first bird reference was used by Hugh Rhodes in a book on good manners: "A byrd in hand is worth ten flye at large." In 1546, John Heywood recorded it in a book of English proverbs as: "Better one byrde in hand than ten in the wood." The current form first appeared in print in an American newspaper, *The Huron Reflector*, in January of 1833: "…bear in mind the good old adage, 'A bird in the hand is worth two in the bush.'"

What is the origin of "What am I, chopped liver?"

"What am I, chopped liver?" means "What am I, insignificant?" Chopped liver is a Jewish culinary tradition. Cooked chicken livers are sometimes ground or chopped then seasoned and made into sandwiches. Chopped liver is also served as a side dish to a main course, but never makes the grade as a main dish, and from this "chopped liver" grew into a metaphor for "unimportant."

What is a "bone of contention"?

The subject or focal point of an ongoing dispute or controversy is often referred to as "a bone of contention." In this case, *contention* means a competition or quarrel over a prize. Being contentious involves presenting an argument within a rivalry. The "bone" in question alludes to two dogs fighting or contending over a single bone. Both this figure of speech and the expression "bone of dissention" entered our language in the sixteenth century.

Why do we define the rat race as "keeping up with the Joneses"?

"Keeping up with the Joneses" has come to mean trying to keep up with your neighbours, in terms of material possessions, at any cost. The expression comes from the title of a comic strip that ran in newspapers between 1913 and 1931 and chronicled the experiences of a newly married man in Cedarhurst, New York. Originally titled "Keeping Up With the Smiths," the cartoon was changed to the "Keeping Up With the Joneses" because it sounded better.

What's the origin of the phrase "busting your chops"?

"Busting your chops" means "in your face"! It's an intention to call a bluff or challenge your integrity. It comes from the end of the nineteenth century when it was fashionable for men to wear long sideburns called mutton chops. A "bust in the chops" was literally a punch in the face. The fashion has changed, but the figurative expression lives on after resurfacing during the 1960s when long hair and sideburns made a comeback.

What are the "cockles of your heart"?

A feeling of pleasure or affection is often said to "warm the cockles of your heart." The heart was long considered the centre of these warm emotions. A cockle is a marine mollusk, and during the seventeenth century the shape of the heart ventricles was likened to the shape of the little sea creature's shell.

What do I mean by saying, "If I had my druthers"?

"If had my druthers" means, of course, "If I had my way." *Druthers* is always plural and indicates that there are a number of options other than what is offered. It's rural American slang; it began as "I'd rather," which, when shortened by dropping the "I," becomes "drather." With a country accent, "drather" becomes "druther," which when pluralized and extended becomes "druthers," meaning "choices."

Where did the expression "I've got to see a man about a dog" originate?

It's the room we most often frequent, but good manners dictate that we avoid direct references to the toilet at all costs. It's a restroom, a powder room, a washroom, and a loo, which is derived from the French word *l'eau*, or water, as in water closet. "Seeing a man about a dog" comes from the 1866 play *Flying Scud*, where a character says, "Excuse me Mr. Quail, I can't stop; I've got to see a man about a dog" meaning he needs to leave the room — and fast.

Flying Scud was written by Irish-born playwright Dion Boucicault.

Modern-Day Bumper Stickers

- Gravity doesn't exist. Earth sucks.
- I almost had a psychic girlfriend but she left me before we met.
- Hire a teenager now — while they still know everything.
- I child-proofed my house but they still get in.
- If a mute child swears, does his mother wash his hands with soap?
- I need someone really bad … Are you really bad?
- Individualists — unite!
- Jesus is coming — look busy.
- Keep honking … I'm reloading
- If you want breakfast in bed, sleep in the kitchen.
- How can I miss you if you won't go away?
- I am only horny on the days that end in *y*.
- Sex on television can't hurt you unless you fall off.
- Never hit a man with glasses. Use your fist.
- Beer — helping white people dance since 1837.
- Our drinking team has a hockey problem.
- The rich get richer. The poor get babies.
- The problem with the gene pool is that there is no lifeguard.
- Suicidal twin kills sister by mistake!
- To err is human. To moo is bovine.
- Women who seek equality with men lack ambition.
- You're just jealous because the voices are talking to me!

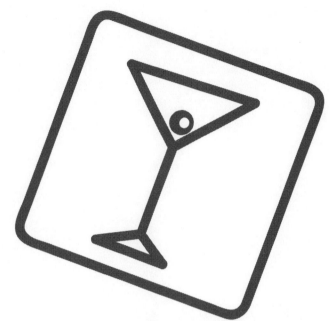

from the bar to the morning after

Why is taking the "hair of the dog" a hangover cure?

In the Middle Ages, people treated a dog bite with the ashes of the canine culprit's hair. The medical logic came from the Romans, who believed that the cure of any ailment, including a hangover, could be found in its cause. It's a principle applied in modern medicine with the use of vaccines for immunization. The "hair of the dog" treatment for hangovers advises that to feel better, you should take another drink of the same thing that made you feel so bad.

Why is the final drink before a journey called "one for the road"?

"One for the road" can be dangerous if you intend to drive, but the expression was coined long before the automobile. It comes from the ancient English tradition of offering condemned felons a final drink at all the pubs on the route to the Tyburn Tree where they were about to be publicly executed by hanging

Why is cheap whiskey called "hooch"?

Hooch is a short form of *Hoochinoo*, a liquor distilled by the natives of Alaska and discovered by American soldiers when they were stationed there in 1867. It became a favourite among the miners during the 1898 Klondike gold rush. The name *Hoochinoo* was taken from the Alaskan tribe's name, *tlingit Hutsnuwu*, which means "Grizzly Bear Fort."

Who invented the cocktail?

No one knows the origin of the word *cocktail*, but we accept the definition as being any one of a number of mixtures of alcoholic drinks, each with a different recipe. Archaeological evidence of the first known cocktail dates back to 3000 B.C. Terracotta vases have been uncovered under the banks of the Tigris River between Iraq and Iran with traces of tartaric acid (indicating wine) along with fermented barley (beer), honey, and apples — proof that the ancients enjoyed mixed drinks.

Today the city with the largest number of bars per capita in the world is Halifax, Nova Scotia, Canada.

Why is a long drinking spree called a "bender"?

A "bender" is a prolonged, irresponsible, and dangerous bout of drinking, which took its name from the patrons of London, England, alehouses during the 1850s. To promote drinking, it was common for a tavern to offer patrons all they could drink for a tuppence a day, so sixpence was good for three days. The sixpence coin, which was worth about a quarter, was nicknamed a "bender" because if it wasn't phony it could be easily bent. Since this bendable coin guaranteed three days of libation, the subsequent binge became known as a bender.

Why is a type of beer called "India pale ale"?

India pale ale dates from the late eighteenth century and was developed by the Hodgson's Company to solve the problem of getting fresh-tasting beer to soldiers and sailors in India and other British colonies in sailing ships that had to navigate hot, tropical waters. Unlike most British beers of the time, India pale ale had a very high hop and alcohol content, which countered bacteria that made beer taste sour. The original India pale ale was copper-coloured. It was called pale because it was lighter than brown, porter, or stout ales. The servicemen appreciated no longer having to drink "skunky" beer.

What does the phrase "Eat, drink, and be merry" tell us?

Today we use "Eat, drink, and be merry" as an invitation to party, but to be merry originally meant to be content or self-satisfied. The phrase is from a parable in the Bible that tells the tale of Epicurious, a man who worked hard all his life to accumulate goods and money and believed that he should take time to "eat, drink, and be merry, for tomorrow we die." When Epicurious died he was remembered as a fool because he did not live for anything but the material.

The phrase also appears in Luke 12:19: "Soul, you have so many goods laid up for years to come; take your ease, eat, drink, and be merry."

Why does "XXX" warn us about both alcohol and sexually explicit material?

The first use of the *X* brand was on casks of English beer and indicated that the contents had been properly aged and had passed government approval after paying a ten-shilling duty, illustrated by the Roman numeral X. Some brewers added extra *X*s to suggest a more potent content, and smut peddlers followed suit. When something is X-rated by the censors, its naughtiness is enhanced if more *X*s are added.

Why do we call someone who sells illegal alcohol a "bootlegger"?

During the prohibition period of the 1920s, those who sold illegal booze became very wealthy, but the term *bootlegger* came out of the nineteenth century, when it was the fashion for horsemen to wear very high boots. These boots were commonly used to conceal pints of illegal bottled moonshine by both the purveyor and the customer and gave us the term *bootleg*, which now means anything sold outside the law.

Why is a bootleg joint called a "blind pig"?

In 1838, Massachusetts outlawed the sale of hard liquor, causing drinkers to find creative ways to buy and sell booze. One entrepreneur set up a booth with a sign offering, for a small fee, a glimpse of an amazing striped pig. Those who paid to enter found a glass of rum standing next to a painted clay pig. The pig saw nothing, so the transaction was safe, and the expression "blind pig" was born.

Why do we say that someone intoxicated is "three sheets to the wind"?

Sailing ships are controlled with an intricate system of ropes, called "halyards," "lines," and "sheets," whose function it is to move or hold things in place. Sheets

are the ropes that control the sails. If one is loose, the sails will flap in the wind. Two loose sheets will affect the ship's steadiness. Three sheets to the wind and the vessel will reel off course like a drunken sailor.

What people make the best tippers?

A recent survey of North American service workers rated the best tippers in this order: (1) Other restaurant workers (2) Regular customers, especially cigarette smokers (3) Young male wannabes (4) Small business owners (5) Tavern owners (6) Hairdressers (7) Liquor salesmen (8) Taxi drivers (9) Salesmen (10) Musicians.

The same survey identified these categories as the worst tippers: (1) Senior citizens (2) People between twenty-one and twenty-four years old (3) Tourists (4) Teachers (5) Women (6) Lawyers (7) Doctors (8) Computer nerds (9) Bankers (10) Pipe smokers.

Waiters, waitresses, and bartenders identify good tippers from best to worst by what they drink in the following order: (1) Vodka (2) Rum (3) Beer (4) Tequila (5) Bourbon (6) Scotch (7) Wine (8) Gin (9) Whiskey (10) Non-alcoholic and creamy or fancy drinks with umbrellas, or frozen, layered, or flaming drinks.

Why is a party bowl of mixed drinks called "punch"?

Punch is usually a mixture of fruit and soda drinks combined with alcohol and served at large gatherings. It originated from the British colonization of northern India after the colonizers discovered a refreshing native drink made from five ingredients: rice alcohol blended with tea, sugar, and lemon, then diluted with water. The Hindi word for *five* (the number of ingredients) is *punch*.

Where did the drinking expression "Bottoms up" originate?

"Bottoms up" means more than "lift your drink." When press gangs cruised dockside English taverns preying on drunks for naval duty, one of their tricks was to drop a shilling into an unsuspecting target's pewter ale jug. When the drink was empty, the gang would tell him that he had accepted the king's shilling and then drag him off to sea. Wary drinkers began using glass-bottom tankards, and "bottoms up" meant to check for the shilling.

Why were dancers in the thirties and forties called "jitterbugs"?

Bandleader Cab Calloway coined the word *jitterbug* as a description of both the music and the dancers during the big band era. It came from a time when drinking alcohol was prohibited by law, giving rise to the popularity of illegal booze. Because of its hangover effect, moonshine had long been called "jitter sauce," and Calloway, while watching the intoxicated dancers, labelled them "jitterbugs."

Why is alcohol called "spirits" and empty beer bottles "dead soldiers"?

After a bachelor party there are a lot of "dead soldiers," or empty beer bottles, lying around. They are dead because the alcohol, or spirit, has left their bodies. The spirit, like the soul, was considered the independent and invisible essence of everything physical and is quite separate from the material fact. A beer bottle without its alcohol has lost its spirit and, just like any other creation human or otherwise, is dearly departed

Why is someone with a drinking problem called a "lush"?

In eighteenth-century London there was an actors' drinking club called the City of Lushington, which may have taken its name from Dr. Thomas Lushington, a prominent drinker from the seventeenth century whose descendants became brewers of fine ale. *Lush*, the abbreviation of *Lushington*, became a common slang reference for beer in early England. It later crossed the ocean, where in America the term *lush* became a reference to a heavy drinker.

Where did the expression as "drunk as blazes" come from?

To be drunk as blazes comes from a feast day created by the Orthodox church to honour a sainted Armenian bishop named Blais who was beheaded by the Roman Emperor Licinius for refusing to deny his faith in A.D. 316. The excessive drinking on St. Blais's day caused the revellers to be referred to as "drunken Blaisers," and soon anyone anywhere who was overly intoxicated was said to be as drunk as blazes.

Who were the first people to establish a legal drinking age and why?

In eleventh-century Europe, Asia, and the Middle East, thirteen was the age a person could hold property, drink legally, and, of course, serve in the military. It was the Normans who changed the age to nineteen after realizing that thirteen-year-olds were simply not strong enough for warfare. Today's drinking ages vary from no minimum in China to twenty-one in the United States, but all agree that eighteen is old enough for the military.

Why is an altered alcoholic drink called a "mickey"?

A mickey is an alcoholic drink that's been altered to incapacitate the person who drinks it. It's become a very dangerous idea, especially for young women, but it started out innocently enough in a Chicago bar owned by a man named Mickey Finn. Around the turn of the twentieth century, Finn discovered that he could get rid of an obnoxious customer by slipping a diarrheic into his drink. Within minutes the troublesome drinker would have urgently left the bar.

Why do we say a corrupt or drunken person has "gone to the Devil"?

In Victorian times, to "go to the Devil" was to visit a bar on Flat Street near the London Civil Courts. The Devil was a favourite pub for lawyers, who seemed to spend more time in that bar than in their offices. If a client thought his money had gone to the Devil to pay for his lawyer's drinks, he might visit the legal offices to ask for an explanation, where he would be told that the absent lawyer had indeed gone to the Devil.

Why is someone who is dazed or confused (or drunk) said to be "groggy"?

If you're in a haze you might be groggy, but you're more likely to be drunk because of the grog. Back in 1740, British Admiral E. Vernon changed the drinking habits of his sailors by issuing their rum ration diluted with water and lime juice to prevent scurvy (which is the origin of the label *limey* for an Englishman). The admiral always wore a grogram coat and was known to the men as "Old Grog," which is why the word *grog* is used to describe rum.

A grogram coat is made from a weave of a coarse waterproof fabric (from the French *gros-grain*) made from silk, mohair, and wool and stiffened by gum.

Why should heavy drinkers wear an amethyst?

An amethyst is a pale blue to dark purple crystallized quartz and is a precious stone found in modern-day Iran, Iraq, India, and some parts of Europe. It was worn on the breastplates of high priests because the ancients believed that wearing or even touching an amethyst kept people from getting intoxicated no matter how much they drank. In Greek the word *amethyst* literally means "not intoxicating."

Quickies

Did you know...
- that Daiquiri is the name of a village in eastern Cuba?
- that tequila is a liquor named after a town in west-central Mexico?
- that the word *rum* is an abbreviation of *rumbullion*?
- that the word *whiskey* comes from Gaelic and literally means "water of life"?
- that the word *aquavit* is derived from the Latin *aqua vitae* and also means "water of life"?
- that the word *vodka* in Russian literally means "little water"?
- that the word *gin* is a shortened form of the Swiss city Geneva, which in Middle Dutch is *Geniver*, which is also a name for the juniper tree that grows the berries that give gin its flavour?
- that the word *lager* in German means "storehouse," therefore *lager beer* means "beer brewed for keeping"?

What is the difference between brandy and cognac?

There is no difference in formula. *Brandy* is an abbreviation of *brandywine* and is any spirit distilled from either wine or fermented fruit juice. The word *brandywine* comes from the Dutch *brandewijn*, which means "burnt wine," because the drink is distilled. All brandywine or brandy is burnt or distilled wine. Cognac is also a brandy but is so called because it is exclusive to the Cognac region of France.

Some types of brandies include ouzo, flavoured with anise and originating in Greece; grappa, distilled from the crushed residue from wine-making and originating in Italy; kirsch, distilled from cherries and originating in Germany; slivovitz, produced from crushed plums and originating in the Balkans; and calvados, created from fermented apple cider and originating in France.

Lofty Origins of Overused Phrases

- Power tends to corrupt and absolute power corrupts absolutely.
  — Lord Acton, 1887
- It is necessary only for the good man to do nothing for evil to triumph.
  — Edmund Burke
- The best laid schemes o' mice an' men Gang aft a-gley [go awry].
  — Robert Burns, 1796
- Music hath charms to sooth a savage breast.
  — William Congreve, 1697
- Mad dogs and Englishmen Go out in the midday sun.
  — Noël Coward, 1931
- Variety's the very spice of life. — William Cowper, 1785
- Genius is one percent inspiration, ninety-nine percent perspiration
  — Thomas Alva Edison, c.1903
- A thing of beauty is a joy for ever. — John Keats, 1818
- Hope springs eternal (in the human breast). — Alexander Pope, 1733
- Timeo Danaos et dona ferentes [I fear the Greeks even
  when they bring gifts]. — Virgil, first century B.C.
- I disapprove of what you say, but I will defend to the death your right
  to say it. — Evelyn Beatrice Hall, *The Friends of Voltaire*, 1906
- O what a tangled web we weave, when first we practice to deceive.
  — Sir Walter Scott, 1808
- "...but when we've practised quite a while,
  how vastly we improve our style." — anonymous

work and career

What is the difference between a job and a career?

The noun *job*, meaning "a piece of work," was first recorded in the mid-sixteenth century. By the mid-seventeenth century, the word had also come to mean "continuous labour for pay." The term began as *jobbe*, which is a variant of *gob* or *lump* and means specific work for money. *Career*, on the other hand, started out as the Latin noun *carrus*, or "chariot," and evolved into several meanings, including "to speed." Generally, during the Middle Ages, *career* was employed to describe a running course such as the sun's transit across the sky or even a racecourse. In the sixteenth century, a track on a jousting field was called a career. In the early twentieth century, *career* began to mean the progression of a life's work, while *job* remained a particular piece of work or a paid position of employment. *Career* can still mean a racecourse, only today it is run by rats.

Why is a self-employed professional called a "freelancer"?

The word *freelance* came out of the period between the fourteenth and sixteenth centuries, when mercenary knights with no particular allegiance would take their lances into battle for the prince or state that paid them the most money. They were referred to as freelancers by authors in the nineteenth century and operated much like the gunfighters in the American West. Now, a freelancer is anyone who works independently.

Why are skilled computer fanatics called "geeks"?

Since the fifteenth century, *geek* or *geck* has described a low-life fool. For example, a geek is, in carnival slang, someone who bites off the heads of chickens or snakes. At the beginning of the computer age, the word *geek* took on the meaning of a socially awkward intellectual. But through accepting and celebrating their geek status, skilled computer operators have managed to change the meaning of the word, so that a geek is someone to be admired.

Why do we say someone has been "fired" when he or she is forced out of a job?

Being fired is usually unpleasant, and even though it's sometimes a disguised blessing, it never reaches the cruelty of its medieval Celtic origins. If a clan leader wanted to get rid of a petty criminal without killing him, or if someone was found guilty of stealing from his employer, especially from the mines, he was taken to his home along with all his tools and placed inside, after which the house was "fired" or set on fire. If he escaped, he was banished from the clan.

When someone loses his job, why do we say he "got the sack"?

"Getting the sack" has come to mean getting fired or dismissed from anything, including a love affair. The expression entered the language long before the industrial era, at a time when workers carried their tools from job to job in a sack. When the job was done, or the labourer was discharged, the boss or employer would simply hand the worker his tool sack. He was literally "given the sack."

Why is the night shift called "the graveyard shift"?

During the Victorian era — before embalming — there was a great fear of being buried alive. Wealthy men and women arranged to have a string tied to their hands that ran from the buried coffins to bells on the surface, so that if they awoke they could sound the alarm. The cemetery was busy during the day, but someone was needed to wander the grounds and listen for the bells during the night. This was called the graveyard shift.

Why if someone isn't up to the job do we say he isn't "worth his salt"?

Thousands of years ago, before money was introduced, workers and soldiers were often paid with a negotiated quantity of salt. More than as a seasoning, salt's value was in its use as a preservative or cure for meat, as well as a medicine. The early Romans called this payment a *salarium*, which gave us the word *salary*. If a man wasn't "worth his salt," he wasn't worth his salary.

Why is the head office called the "flagship" of a corporation?

We often use the word *flagship* to indicate the most important or largest component or unit within an industrial complex. This derives from the navy where a flagship carried the admiral and flew his flag. The admiral's ship was the largest in the fleet, and just like today's CEO, the admiral required larger quarters and rooms to conduct strategy meetings.

Why do we say that someone has "knocked off work" for the day?

To "knock off work" might be for any length of time, but it usually means for the day. The expression certainly had significance to those who first used it, because they were the oarsmen of a slave galley. To keep the ship on course, the slaves were kept rowing in unison by a drumbeat pounded out rhythmically on a block of wood. Different beats had different meanings — the left or right side only, or both together. These beats also signalled rest breaks and the end of a shift, when the slaves were "knocked off" for the day.

Why do we call leisure work a "hobby"?

Hobby is a word used to describe an avocation done for diversion or self-pleasure. Few people find fulfillment working for someone else, and so many express their individuality within a hobby. The word comes from a toy made from a stick with a horse's head that children used to ride. It was called a hobby horse, and, like the child at play, anyone pursuing a hobby was doing it for escapism and pleasure, not money.

Why is the person who fixes your pipes called a "plumber"?

A *plumb* or *plumb bob* is the lead weight at the end of a line used to determine the depth of water. It was sailing ships' precursor to sonar. In the fourteenth century, when indoor plumbing was introduced, the pipes were made of lead, and the artisans who installed the pipe systems to buildings took their professional name from what had previously been the metal's main nautical function: they were "plumbers."

Why are men who work on the docks called "longshoremen"?

The title *longshoreman* goes back to a time when there was very little mechanical help to unload a great sailing vessel, and often there were no port or docking facilities either. Everything was done by hand. Unloading the big ship into smaller rowing boats, then unloading these onto the shore, was hard work and needed a lot of strong men. Because these men would line up on the water's edge, they were called "along the shore men" which in time became simply "longshoremen."

Where did the words *steward* and *stewardess* originate?

A steward or stewardess is usually employed as a caretaker in a variety of circumstances, including at sea and in the air. Although the position carries great responsibility, working conditions are often unpleasant. The title of steward was originally given to someone who took care of the cattle and pigs. It derives from the Anglo-Saxon word *stig-weard*, meaning "sty-keeper." No wonder they want to be called flight attendants.

Why is a cowboy called a "cowpoke"?

The word *cowboy* is from England and entered the language in 1725 as a simple description of a young boy who tended to the cows. It was also a reference to terrorists on both sides of the American Revolutionary War, because they stole and killed the enemy's cattle. When *cowboy* became a western U.S. reference to a ranch hand in 1849, its meaning by association was someone reckless or irresponsible. By 1881 the word *cowpoke* was restricted to those young cowboys who poked and prodded cattle into railway cars using long poles.

What kind of a job is created by "featherbedding"?

About sixty years ago, when a group of railroad men complained about being unable to sleep on their hard bunks, the boss asked, "What do you want … feather beds?" At the time a feather bed was the warmest and coziest place to curl up and sleep, and so companies began calling the union practice of creating unnecessary soft jobs requiring little or no work, for members who would otherwise be laid off, "featherbedding."

Why is a lazy, irresponsible person called "shiftless"?

The word *shift* means to change or rearrange, which is why we call those who work during differing blocks of time "shift workers." This use of the word *shift* also applies to an individual's ability to change or adapt. Therefore, if you're "shiftless" you lack the initiative or resources to change with the circumstances. On the other hand, someone who is "shifty" is too adept at change and isn't to be trusted.

Why is something of little value called "fluff" and poor workmanship called "shoddy"?

The word *shoddy* is used to describe both poor workmanship and poor character, while *fluff* means of little value. *Shoddy* is derived from *shode*, meaning "shed" or "thrown off," and refers to the excess tossed from the good cloth during the process of weaving. This fluff is re-spun and used to make similar but cheaper wool products, which, although they look good, through time reveal their poor quality.

Why are construction cranes and the mechanisms used for drilling oil called "derricks"?

A derrick, an instrument used for heavy lifting, got its name from a famous London hangman. In the early 1600s, Godfrey Derrick built a sturdy gallows from which he executed some three thousand souls by hanging. Because items hung and swayed from the cranes used to load ships, longshoremen called them "derricks" after the executioner's infamous device.

Why is a practice session called a "dry run"?

A "dry run" is firefighter jargon. It was once common for firemen, especially volunteers, to hold public exhibitions of their skills and to compete with other companies at fairs and carnivals. This dry run gave the firemen practice and was so called because no water was used. A "fire run" or "wet run" is a call to an actual blaze.

Why do we use the word *glitch* to define an unknown computer problem?

Along with space exploration came new expressions that are now everyday language. Astronauts said "affirmative" for yes, "check" to confirm a completed task, and "copy" to indicate that an instruction was understood. "Glitch," an unexplained computer malfunction, was first used to describe the Mercury space capsule's frustrating tendency to signal an emergency when none existed.

Where did the insult "couldn't hold a candle" come from?

The derogatory expression "couldn't hold a candle" is from the sixteenth century. Before electricity, experienced workers needing light to work by would have a young apprentice hold a candle so that they could see to complete a complex job. Holding a candle for a skilled tradesman gave the apprentice a chance to watch and learn, but if he couldn't even do that properly, it was said disparagingly that "he couldn't hold a candle" to the tradesman.

Why is buttering up a boss said to be "currying favour"?

If you are trying to get on someone's good side with insincere behaviour, your actions are "currying favour" from that person. *Curry* is a horse-grooming term for cleaning and rubbing down an animal. *Favour* in this expression was originally *Fauvel*, the name of the centaur in the fourteenth-century satire *Le Roman de Fauvel*. Fauvel was very evil and cunning, and it was a good idea to get on the centaur's good side. You could do this by pampering or grooming or "currying Fauvel."

place names
and nicknames

Why are citizens of the United States the only North Americans called "Americans"?

After discarding dozens of suggestions, Canada took its name from the Native American word *kanata*, meaning "a collection of huts." The most popular of the names considered by the United States was Columbia, which is why the nation's capital is located in the District of Columbia. But because they couldn't make a final decision, the people of the United States have accepted the unofficial name given to them by the British during the Revolutionary War. They are, simply, Americans.

Odds & Oddities

- Brazil was named after the nut, not the other way around.
- Damascus, Syria, was flourishing a couple of thousand years before Rome was founded in 753 B.C., making it the oldest continuously inhabited city in existence.
- Los Angeles's full name is El Pueblo de Nuestra Senora la Reina de los Angeles de Porciuncula — its abbreviation (L.A.) is 3.63 percent of its name's length

Why are the southern United States called "Dixieland"?

The nickname "Dixieland" didn't come from the Mason-Dixon Line, the boundary between the free and the slave states. Rather it's from the word *dixie*, which was what southerners called a French ten-dollar bank note of New Orleans that was already in use in 1859 when Daniel Emmet, a northern black man, wrote and introduced his song "Dixie," which spread the South's nickname and somehow became a battle song for the Confederacy.

Buffalo, New York

The buffalo is associated more with the western plains, so it seems an odd name for New York State's second largest urban area until you realize that it came not from the prairie bison but instead from a French missionary's description of the Niagara River. He called the region Beau Fleuve, which in French is "beautiful running water." In time, the English-speaking locals simply mispronounced Beau Fleuve until it became as it sounded to them — "Buffalo." Buffalo is known as "the City of Good Neighbours."

Detroit, Michigan

During the seventeenth century, France established a number of strategic trading posts in defence of the advancing British. One of these, Fort Ponchartrain, was built in 1701 by Antoine de la Mothe Cadillac in an area where the river narrowed, which had become known in French as *le detroit*, "the straits." Of course the founder of Detroit, the motor city, or "Motown," Antoine Cadillac, has his name on a luxury car, so it seems only logical that to keep the automotive theme alive, Detroit's sister city is Toyota City, Japan.

Michigan is derived from *Meicigama*, an Algonquian word for the Great Lakes.

Why do we call New York "the Big Apple"?

During the 1940s, Robert Emmerich, who played piano in the Tommy Dorsey Band, wrote an obscure song called "The Big Apple." It was soon forgotten by everyone except the legendary reporter Walter Winchell, who liked the song so much that in his daily column and on the air he began referring to his beat, New York City, as "the Big Apple," and soon, even though Emmerich's song was long forgotten, its title became the great city's nickname.

Why is the city of New Orleans called "the Big Easy"?

It was the jockeys of New Orleans who first began referring to the big-time racetrack in New York as the Big Apple, a phrase popularized as the city's nickname by gossip columnist Walter Winchell. Possibly in response to this, during the 1970s New Orleans gossip columnist Betty Guillaud began referring to her city as the Big Easy — originally the name of a long-forgotten jazz club called the Big Easy Hall.

How did the city of Calgary, Alberta, get its name?

In 1875, during trouble with the First Nations, the local North-West Mounted Police sent E Troop under Inspector E.A. Brisebois to erect a barracks on the Bow River. When Brisebois wanted to name the new structure after himself, his commander, Lieutenant-Colonel James Macleod, overruled him and named the settlement Fort Calgary, after the ancestral estate of his cousins, the MacKenzies, in Scotland. The Gaelic translation of Calgary is "clear running water," which certainly describes the Bow River. The translation of the Blackfoot name for the area was "elbow many houses." The translated Cree name for the area was "elbow house." Both Native references are to the Elbow River.

Why is Chicago called the "Windy City"?

Most people believe that Chicago got its nickname from its prevailing winds, but that isn't the case. In 1893, Chicago hosted the World's Columbian Exposition, celebrating the four hundredth anniversary of America's discovery. The city's aggressive promotional campaign offended the people of New York, whose press nicknamed it the Windy City to mock its bragging ways. The moniker stuck, but, fortunately for Chicago, its original meaning has been forgotten by most.

Niagara Falls, New York, and Niagara Falls, Ontario

In 1641, the first reference to the mighty falls was written down as *Onguiaahra*, which is how it sounded in the local dialect, and because the natives had no written reference it was soon after abbreviated to *Ongiara*. Both words were interpreted as meaning "thunder of waters." Word of the amazing natural wonder was spread orally, and through telling rather than writing, *Ongiara* became *Niagara*.

Who was the first Niagara Falls daredevil?

In October of 1829, "the Yankee Leaper," Sam Patch, became the first of the Niagara daredevils by surviving a jump off the main 110-foot Canadian Falls. The twenty-two-year-old Patch then went to Rochester the following month and jumped from the 99-foot Upper Falls. Disappointed in the small crowd, he chose to repeat the stunt a week later on Friday, November 13. After a pre-jump celebration at several local taverns and in front of ten thousand spectators, Sam Patch climbed a tower he had built at the brink of the falls, but as he jumped he slipped, causing his feet to miss his planned vertical entry. The crowd heard a very loud noise as he hit the water. His body was found four months later frozen in the ice of the Genessee River. His grave is marked by a simple wooden board with the inscription: "Sam Patch — Such is Fame."

Who was the first person to go over Niagara in a barrel?

The first person to go over Niagara Falls in a barrel was a woman. Bored with teaching school, and desperate for money, Annie Edison Taylor, a sixty-three-year-old widow (she claimed to be in her forties) chose her birthday, October 24, 1901, to challenge the Canadian Falls, and she did it in a wooden pickle barrel made from oak and iron and padded inside with a mattress. When she emerged from her plunge battered and bruised with only a minor cut on her forehead she exclaimed, "No one ought ever to do that again." Unfortunately, her dreams of fame and fortune never materialized. A speaking tour didn't work out, and in 1921, the now eighty-three-year-old Annie Nelson (she had since remarried) died a pauper at the Niagara County Infirmary in Lockport, New York. She's buried in the Stunters Section of Oakwood Cemetery in Niagara Falls, New York.

Of the sixteen known attempts to go over the falls in a barrel or enclosed device, six have died and ten have survived.

Quickies

Did you know...

- 25 percent of the territorial United States once belonged to Mexico?
- twenty-four American states have Native American names, and six have Spanish origins?
- when Spain sold Florida to the United States in 1821 for $5 million it was known in Spanish as *Pascua Florida*, which was a tribute to Easter and means "feast of flowers"?
- that in 1867 the United States bought Alaska from the Russians for 2 cents an acre? (*Alaska* is from the Aleut word for "Great Land.")

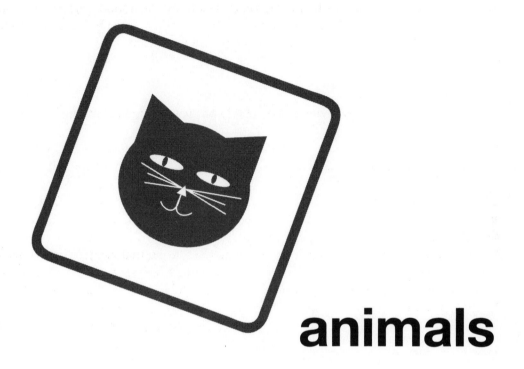

animals

How did the Australian kangaroo get its name?

Captain James Cook introduced *kangaroo* into the English language when he entered it in the ship's log on June 24, 1770. The explorer got the name from a local Aboriginal who didn't understand English. A myth grew that in the local language, *kangaroo* meant, "I don't know," but that legend has recently been dismissed by the discovery through linguistic research that in the Aboriginal language from the region of Australia where Cook first made his sighting, the word for what we call a kangaroo is, in fact, *gangurru*.

Why is one breed of dog called a "Boxer"?

The Belgian breed of dog known as the Brabanter Bullenbeiser was a cattle dog and an enthusiastic family pet even though it was used by the gentry for hunting wild boar. Around 1830 it was crossbred with an English bulldog (bred for bull fighting), and the Boxer breed was initiated. The dog flourished during the nineteenth century under the guidance of the German Boxer Klub, who gave it the English name Boxer because of its fighting tenacity and its unique use of its front paws while in combat or playing.

When we want a dog to attack, why do we say, "Sic 'em"?

Dogs are descended from wolves and interact with humans the same as they would with other dogs within a pack. They are protective of their family or pack and instinctively attack only when hunting or frightened. This behaviour can be altered in some dogs through aggressive training. Guard dogs have to learn to attack on command from the human alpha dog, their trainer. "Sic 'em," a very old command, is an abbreviation of "seek him."

Why do the Chinese name each year for an animal?

The Chinese have tied animal names to calendar years for centuries. According to the myth, Buddha invited all the animals on Earth to visit him on New Year's Day, but only twelve arrived. They were the rat, the ox, the tiger, the hare, the dragon, the snake, the horse, the sheep, the monkey, the rooster, the dog, and the pig. As a reward, Buddha honoured each of these twelve with a year of its own.

What's the story behind the expression "It's a dog-eat-dog world"?

In the year 43 B.C., Roman scholar Marcus Tarentius Varro observed humanity and remarked that even "a dog will not eat dog." His point was that humans are less principled in the matter of destroying their own kind than other animals. By the sixteenth century, the phrase became a metaphor for ruthless competition, and during the Industrial Revolution the expression "It's a dog-eat-dog world" became commonplace.

Why does shedding crocodile tears mean that you're faking sadness?

Crocodiles have a nasty habit of sounding like a baby crying, which can attract naive human prey. While lying motionless in the sun, often hidden by tall grass, a crocodile waiting for lunch might leave its mouth open, which puts pressure on its tear glands, causing the illusion of crying. Like their phony human counterparts, they shed tears without any sense of contrition or sadness.

Where did we get the saying "Not enough room to swing a cat"?

This colourful phrase evokes strange images of feline cruelty. In fact, it has nothing to do with cats, but the real story is at least as cruel. The "cat" is a cat-o'-nine-tails, a type of whip used to discipline sailors on old sailing ships. The cat-o'-nine-tails has one handle attached to nine thin strips of leather, each perhaps three feet long. The cat-o'-nine-tails would be used to administer lashings that would sting and leave welts on the recipient. The whippings would take place on the deck, because below deck there was not enough ceiling height to swing a cat (o'-nine-tails).

Why does "letting the cat out of the bag" prevent you from buying "a pig in a poke"?

A *poke* has the same origins as *pocket* and *pouch* and is a small bag within which a young pig could be packaged after being sold at a farmers' market. In 1540, it was recorded that unscrupulous farmers would sometimes replace the pig with a cat and advise the purchaser not to open the bag until they reached home or the pig might escape. If the poke was opened, then the cat was out of the bag and the seller had been caught cheating.

Why is a leader of a trend called a "bellwether"?

The metaphorical use of *bellwether* to mean a human leader dates back to the fifteenth century; its modern use usually means a company that sets an industry standard. A *wether* is in fact a castrated ram or male sheep, and a *bellwether* is the leader of the flock. He knows the routine, and he wears a bell so that the shepherd knows where his sheep are, because all the others will follow the bellwether anywhere without hesitation.

Why are Dalmatians used as mascots by firefighters?

Ancient Egyptian hieroglyphs show Dalmatians running with chariots. In Britain, they were used to escort carriages over hundreds of miles before standing guard while travellers stopped to eat or rest. Throughout the centuries the breed developed an affinity with horses, which is why they were a natural for early firefighters. The Dalmatians ran with the fire wagon and then kept the horses in line while the firefighters fought the blaze.

Dalmatians are from Dalmatia in a region of what is now Croatia. They were spread across Europe by the Roma people. Endurance, strength, and loyalty are their greatest characteristics.

Why do we call male felines "tomcats"?

A 1760 book titled *The Life and Adventures of a Cat* became so popular that from then on, all un-neutered male cats were called "Tom" after the book's feline hero. A female cat that has procreated is called a "queen," a title easily understood by any cat lover. Legend has it that one such cat lover, the great prophet Mohammed, once cut off the sleeve of his shirt before standing rather than disturb a sleeping kitten.

Why do we say that something worthless is "for the birds"?

In the days before automobiles, the streets were filled with horse-drawn carriages, and these animals quite naturally left behind deposits from their digestive systems. These emissions contained half-digested oats that attracted swarms of birds, which took nourishment from the deposits. The people of the time coined the expression "for the birds" as meaning anything of the same value as these horse-droppings.

Why is something useless and expensive called a "white elephant"?

The term *white elephant* comes from ancient Siam, where no one but the king could own a rare and sacred albino elephant without royal consent. The cost of keeping any elephant, white or otherwise, was tremendous, and so when the king found displeasure with someone he would make him a gift of a white elephant, and because the animal was sacred and couldn't be put to work, the cost of its upkeep would ruin its new owner.

Why is the height of a horse measured in hands?

For five thousand years, the height of a horse has been measured in hands. Body parts were our first points of reference for measurement. For example, a foot was exactly that: the length of a Roman foot. A hand was measured with the thumb curled into the palm, a distance now standardized as four inches. A horse's height is measured in a straight line from the ground to the withers (the top of the shoulders between the neck and the back).

A horse of 15.2 hands measures 15 times 4 inches, plus 2 inches, or 62 inches. It's important to keep in mind that you can have 15.3 hands, but after the next full inch the height is taken as 16 hands, not 15.4.

The hand is a tradition of British measurement. In the rest of Europe a horse's height is measured in metres and centimetres. In some places, like Europe and South Africa, they measure in both hands and centimetres.

Why do geese fly in a *V* formation?

When geese fly in either a *V* formation or a single line, they are drafting off the one in front in the same way that racecar drivers use each other to pick up speed. The lead, or dominant, bird, which is always a female, begins a turbulence wave that helps lift the birds behind her. The farther back in the flock, the less energy they need to fly. The lead bird rotates position to fight exhaustion. The Wright brothers were inspired by the same principle of flight!

What is the difference between a "flock" and a "gaggle" of geese?

Any group of birds, goats, or sheep can be referred to as a flock, but each feathered breed has its own proper title. Hawks travel in *casts*, while it's a *bevy* of quail, a *host* of sparrows, and a *covey* of partridges. Swans move in *herds* and peacocks in *musters*, while a flock of herons is called a *siege*. A group of geese is properly called a *gaggle*, but only when they're on the ground. In the air they are a *skein*.

Why is an innocent person who takes the blame for others called a "scapegoat"?

The term *scapegoat* or *escape goat* entered the English language with William Tyndale's translation of the Hebrew Bible in 1525. Under the Law of Moses, the Yom Kippur ritual of atonement involved two goats. One was sacrificed to the Lord, while all the sins of the people were transferred to the other. The scapegoat was then led into the wilderness, taking all the sins of the Israelites with it.

Why are long, rambling, and unfunny stories called "shaggy dog stories"?

A shaggy dog story usually takes forever to tell and has a clever (if not funny) ending. The joy is found within the skill and craft of the narrator. During the 1930s and '40s a series of such jokes involving shaggy dogs circulated as a fad. A collection of these stories was published in 1946. Today, any rambling story ending in a pun is called a "shaggy dog story."

Here's one of the original shaggy dog stories: A grand householder in Park Lane, London, lost his very valuable and rather shaggy dog. The owner advertised repeatedly in the *Times*, but without luck, and finally he gave up hope. When an American in New York saw the advertisement, he was moved by the man's devotion and took great trouble to seek out another dog that matched the one in the advertisement. He found a perfect match. During his next business trip to London, he sought out the grieving owner's impressive house, where he was received in the householder's absence by a very English butler, who glanced at the dog, bowed, and exclaimed, in a horror-stricken voice, "But not so shaggy as that, sir!"

How did an American bird get named after the distant country of Turkey?

In 1519, conquistador Hernando Cortez returned to Spain with a bird introduced to him by the Native Americans of Mexico. The peculiar bird confused all of Europe. The French thought it was from India and so named it *dindon* (from *pouletes d'Inde*). Although the Germans, Dutch, and Swedes agreed that the bird was Indian they named it *kilcon* after Calcutta. By the time the trend reached England, rumour had it that the bird was from Turkey, and so that became its name.

How many native wild jackrabbits are born each year in North America?

This North American animal is properly classified as a hare, not a rabbit, so the answer to the above question is really zero. Early North American settlers dropped the word *hare* from their vocabulary. The American term *jackrabbit* is an abbreviation of the original name *jackass-rabbit*, so named because of its long ears.

A "rabbit punch," describing an illegal action in boxing, comes from a gamekeeper's method of dispatching an injured rabbit by chopping it on the back of its neck with the side of the hand.

Why are some schemes called "hare-brained"?

The adjective *hare-brained* usually refers to a plan or action that is unexplainably preposterous. If there is any confusion about this word's meaning, it lies in the sixteenth-century dual spelling as both *hare-brained* and *hair-brained*. In any case, the word is a reference to the wildly odd mating season practices of hares, which are so bizarre that they are the origins of the expression "mad as a march hare."

Why do we say that a different subject is "a horse of a different colour"?

"A horse of a different colour" is a separate issue from the business at hand and comes from horse trading. When horses are born, their official registration includes a record of their colour. To make sure they were buying the horse pedigree as advertised, traders learned to check this registration to ensure that the colt's colour was the same as the one for sale, otherwise they were being cheated with a "horse of a different colour."

How did the beaver get its name?

A beaver is an industrious little rodent whose fur was the foundation of an industry that helped create Canada. The furry little creature got its name from the Welsh *befer*, meaning "bear." Another definition of the word came at a time in history when knights wore armour. The hinged bottom portion of the helmet was called the "beaver," although in this sense the word is derived from the Latin *bevere*, meaning "to drink."

Why do dogs circle so much before lying down?

Dogs turn around several times before lying down. They appear to be trying to make themselves comfortable, though it has been facetiously suggested that they are looking for the head of the bed. The fact is that dogs have maintained this habit from their origins in the wild. Like their ancestors and cousins, such as wolves, coyotes, and foxes, domesticated dogs still turn circles to beat down a bed of tall grass.

What does the "grey" mean in "greyhound"?

Greyhound dogs have been bred for hunting and racing and have extremely keen eyesight. They are one of the fastest land mammals and can reach speeds up to forty-five miles per hour. They were introduced to England from mainland Europe in the sixth century B.C. The dogs come in a wide variety of colours, which indicates that the "grey" in their name has nothing to do with their hue. *Hound* is from the Old English word *hund*, and *grey* derives from the Old Norse *grig*, which was used generically for any fair or light-coloured dog. Greyhounds make wonderful pets and have been nicknamed "forty-five-mile-an-hour couch potatoes."

All ancient variations of the word *grey*, as in *greyhound*, have the common meaning of "shine" or "bright."

Why is a species of whales called "sperm whales"?

The *sperm* in *sperm whale* is an 1830 abbreviation of *spermaceti*, which means "sperm of a whale." It was once believed that the waxy, gel-like substance in the snouts of these aquatic mammals was the seed of the male whale. Spermaceti was prized for its medicinal properties and was also used for candle oil. The material is, in fact, used by the whale to cushion its sensitive snout as it dives and has nothing to do with the animal's reproductive functions.

In 1471 the English alchemist Sir George Ripley (*c.* 1415–1490) suggested in "The Compound of Alchemy" that drinking a mixture of "whale sperm" and red wine would fight the chronic ills of growing old.

When and why do cats purr?

One of the great and endearing mysteries about cats is their use of purring to show affection; but they also purr when in danger or while giving birth or dying. Feral cats will even purr during a standoff with another cat. Cats only purr in the presence of humans or other cats. Because they are born blind and deaf, kittens depend on feeling the purring of their mothers to find comfort and a place to nurse. The kittens themselves start purring at one week. The purring of all adult cats derives from this mother-kitten experience, a form of communication often accompanied by kneading the paws as they did while nursing. Purring is by choice and is exclusive to domestic cats in that it occurs uninterrupted both during inhaling and exhaling. Big cats make a similar noise, but only while exhaling. Raccoons also produce a purring sound, but again only while exhaling. Cats choose to purr, but how is another question still a mystery to science.

How did "hightailing it" come to mean a rushed exit?

When people leave in a frantic hurry, they are "hightailing it." The expression grew out of America's Old West after cowboys noticed that both wild horses and deer would jerk their tails up high when frightened as they dashed to safety. The lifting of the tail by both animals was a signal to the rest of the herd that humans, and therefore danger, were near and that the creatures needed to run for their lives.

Quickies

Did you know...
- there have been no new animals domesticated in over four thousand years?
- the NFL use the skin of roughly three thousand head of cattle to supply enough leather for a one-year supply of footballs?
- dogs communicate with roughly ten different vocal sounds, while cats use over one hundred?
- Border Collies are the most intelligent dog breed, while Afghan Hounds are the least?
- a bee's honey is the only natural food that doesn't spoil?
- a snail can sleep for three years?
- all polar bears are left-handed (left-pawed)?
- butterflies taste with their feet?
- elephants are the only land animals that can't jump?
- rats multiply so quickly that in eighteen months, two rats could have over a million descendants?
- 85 percent of all Earth's plants and animals live in the sea?

baseball

Why is the Cleveland baseball team called the Indians?

Controversy generally surrounds the choice of Native American names for sports teams, but not in Cleveland. That city's baseball team is named in honour of one of their star players from the 1890s. He was Alex Sophalexis, a Penobscot Indian so respected that in 1914, one year after his death, Cleveland took the name "Indians" to commemorate Alex and what he had meant to their team.

Who is featured on the world's most valuable baseball card?

The most valuable baseball card in history was issued in 1909 and features Honus Wagner. One in mint condition sold for $110,000 in 1988. The reason it became so valuable is its scarcity — it was issued by the Sweet Caporal Cigarette Company, but Wagner, an eight-time National League batting champion, had it discontinued because he didn't want to promote smoking among children.

What number has been retired by every Major League baseball team and why?

In 1997, fifty years after he broke the colour barrier, every Major League baseball team retired Jackie Robinson's number 42. Active players who had the number before 1997 were allowed to wear it until they retired, but after that the number will never be worn again. Two who kept wearing number 42 are Mo Vaughn and Butch Huskey, both of whom chose the number as a tribute to Robinson.

Why do we say that someone in control has "the upper hand"?

Someone with the "upper hand" has the final say over a situation. When a group of youngsters gather to pick sides at a game of sandlot baseball, the two captains decide who chooses first when one of them grasps the bat at the bottom of the handle. The captains take turns gripping the bat one fist over the other until there is no more room. The last one to fully grip the bat handle has first choice. He has the upper hand.

Why do we say that someone who is sharp is "on the ball"?

To be "on the ball" means to be at the top of your game. We have all heard a pitcher's excuse of not having his "stuff" after a bad outing and wondered how that excuse would work with our bosses if we had a bad day. From the early days of baseball, when a pitcher couldn't find the spin and lost control, it's been said he had "nothing on the ball," which gave us "on the ball," meaning "he's in control."

What does the sign "No Pepper" mean at a baseball park?

The sign "No Pepper" is seen in many baseball dugouts and refers to a game played to warm up the players. During pepper, one player bunts grounders and hits line drives to a group of infielders standing about twenty feet away. The fielders play the ball then throw it back to the batter as quickly as possible, and he then attempts to hit those return throws. Pepper is banned when spectators are in the park for fear of injury.

Why is the L.A. baseball team called the Dodgers?

Before moving to Los Angeles, the Dodgers were based in Brooklyn, New York. The team originated in the nineteenth century when, because of the dangers of horse-drawn trolleys and carriages, the pedestrians of Brooklyn called themselves "trolley dodgers." Because most of their working-class fans had to dodge traffic on their walk to the games, the Brooklyn baseball team named themselves the Dodgers in their honour. When the team moved to L.A. in the 1950s, they took the name with them.

What are the seven different ways a baseball batter can reach first base?

In baseball, a batter can reach first base with a hit, or by being walked with four balls. He also goes to first if he is struck by a pitch, if the catcher interferes with his at bat, if the catcher drops the ball on strike three, or if the pitcher throws the ball out of the playing area. Finally, the seventh way a batter can get on base is if the baseball becomes stuck in the umpire's mask or equipment.

Why do the New York Yankees wear pinstripe baseball uniforms?

In 1925, thirty-year-old Babe Ruth was suffering from an intestinal disorder, and his weight ballooned to over 260 pounds. This embarrassed Yankees owner Jacob Rupert so much that he ordered the team to wear pinstripe uniforms in order to make the Bambino look thinner. Limited to 98 games that season because of surgery and suspensions, Babe Ruth still managed to hit .290 with 25 home runs.

Why is the warm-up area for baseball pitchers called a "bullpen"?

As early as 1809, the term *bullpen* referred to a stockade for holding criminals. In the 1870s, a roped-off area in the outfield for standing room was nicknamed the bullpen by the *Cincinnati Enquirer*. When relief pitchers were introduced into the game they took over that area to warm up, and in a stroke of brilliance the Bull Durham Tobacco Company erected a sign overhead to confirm it as the bullpen.

Why do we call a leg injury a "charley horse"?

The phrase *charley horse* has its roots in baseball. At the beginning of the twentieth century, groundskeepers often used old and lame horses to pull the equipment used to keep the playing field in top condition. The Baltimore Orioles had a player named Charley Esper, who, after years of injuries, walked with pain. Because his limp reminded his teammates of the groundskeeper's lame horse, they called Esper "Charley Horse."

Why is an erratic person called a "screwball"?

In baseball, when a pitcher throws a curveball, it breaks to a right-hander's left and a left-hander's right. Early in the twentieth century, the great Christy Mathewson came up with a pitch that broke in the opposite direction and completely baffled opposing batters, who called it a "screwball." It became a word used to describe anything eccentric or totally surprising — including the behaviour of human "screwballs."

Why is there a seventh-inning stretch during a baseball game?

While attending a baseball game in 1910, American President William Howard Taft stood up to stretch his legs between the top and bottom of the seventh inning. The crowd stood out of respect because they thought the president was leaving, then as he sat back down so did the crowd, and a tradition was born. The stretch became popular with vendors because it became a last chance to sell off their hot dogs and french fries before fans started drifting home.

Why is the position between second base and third base called "shortstop"?

Baseball began with four outfielders and only three infielders to guard the bases. In 1849, D.L. Adams (1814–1899) realized that three men could cover fly balls in the outfield and that by moving one of these outfield players to the infield he could keep a lot of ground balls from getting through by stopping them short, thus giving the new position its name: shortstop. Technically, this position is still an outfielder.

Why is an easily caught pop fly in baseball called a "can of corn"?

The legend is that in the days before supermarkets, small grocery store owners placed their tins of canned corn on the top shelves because they stored well and didn't sell as quickly as fresh corn. For most customers this system put the cans out of reach. The store owner or clerk needed a broomstick to reach up and topple the can of corn from the shelf and easily catch it by hand or in an apron.

Why are the pitcher and catcher collectively called "the battery"?

A *battery* is a military term for artillery and its use in baseball to describe a pitcher and a catcher alludes to the fact that the battery is the principal attack force for the small army of nine players on a baseball diamond. There is also an earlier theory that the baseball term derives from telegraphy where the word *battery* (also borrowed from artillery) defines the sender (pitcher) and the receiver (catcher).

How did the World Series get its name?

There is a myth that the World Series was named after the *New York World* newspaper, which was established in 1860 and was sold in 1930 after merging with the *Evening Telegram*, becoming the *New York World Telegram*. However, the *World* had nothing to do with naming baseball's annual classic. In 1884 a series of games between the National League and American Association champions was reported by the press as a contest to decide baseball's "World Champions." When the modern series began in 1903, the reference evolved (within all newspapers) into the "World Series" simply to hype the contest.

Who introduced the first catcher's mask?

The first baseball catcher's mask was a fencer's mask introduced by Harvard University's Fred Thayer in 1877. It wasn't until 1890 that the major leagues adopted the idea that all catchers should wear protective masks.

Who invented baseball's hand signals?

Baseball's hand signals evolved from the earliest days of the game. Consequently, there are many moments and persons involved in their development. For instance, in 1869, the Cincinnati Red Stockings began utilizing a system of hand signals based on military flag signals that soldiers had used while playing baseball during the Civil War. However, no one was more important to the development of these signals than a five-foot-four-inch, 148-pound centre fielder named William "Dummy" Hoy (1862–1961). Hoy was the first deaf baseball player to make the major leagues. One afternoon in 1889, as a centre fielder with the Washington Senators, Hoy set a major-league record by throwing out three base runners at home plate. His is a fascinating story, although not recognized in baseball's Hall of Fame. Hoy and his coaches and teammates developed an advanced system of hand gestures to overcome Hoy's deafness, which was a key impetus in the evolution of hand signals. Even umpires started physically indicating the batting count to communicate with Hoy. He couldn't hear the crowd, but Hoy's legacy is a major part of each and every ball game played to this day.

William Hoy played fourteen years in the majors, retiring in 1902 with a .288 lifetime batting average, 2,054 hits, and 726 runs batted in. His 597 career stolen bases still rank seventeenth in history.

During a regular nine-inning baseball game, more than a thousand silent instructions are given — from catcher to pitcher, coach to batter or fielder, fielder to fielder, and umpire to umpire.

What is a corked bat?

Some baseball players, like Sammy Sosa, believe that the spring from a corked bat adds distance to a struck ball. Even though physicists say this notion is nonsense, occasionally someone will try to use one. The basic method of corking a bat is to drill a straight hole into the top about one inch wide and ten inches deep. Then, after filling the cavity with cork, the player plugs the hole with a piece of wood and sands it smooth. A corked bat is illegal only if used in play.

Why does the letter *K* signify a strikeout on a baseball score sheet?

Early in baseball history, a man named Henry Chadwick designed the system we still use for keeping score. Because his system already had an overabundance of *Ss* scattered throughout his score sheet — safe, slide, shortstop, sacrifice, second base, etc. — he decided to use the last letter of *struck*, as in, "he struck out," rather than the first. And that's why *K* signifies a strikeout in baseball.

Why do we call someone who is left-handed a "southpaw"?

When the first baseball diamonds were laid out there were no night games. To keep the afternoon or setting sun out of the batters' eyes, home plate was positioned so that the hitter was facing east, which meant the pitcher was facing west. Most pitchers threw with their right arm, but the rare and dreaded left-hander's pitching arm was on the more unfamiliar south side, and he was referred to, with respect, as a southpaw.

What is the origin of the term *grand slam*?

Although in North America and Japan a grand slam is best known as a baseball homerun with the bases loaded, the term originated in the game of bridge, where it means winning all thirteen tricks in one hand. It's also used today when you win all four major tennis tournaments (Australian Open, French Open, U.S. Open, and Wimbledon) in one year. This application of "grand slam" was first used by sports journalist Allison Danzig in 1938 when he referred to the achievement of Australian Donald Budge, who had won all that season's major tennis tournaments.

How did *rhubarb* become baseball slang for a fight or argument?

Legendary Brooklyn Dodgers broadcaster Red Barber first used *rhubarb* on-air to describe a baseball altercation in 1943. He said he heard it from reporter Garry Shumacher, who picked it up from another reporter, Tom Meany, who learned it from an unnamed Brooklyn bartender. The anonymous bartender used it to describe an incident in his establishment when a Brooklyn fan shot a Giants fan.

Why don't baseball coaches wear civilian clothes like those in every other sport?

In the 1800s, baseball managers looked after travel and logistics, while a uniformed playing captain guided the team on the field. Captains who had retired from playing kept their uniforms on in case they were needed as a player. Eventually the manager's job expanded to include coaching, but tradition and a 1957 rule insisted that no one without a uniform could enter the playing area, including base coaches and the managers.

During the early twentieth century, the legendary Connie Mack managed the Philadelphia Athletics while wearing a suit and tie and never left the dugout.

Why is someone out of touch said to be "out in left field"?

"Out in left field" can mean to be misguided or lost, but it generally means to be out of touch with the action. In baseball, left field is generally no more remote then centre or right field, but in Yankee Stadium, when right fielder Babe Ruth was an active player, the choice outfield seats were near the Bambino. Fans in the right field stands derided those "losers" far from the action as being out in left field.

Why are extra seats in a gymnasium or open-air benches in a stadium called "bleachers"?

Quickies

Did you know ...
- that the Detroit Tigers baseball team acquired its name in 1901 when the club's ball players wore yellow-and-black socks? Sports editor Philip Reid thought the socks were similar to those worn by the Princeton University Tigers football team.
- the odds of becoming a professional athlete are 22,000 to 1?
- the odds of catching a ball at a major-league baseball game are 563 to 1?

Bleachers were used in a pinch as uncovered overflow seating from the grandstand before they became common at baseball and football games. The first recorded printed reference was in the *Chicago Tribune* on May 6, 1889. They were called "bleachers" because of their exposure to the sun. The folding seating at an inside gymnasium simply took its name from the open seating outside.

What is the advantage of "sitting in the catbird seat"?

"Sitting in the catbird seat" means you have an advantage over the opposition. The catbird is a thrush and, like its cousin, the mockingbird, perches among the highest branches of a tree and has a warning cry that resembles that of a cat. "Sitting in the catbird seat" originated in the American South in the nineteenth century and was regularly used on radio by Red Barber (1908–1992), the Brooklyn Dodgers' baseball announcer. Amused by the expression, Dodgers fan and humorist James Thurber (1894–1961) popularized the expression in a 1942 *New Yorker* story entitled "The Catbird Seat." As Thurber wrote, "'Sitting in the catbird seat' meant sitting pretty, like a batter with three balls and no strikes on him."

Quickies

Did you know ...
- the first humans to fly were the Marquis d'Arlandes and Pilatre de Rozier, who on November 21, 1783, flew over Paris in a hot-air balloon for 20 minutes?
- on July 4, 2002, Steve Fossett became the first solo balloonist to circumvent the globe when he landed in Australia?

the human
condition

Why are the derelicts of "skid row" said to be "on the skids"?

To be "on the skids" means to be down on your luck and still falling. In the early twentieth century, skids were greased wooden runways used on dirt roads by the forest industry to make it easier to move logs from the bush to the river or the sawmill. The depressed street these skid roads passed through in a lumber town were lined by bars and flophouses where the transients looking for work lived, and so it was called "skid row."

If you're being driven to "rack and ruin" where are you going?

Being driven to rack and ruin is sometimes expressed as "wreck and ruin," but either way you're in big trouble. *Rack* was the original reference and first appeared in the fifteenth century as a torture machine that encouraged victims to "rack their brains" to come up with the answers the inquisitors desired — otherwise they would be torn apart. So whether you're being driven to rack and ruin or wreck and ruin, unless you come up with the right answers, you're on your way to total destruction.

Why does the word *bully* have both good and bad meanings?

Today a bully is generally a description of a brute who intimidates someone weaker or more vulnerable, but in the United States the positive power of the presidency is often referred to as the "bully pulpit." In the 1500s, the word in its positive sense entered English from the Dutch *boel*, meaning "sweetheart" or "brother," but by the 1700s, the word's meaning deteriorated when it became the popular description of a pimp who protected his prostitutes with violence.

In North America, separated by the ocean, the word stayed closer to its positive origins and gave rise to the expression "bully for you," meaning "admirable or worthy of praise."

Why is a sleazy area of town known as the "red-light district"?

In the early days of the railroad, steam trains made quick stops in small towns for water or to pick up passengers and cargo. The crew would use this time to dash to the saloon or to make a quick visit to the local brothel. While doing their business, the trainmen would hang their lit red kerosene lanterns outside, so that the train wouldn't leave without them, and this is how areas practising prostitution became known as red-light districts.

Why are men and boys called "guys"?

Every November 5, the British celebrate the 1605 foiling of a plot to blow up the Parliament buildings by Guy Fawkes. As part of the festivities, an effigy of Fawkes dressed in rags and old mismatched clothes was paraded through the streets and then burned on a bonfire. By 1830, any man who was badly dressed was being referred to as a "guy," meaning he looked as dishevelled as the effigy of Guy Fawkes.

Why were young women from the Roaring Twenties called "flappers"?

The 1920s was a breakout decade for young women who'd just won the right to vote. The era evokes images of young flappers like the cartoon character Betty Boop, who was only sixteen, wildly dancing to the Charleston. They were called "flappers" because of the way they resembled a baby duck flapping its wings before being able to fly. *Flapper* is also a very old word meaning a girl too young to conceive.

Why is suddenly stopping a bad habit called "cold turkey"?

"Cold turkey" had the folk symbolism of stark circumstances without the trimmings (such as an unadorned sandwich made from the leftovers of a feast as a symbol of having seen better times) before it first appeared in print as a reference to drug withdrawal in 1921. The expression gained credence from withdrawing addicts' desperate appearance — cold, pale, pimply skin, making them resemble a cold, uncooked turkey.

Why are slaves to substance abuse called "addicts"?

After the Romans conquered most of Slavonia, the word *Slav* became synonymous with subjugated people. *Slav* gave us the word *slave*. Slavs were given as rewards to Roman warriors and were known by the Latin word for slaves — *addicts*. If your life is controlled by anything other than your own will, you are a slave to those circumstances. Eventually a person who was a slave to anything was called an addict.

Why do we say that something deteriorating is either "going" or "gone to pot"?

If a relationship or a career is going to pot, it means its glory days are over. The expression originated in 1542, long before refrigeration, and came from the urgency to save leftovers from a substantial meal before they went bad. As a metaphor, "going to pot" means that like the leftovers from a great meal, circumstances now assign the subject to something more humble, like a stew.

What does it mean to be "footloose and fancy-free"?

To be "footloose and fancy-free" means to be free from any responsibilities, or in other words, to be single. The expression started appearing in print around 1700 with *footloose* simply meaning your ankles were unshackled so you could go anywhere you wanted. *Fancy* was a sixteenth-century word for being attracted to someone of the opposite sex. If you weren't in love, you were fancy-free.

Why do we say that someone grieving is "pining"?

If a person is "pining away," he or she is tormented by longing or grief, because *pine*, in this case, has the same meaning as *pain*. In the early English language, Christians referred to the consequence of the tortures and punishment of hell as *pinian*. *Pinian* became both *pine* and *pain*. As time went on, *pine* acquired a softer meaning, more associated with Purgatory, that suggested languishing or wasting away, while *pain* retained its "hellish" origins. Today *pine* usually has a romantic context, such as pining for a lost love.

Why are young women and girlfriends sometimes referred to as "birds"?

Referring to young women as birds dates back to the Anglo-Saxons, who used the endearment *brid*, meaning "baby animal." *Brid* is the derivative of *bride*, and over time, the term created a number of similar words, all of them having to do with young women. During the 1920s, the flapper look was named after a baby duck. The cancan, popular in France in the 1890s, took its name from *canard*, which is French for "duck." When they danced, the girls displayed their tail feathers. The original dancers wore no underwear.

Why did Sinatra and the rest of the Rat Pack call women "broads"?

In the eighteenth century, poker cards were called broads because they were wider than those used for other card games. Around 1912, because they resembled poker cards, tickets of admission, meal tickets, and transit tickets were being called "broads." By 1914, because they were a different kind of meal ticket, pimps began calling their prostitutes "broads." Soon the term entered the underworld and was eventually picked up by entertainers.

How did the word *gay* come to mean "homosexual"?

The word *gay* is from the Old French *gai*, meaning "merry." It came to mean reckless self-indulgence in the seventeenth century, and it wasn't until the 1930s that its homosexual connotation came out of the prison system, where the expression "gay-cat" meant a younger, inexperienced man who, in order to survive, traded his virtue for the protection and experience of an older convict.

Why are homosexual men sometimes called "fags"?

"Faggot," the cruel label for homosexuals, actually began as a contemptuous slang word for a woman, especially one who was old and unpleasant. The reference was to a burden that had to be carried in the same manner as baggage and harks back to the word's original meaning. In the thirteenth century, a faggot was a bundle of wood or twigs bound together (derived from the Latin *fasces* via the French *fagot*, meaning "a bundle of wood"), such as the ones carried by heretics to feed the fires that would burn them at the stake. Heretics who recanted were required to wear an embroidered figure of a faggot on their sleeves. It wasn't until 1914 that the slang word *faggot* first appeared in the United States as a reference to a male homosexual, probably derived from the earlier reference to an annoying woman. The abbreviation *fag* surfaced in 1921.

There is a misconception that male homosexuals were called faggots because they were burned at the stake, but this notion is an urban legend. Homosexuals were sometimes burned alive in Europe, but by the time England made homosexuality a capital offence in 1533, hanging was the prescribed punishment.

The Yiddish word for male homosexual is *faygele*, which literally means "little bird."

Why do we say we have a "yen" for something that we crave?

Although a yen is also a type of Japanese currency, that meaning has nothing to do with an overwhelming urge; instead, the yen in question is from the Cantonese Chinese *yin-yan*. *Yin* means opium, and *yan* means craving. Brought to America in the mid-nineteenth century, the phrase entered English slang as "yen yen" and eventually just "yen," which early in the twentieth century took the meaning of a craving for anything.

Why are unrealistic fantasies called "pipe dreams"?

Pipe dreams are often schemes that just won't work. Like daydreams, pipe dreams dissolve like smoke rising into the air — which is appropriate, because the metaphor comes from smoking opium. It can be traced to print in the late nineteenth century, when it was fashionable for hedonists and the upper classes to escape reality through an opium pipe. Those "on the pipe" were experiencing opium-induced "pipe dreams."

How did teenagers become a separate culture?

The word *teenager* first appeared in 1941, but the emancipation of that age group began forty years earlier when new laws freed children from hard labour and kept them in school. Until then, there was only childhood and adulthood. At the age of thirteen, a girl became a woman and could marry or enter the workforce and a boy became a man. Today, a young adult or teenager is treated as a child with suppressed adult urges.

Why do we call tearful, overly sentimental people "maudlin"?

A lot of drinkers are referred to as "maudlin" when they become weak and overemotional and "cry in their beer." The word is a common British alteration of Magdalene, the surname of Mary, the woman who repented and was forgiven by Jesus Christ in Luke 7:37. In medieval paintings, as a sign of repentance, Mary Magdalene is most often shown with eyes swollen from weeping. The use of her name in terms of being maudlin, meaning "tearful sentimentality," was first recorded in 1631.

Why is someone susceptible to deception called a "sucker"?

A "sucker" is someone who is easily tricked or deceived, and the use of the word for this purpose dates from 1753 when settlers in the New World discovered a large-lipped tasty fish that was so easy to catch during their annual migrations that all you had to do was throw a hook into the water. This led to similarly easily "caught" naive humans being called "suckers."

What was the original "fate worse than death"?

Although today a "fate worse than death" could have many meanings, it began as a euphemism for rape or at least the loss of virginity. In 1781 Gibbon wrote in *The Decline and Fall of the Roman Empire*, "The matrons and virgins of Rome were exposed to injuries more dreadful, in the apprehension of chastity, than death itself." This suggests that the culture of the time considered that a victim of such a sexual crime had been dishonoured and was better off dead. The word *rapture*, meaning "ecstatic joy" is related to the word *rape* through the Latin *raptus*, meaning "carrying off" or "kidnapping."

Why do we call prostitutes "hookers"?

It's a myth that the camp followers of Union General Joseph Hooker gave us the popular euphemism for a prostitute. It's true they were called "Hooker's division," or "Hooker's reserves," but the word predates the American Civil War, as, of course, does the profession. It first appeared in 1845 as a reference to an area of New York known as "the Hook," where ladies of the night could be found in abundance.

What is the original meaning of the word *sex*?

The word *sex* is used in many different ways, and it seems somehow appropriate that it was introduced into English by the French as *sexe* during the fourteenth century. The Latin origin is *sexus* and was derived from the verb *secare*, meaning "to cut." The reason is that the Romans simply saw the world as cut or divided into two genders.

Why is a homeless women called a "bag lady"?

The homeless women who pick through garbage cans or roam the streets and subway stations searching for useful items have become a curious symbol of fierce independence within the urban areas of North America. Although they sleep in doorways or in makeshift shelters they are almost never beggars. The term *bag lady* is an abbreviation of "shopping bag lady," because that's where she carries most of her worldly possessions.

Why is a frightening or dishevelled old woman called a "hag"?

It would be simple to say that *hag* is just an abbreviation of *haggard*, which surfaced in 1567 as meaning "wild or unruly," but it's more interesting than that. Witches, who were usually homeless and gaunt and sometimes crippled, were said to be hedge-riders; they roamed the darkened roads by the edge of town and were reputed to live in two realities by straddling the hedges between the civilized safety of a small village and the real and imagined dangers from ghosts and demons who dwelled beyond. *Haga* is the original pronunciation of the "haw" in *hawthorn*, which is a major ingredient for pagan rituals and so was associated with witches or "hags," who often slept under the hedges.

Why are strangers who plead for help called "beggars"?

The name of a twelfth-century monk, Lambert de Begue, whose followers wandered the French countryside depending on handouts, gave us the verb *to beg*. When in A.D. 555 the Roman General Belisarius was stripped of his rank and wealth, he became one of history's most notable beggars, and his frequent cry, "Don't kick a man when he's down," gave us a maxim for all who are on very hard times.

Why do we say, "Beggars can't be choosers"?

The meaning of "Beggars can't be choosers" is clear: "Take it or leave it"! The proverb is ancient and first appeared in writing in 1546 in a book compiled by John Heyword as, "Folk always say beggars should be no choosers." Another related proverb in Heyword's book was "If wishes were horses, then beggars would ride."

Why are inhabitants of the Appalachian and Ozark mountains called "hillbillies"?

The term *hillbilly* generally describes an uneducated or rough-hewn inhabitant of the Ozark and Appalachian mountains of the United States. Hillbillies are a proud culture unto themselves with amazing music that reflects their harsh, isolated existence and the origins of their forefathers. The first hillbillies were the Scottish-Irish followers of Britain's King William III (1650–1702) whose Protestant Orangemen defeated the Roman Catholic allies of the former British king James II (1633–1701) at the Battle of the Boyne in Ireland in 1690. William III's followers were known as Billy Boys, and many of them immigrated to the hills of Appalachia before the American Revolution. It was during this time that British soldiers gave these people the name hillbillies, an informal reference to their previous history as supporters of King William of Orange.

In 1900 an article in the *New York Journal* described a hillbilly as a "free and untrammelled white citizen of Alabama who lives in the hills, has no means … drinks whiskey … and fires off his revolver."

In many remote Ozark areas, it is still possible to find people who speak English with a dialect that can be traced back to pre–American Revolution days.

Who were the first "rednecks"?

The concept of a redneck being a poor white farmer or labourer from the American South dates back to the late 1800s, but two hundred years earlier Scottish and Northern Irish Presbyterians were also known as rednecks. To show their rejection of the Church of England, they wore red cloths around their necks. The South African Boers called British soldiers rednecks for the same reason Southerners got the title. Only the fair skin of their necks was exposed to the burning sun.

How valid is the theory of six degrees of separation?

Six degrees of separation is the theory that anyone on Earth can be connected to any other person on the planet through a chain of five acquaintances. The phrase was inspired by an

article in Psychology Today that reported a 1967 study by Stanley Milgram (1933–1984), an American social psychologist who tested the theory by having strangers randomly send packages to people several thousand miles away with only the intended recipient's name and occupation as an address. They were instructed to pass the package on to someone they knew on a first-name basis who was most likely personally familiar with the target. That person would do the same and so on until the package was delivered to the intended recipient. The result was that it took between five and seven intermediaries to get a package delivered.

The theory was first proposed by Hungarian writer Frigyes Karinthy (1887–1938) in a 1929 short story called "Chains." After a twenty-year study begun in 1950, mathematicians from IBM and the Massachusetts Institute of Technology were unable to confirm the theory to their own satisfaction.

In 2001, Duncan Watts of Columbia University researched the six-degree theory using email as the package. When he reviewed the data collected by 48,000 senders and 19 targets in 157 countries, Professor Watts found that the average number of intermediaries was six.

In 1990, American playwright John Guare had his play *Six Degrees of Separation* produced on Broadway. Starring Swoozie Kurtz and Courtenay B. Vance, it dramatized the true-life story of a young black man who conned upper-middle-class couples in Manhattan into believing he was the son of actor Sidney Poitier. The story was later turned into a movie starring Donald Sutherland and Will Smith. Around the same time a trio of college buddies, inspired by the six-degree theory, dreamed up Six Degrees of Kevin Bacon, the vastly popular trivia game.

Why is an effeminate man called a "sissy" or a "priss"?

Odds & Oddities
- The chance of giving birth to a genius is 1 in 250.
- The odds of dating a supermodel are 88,000 to 1.
- The odds of dating a millionaire are 215 to 1.
- The odds of becoming a saint are 20,000,000 to 1.
- The odds that a first marriage will survive without separation or divorce for fifteen years are 1.3 to 1.
- The chance of being audited by the tax department is 1 in 100.

Since 1887, when a male is unwilling or fails to meet the challenges of being a robust young man, he has sometimes been called a sissy. The word *sis* is an abbreviation of *sister*. *Sissy* was often used as an endearment for a female sibling. On the other hand, *priss* is an 1895 merger of the words *precise* or *prim* and *sis*.

lovers and loving

How did Valentine become the patron saint of lovers?

In A.D. 270, the mad Roman emperor Claudius II outlawed marriage because he believed married men made for bad soldiers. Ignoring the emperor, Bishop Valentine continued to marry young lovers in secret until his disobedience was discovered and he was sentenced to death. As legend has it, he fell in love with the jailer's blind daughter, and through a miracle he restored her sight. On his way to execution, he left her a farewell note ending, "From Your Valentine."

Why is a small personal case for mementos called a "locket"?

Lockets are usually worn on chains around the neck and carry small personal items, photos, or memories of a loved one. They are the reason a small clipping or tress of hair is called a "lock of hair." The word *locket* probably arrived in England in 1066 with the invasion of William the Conqueror (*c.* 1028–1087), who would have used the Old French word *loquet* to describe a small lock or latch. The small ornamental case with a hinged cover and latch, as we know it today, surfaced in 1679.

Why do some women wear beauty marks?

Beauty marks highlight facial features, but they began as beauty patches to cover the scars left by a seventeenth-century smallpox epidemic. As the epidemic subsided, women continued using beauty marks as a silent language aimed at potential suitors. One near the mouth signalled a willingness to flirt, one on the right cheek meant she was married, one on the left cheek meant she was engaged, while a beauty mark near the corner of the eye meant "Let's do it."

What does a handkerchief have to do with "wearing your heart on your sleeve"?

When fifteenth-century French sailors brought back linen head coverings worn by Chinese field workers as protection from the sun, they called them *couvrechef*, or "head covering," which when Anglicized became *kerchief*. Because they were carried in the hand, they became hand kerchiefs. Women began giving scented handkerchiefs to suitors, which the suitors then tucked under their sleeves in a ritual known as "wearing his heart on his sleeve."

Why is the word *cuckold* used to describe the husband of an unfaithful wife?

Cuckold is a centuries-old metaphor for a deceived husband and is taken from the habits of the European cuckoo bird, which, in the spring, lays a single egg in the nest of some other unsuspecting bird to be hatched and then fed among its own chicks. When a husband has been cuckolded, his nest has been violated by another, who might well have left behind his own offspring.

Why do we say that someone special is "the apple of your eye"?

For centuries it was believed that the pupil of the eye was solid and spherical like an apple, so that's what they called it. Therefore, anything or anyone compared to it would indeed be very special. In the Bible, the expression is part of this song spoken by Moses: "He found him in a desert land, and in the howling waste of the wilderness; he encircled him, he cared for him, and kept him as the apple of His eye."

Why do we say that someone seeking favour has put his or her "best foot forward"?

If you're trying to impress someone it's wise to put your "best foot forward." This means you are on your best behaviour and your manners, charm, and deportment have been arranged and calculated to win favour. When European men wore short pantaloons with tight stockings conforming to the muscular shape of their legs they would vainly stand with their most attractive leg in a forward position to interest women and impress other men with their strength. They would place their best foot forward.

Why do we use Xs as kisses at the bottom of a letter?

During medieval times, most people could neither read nor write, and even those who could sign their names were required to follow it with an X, symbolizing the cross of St. Andrew, or the contract would be invalid. Those who couldn't write their names still had to end the contract with the X to make it legal. To prove their intention, all were required to kiss the cross, which through time is how the X became associated with a lover's kiss.

Why is embracing and kissing called "spooning"?

Spooning may be an old-fashioned word, but it still means "cuddling." This use of the word comes from Wales, where in order to ensure that a young suitor kept his hands off their daughter, her parents required that he carve a wooden spoon while courting. Some of these spoons were quite creative and elaborate, which gave evidence of the young couple's continuing virtue.

The Scots might have considered this custom after an 1868 study revealed that 90 percent of Scottish brides were pregnant the day of their weddings.

Why do humans kiss?

The average person spends two weeks kissing during his or her lifetime. The romantic or erotic kiss is a sensual genetic memory search for compatibility, whether on the lips or elsewhere, and is revealed to the brain through smell and taste. Kissing originated from prehistoric mothers breast-feeding, then chewing and pushing food into their infants' mouths with their tongues. Sigmund Freud (1856–1939) described the kiss as "an unconscious repetition of infantile delight in feeding."

Smell is the primary ingredient of the kissing ritual for some cultures, such as the Inuit, who believe that exhaled breath reveals a person's soul. Exchanging breath in this sense is a spiritual union. This concept has a parallel in Christian dogma (Genesis 2:7), which reveals that God infused the spirit of life into his creatures by breathing into them.

Hygiene has a lot to do with the success of a romantic kiss. In medieval England, it was common during a town fair for a young woman to pick an apple and fill it with cloves. She would then approach a man she had chosen for romance and offer him the apple. After he ate it, the man would have his breath sweetened by the cloves, making a kiss from him at least palatable.

Of the many different kinds of kisses (for lovers, friends, family, or babies), one of the most interesting is the ceremonial kiss. This type is common in European countries or high society, where dignitaries offer each other a quick kiss on each side of the face. This custom isn't simply good manners; it's an ancient political gesture symbolizing goodwill between different peoples or tribes.

Finally, there is the Mafia kiss of death, which was inspired by the New Testament and is related to the kiss Judas gave to Jesus Christ when he betrayed him to the authorities.

Why do we say someone is "head over heels" when in love?

When people fall "head over heels" in love, their world has been turned upside down by romance. The word *fallen* suggests helplessness, and the metaphorical "head over heels" is intended to expand the illusion. However, consider that having your head over your heels is, in fact, the normal standing position! You can blame American frontiersman, congressman, and Alamo martyr Davy Crockett (1786–1836), among others, for turning the phrase around. When the expression first appeared around 1350, it was "heels over head." In his 1834 autobiography, Crockett wrote: "I soon found myself 'head over heels' in love with this girl." So the phrase has been "head over heels" ever since.

Why is unconsummated love called "platonic"?

Greek philosopher Plato observed his teacher Socrates' great but non-sexual love for young men, and concluded that the purest form of love exists only within the mind. Ideal love's perfection is spiritual, and that perfection is often destroyed by a sexual act. Eventually, Plato's philosophy on love was expanded to include women. "Platonic love" entered popular use in English around 1630.

Why do we shake our heads for "no" and nod for "yes"?

According to Charles Darwin, the nodding of our heads forward for "yes" and shaking for "no" comes from our infant nursing habits. When the baby nods forward it's seeking its mother's breast, while turning its head away or to the side says it's not hungry or in need of comfort. Support for this theory comes from the fact that a baby born deaf and blind will follow this same pattern of nodding and shaking the head into adulthood.

How did the terms of divorce evolve?

Divorce to the Athenians and Romans was allowed whenever a man's like turned to dislike. In the seventh century it was recorded that Anglo-Saxon men could divorce a wife who was barren, rude, oversexed, silly, habitually drunk, overweight, or quarrelsome. Throughout history, in societies where men were paid dowries, divorce favoured the husband; however, in matrilineal societies where the woman was esteemed, mutual consent was required. The word *alimony* means "nourishment."

Quickies

Did you know ...
- the longest kiss on record lasted 130 hours and 2 minutes?
- married men tip better than unmarried men?

flowers

How did the Dutch flower the tulip get its name?

Holland is their cultivated home, but tulips originated in Iran. In the sixteenth century tulips were introduced to Europe by the Turks, who gave them their name because the fully opened flower resembles a turban. The Turks called them *tulbent*, a reference to the gauze used to wrap a turban. That word came to English through the French interpretation *tulipe*, which when anglicized became *tulip*.

How did the dandelion and the daisy get their names?

The dandelion and the daisy are both named for a particular physical characteristic. The English daisy, with its small yellow centre and white- or rose-coloured rays, closes at night and reopens with daylight like the human eye, and so it was named the "day's eye." The dandelion, because of its sharp, edible leaves, was named by the French *dent de lion*, the "tooth of a lion."

Who started the custom of giving a dozen roses to a lover?

It was the Persians who initiated the idea of communicating through flowers, and the custom was introduced to Europe courtesy of Sweden's King Charles XII (1682–1718), who lived as an exile in Turkey in the early eighteenth century. In Persia every flower had a meaning. This notion captured the hearts of Europeans, who began carrying out complete conversations by exchanging different kinds of flowers. In the language of flowers, roses are said to communicate love and passion, so a dozen is like shouting out loud!

As important as roses are to Valentine's Day, the real flower of the day ought to be the violet. Legend says that violets grew outside the window area of the prison cell occupied by St. Valentine prior to his martyrdom in A.D. 269. It was said that he crushed up the petals of the violets to make ink for writing letters.

How important is the colour in a gift of flowers?

Throughout time flowers sent as gifts have had unspoken meanings that are steeped in centuries of tradition. For example, red flowers represent love, respect, passion, or courage. Pink flowers express perfect happiness, grace, thankfulness, or admiration and are an appeal for trust. Yellow flowers mean friendship, joy, jealousy, or an appeal for affection. White flowers signify innocence, purity, secrecy, or silence, while those that are peach or coral send a message of enthusiasm, desire, joyful modesty, or shyness. Purple is a declaration of passionate hope and fidelity.

Different kinds of flowers also send the recipient a personal message. Roses say, "Know that I love you." Carnations affirm, "You are beautiful and I am proud of you." Daffodils insist, "You are a brave and good person." Chrysanthemums proclaim, "I am faithful to you." Gladioli admit, "I admire your character." Irises inform, "I send my compliments and congratulations." Orchids declare, "You are in my heart." Snapdragons reveal, "I desire you." Sunflowers broadcast, "My thoughts are pure." Tulips announce, "I am declaring that I love you."

Quickies

Did you know ...

- the most common name in the world is Mohammed?
- that the name of every continent on Earth ends with the same letter it began with?
- the strongest muscle in the body is the tongue?
- it is impossible to lick your elbow?
- that Easter Island is so called because it was discovered by Europeans on Easter Sunday, 1722?
- that "housewarming parties" have their origin in Scotland, where embers from the fireplace of an old home were carried to start the fire in a new house?

home, hearth, and family

What exactly is a family circle?

When the early Normans brought fire indoors they built semicircular open fireplaces. To keep warm at night or when the air was cool, the family would sit in a semicircle opposite the one formed by the hearth, creating a complete circle where they would spend time telling stories or singing songs within what they called the "family circle." When neighbours were included, it became "a circle of friends."

Why do we say, "Goodnight, sleep tight"?

Sometime during the sixteenth century, British farmers moved from sleeping on the ground to sleeping in beds. These beds were little more than straw-filled mattress tied to wooden frames with ropes. To secure the mattress before sleeping, you pulled on the ropes to tighten them, and that's when they began saying, "Goodnight, sleep tight."

What is the difference between a settee, a divan, and a couch?

A settee, a divan, and a couch are all parlour furniture designed for sitting. *Settee* entered the language from the German *setlaz*, which means simply "seat." *Divan* is from the Persian word for "council of rulers" and was given as a name to an armless couch. The word *couch* originally referred to a bed and comes from the French word *coucher*, meaning "to lie in place" … like "Voulez-vous coucher avec moi."

Why is socializing called "hobnobbing"?

When the Normans conquered England, they introduced the open hearth for cooking and heating. At each corner of the hearth was a large container for heating liquids. It was called a "hob." Near the fire was a table where the hob was placed for convenient serving. They called this table a "nob." When friends gathered by the warmth of the fire, they drank warm beer from the hob, which was served on the nob, and so they called it "hobnobbing."

Why is going to bed called "hitting the hay"?

When going to sea, early sailors had to provide their own bedding. This need was catered to by merchants on the docks, who, for a shilling, sold the seamen crude canvas sacks stuffed with hay. When heading off to sleep, a sailor would announce that he was going to "hit the hay." Although less crude than those coarse canvases, early North American settlers also used hay to stuff mattresses and pillows, so when going to bed, they too would "hit the hay."

Why are nightclothes called "pyjamas"?

In the sixteenth century, the first nightgowns appeared as loose-fitting, full-length unisex garments for warmth in bed. In the eighteenth century the negligee became a lounging garment for women, while a nightshirt with loose-fitting pants called pyjamas replaced the long gown for men. Pyjamas were modelled after harem pants and were imported from Iran, using the Persian words *pae*, "leg garment," and *jama*, "clothing."

Why is the entrance to a house called a "threshold"?

Today, crossing the threshold signifies a figurative beginning, but a thousand years ago, a threshold was just the floorboard in the doorway of a country cottage. *Threshing* is the process of separating wheat from the straw. While the wheat was stored, straw, among other things, was used to cover both slate and dirt floors. The board in the doorway that held the straw inside was called the *threshold* — holder of the straw.

How did the expression "dead as a doornail" originate?

When metal nails were introduced to construction, they were hand tooled, which made them very rare and very expensive. When an aging house or barn with metal nails was torn down it was important to collect and reuse the nails. Because previous carpenters had bent the sharp end of the doornails for safety and to stabilize them against constant opening and closing, they were useless for recycling, which made them "dead."

Why is the shelf above a fireplace called a "mantelpiece"?

In the seventeenth century it was both fashionable and practical for men and women to wear sleeveless cloaks for protection from the elements. These cloaks were called *mantles* from the Latin *mantellum,* meaning "cloak." Fireplaces were designed with a shelf and hooks so that these mantels or cloaks, as well as other wet clothes, could be hung and dried by the heat of the flames. First called a *manteltree*, the frame and shelf began being referred to as a mantelpiece in 1686 and have kept that name down through the centuries.

Why is a surplus of anything called a "backlog"?

While a backlog of work might be a burden, it's better than no work at all, and in business it guarantees survival. Before stoves, or even matches, the kitchen fireplace was kept burning around the clock. This was done by placing a huge log, or back log, behind the fire that would keep smoldering once the flames had died down during the night. The embers from the back log could then ignite a new fire in the morning.

How did the word *curfew* come to mean "stay in your homes"?

The word *curfew* comes from the French *couvre-feu,* which means "cover-fire," and was brought to England by William the Conqueror. The original Curfew Law minimized the tremendous risk of fire by ordaining that a bell be rung at eight o'clock each evening, signalling everyone to either extinguish or cover their home fires. During political unrest, the same curfew bell signalled the public to clear the streets and stay in their homes for the night.

What's the origin of the word *window*?

Early Norse homes were simply designed and often included a stable area for livestock under the same roof as the humans. In the winter, because the tightly shut doors trapped stale air and smoke from the indoor fires, they built holes high on the walls and in the roof for ventilation. They called these openings *vindr auga*, which means "the wind's eye." When the British copied this practice they modified *wind's eye* to *window*.

How did the toilet get its name?

Toilet seems an odd name for the bathroom's chief plumbing fixture, but it makes sense when you consider that since the seventeenth century, *toilette* meant a lady's dressing room. The chief purpose of the room was for cleaning up or changing clothes. The other business was done in an "outhouse." When a lavatory became attached during the early nineteenth century and the room changed its main purpose, it not only kept its name, *toilette*, but applied it to the regal new sitting device. The beauty care and implements or "toiletries" assembled there were so named because they were placed on a fabric table cover called a *toile*. A toile, like a doily, is a decorative netted cloth.

Why do wives call money from their husbands "pin money"?

"Pin money" is an English phrase used to describe extra cash set aside for wives to run the household. During the fourteenth and fifteenth centuries, pins were rare enough to be sold on just two days of the year, January 1 and 2. Although through time pins became more commonplace and far less expensive, the British courts still enforce any prenuptial agreement or property lien demanded by the wife as the "pin money charge."

Why is listening in on a private conversation called "eavesdropping"?

In medieval times, houses didn't have roof gutters to carry off rainwater; instead they had "eaves," which are the lower wide projecting edges of a sloping roof. These eaves protected the mud walls from damage from the rain dropping from the roof. If, during a sudden shower, someone sought cover by standing under an eave, they could hear everything that the people inside were saying. They were "eavesdropping."

Why does a man refer to his wife as his "better half"?

Most men call their wives their "better halves" because they believe it, but the expression comes from an ancient Middle Eastern legend. A Bedouin man had been sentenced to death, so his wife pleaded with the tribal leader that because they were married, she and her husband had become one, and that to punish one half of the union would also punish the other half who was innocent. The court agreed, and the man's life was saved by his "better half."

Why are women referred to as the "distaff" side of a family?

In medieval times, the marriage bargain held men responsible for the physical labour outside of the home, while the women provided nourishment and comfort inside. A *distaff* was a rod used to hold wool during weaving and became a symbol of honour and respect to the value of a woman's work toward the family's well-being. The equal to the female "distaff-side" is the male "spear-side."

Why is the family non-achiever called a "black sheep"?

Most families have at least one embarrassing loafer who is referred to by the others, and sometimes by himself, as the "black sheep." A black sheep is considered worthless because, unlike the majority of sheep, its dark wool cannot be dyed. Although it takes as much time and nurturing to raise a black sheep as it does any other, its wool has very little market value, making raising it almost a waste of time to the shepherd.

Why is a vulgar woman called a "fishwife" while a respectable married woman is a "housewife"?

From its Anglo-Saxon root *wif*, *wife* simply means "woman." A woman's profession, such as a policewoman or chairwoman, often acknowledges her gender in her job title. *Housewife* and *midwife* are among the few titles like this to have survived from medieval times, but at one time, an alewife owned a pub, an oysterwife sold oysters, and a fishwife sold fish. She picked up her vulgarity from the men on the waterfront.

What is the difference between a parlour and a drawing room?

If you are invited to a stately home for dinner, you are first directed into the parlour, where, through introductions and conversation, you mingle and become acquainted with your host and other guests. It's called a parlour after the French word *parler*, meaning "to talk." After the meal, you retire to the drawing room for liqueurs and cigars. The name "drawing room" is an abbreviation of "withdrawing room" and was originally for men only.

Why do we call money saved for a rainy day a "nest egg"?

The term *nest egg* usually refers to savings that compounds or grows with interest or through investments. The expression is an old one and comes from a trick poultry farmers use to increase a hen's egg-laying ability. By placing a false egg in her nest, the farmer fools the chicken into laying more eggs than she otherwise would, meaning more money for the farmer, which he credits to his nest egg.

What is the origin of the thimble?

A thimble is more than a token in a game of Monopoly. Its true name is *thumb-bell*, and before the seventeenth century, when it was invented in Holland, pushing a sewing needle through skins or fabric often required the use of a small block of wood or bone. Thimbles have a romantic history, and during the Victorian era thimbles were often love tokens. They were even used to measure drinks, which gave us the expression, "Just a thimbleful."

A person who collects thimbles is a digitabulist.

Quickies

Did you know ...
- the word *bungalow* is from the Hindi word *bangla*, meaning "Bengalese," and refers to a low, thatched house in the Bengal style?
- *Igloo* is a Canadian English word derived from the Inuit word *igdlo*, meaning "house"?
- that in Calcutta, 79 percent of the population live in one-room houses?

everyday customs
and convention

Why do we say "Hello" when we answer the telephone?

The first word used to answer the phone was the nautical greeting "Ahoy" because the first regular phone system was in the maritime state of Connecticut. Alexander Graham Bell, the inventor, answered with the Gaelic "Hoy," but it was Thomas Edison's greeting of "Hello," an exclamation of surprise dating back to the Middle Ages, that caught on, and so we answer today with, "Hello?"

Why do we say "Goodbye" or "So long" when leaving someone?

The word *goodbye* is a derivative of the early English greeting "God be with you," or, as it was said then, "God be with ye." Over the years its abbreviated written form and pronunciation became "goodbye." As for "so long," it came to Britain with soldiers who had spent time in Arabic-speaking countries, where the perfect expression of goodwill is *salaam*. The unfamiliar word to the English men sounded like, and then became, "so long."

What's the origin of the parting wish "Godspeed"?

The word *Godspeed* has nothing to do with haste. The archaic meaning of the word *speed*, as used in this case, meant "succeed" or "prosper." Just as *goodbye* came from "God be with you," *Godspeed* is an abbreviation of "May God speed you" and was first heard in the late fifteenth century. A modern translation might be "May God grant you success."

Why are men's buttons on the right and women's on the left?

Decorative buttons first appeared around 2000 B.C., but they weren't commonly used as fasteners until the sixteenth century. Because most men are right-handed and generally dressed themselves, they found it easier to fasten their buttons from right to left. However, wealthy women were dressed by servants, who found it easier to fasten their mistresses' clothes if the buttons were on her left. It became convention and has never changed.

Why do baby boys wear blue and girls wear pink?

The custom of dressing baby boys in blue clothes began in around 1400. Blue was the colour of the sky and therefore heaven, so it was believed that the colour warded off evil spirits. Male children were considered a greater blessing than females, so it was assumed that demons had no interest in girls. It took another hundred years before girls were given red as a colour, which was later softened to pink.

Why is a handshake considered to be a gesture of friendship?

The Egyptian hieroglyph for "to give" is an extended hand. That symbol was the inspiration for Michelangelo's famous fresco "The Creation of Adam," which is found on the ceiling of the Sistine Chapel. Babylonian kings confirmed their authority by annually grasping the hand of a statue of their chief god, Marduk. The handshake as we know it today evolved from a custom of Roman soldiers, who carried daggers in their right wristbands. They would extend and then grasp each other's weapon hand as a non-threatening sign of goodwill.

Where did the two-fingered peace sign come from?

The gesture of two fingers spread and raised in peace, popularized in the 1960s, is a physical interpretation of the peace symbol, an inverted or upside-down *Y* within a circle, which was designed in 1958 by members of the anti-nuclear Direct Action Committee. The inverted *Y* is a combination of the maritime semaphore signals for *N* and *D*, which stood for "nuclear disarmament."

Where did the rude Anglo-Saxon one-fingered salute come from?

When the outnumbered English faced the French at the Battle of Agincourt, they were armed with a relatively new weapon, the longbow. The French were so amused that they vowed to cut off the middle finger of each British archer. When the longbows won the day, the English jeered the retreating French by raising that middle finger in a gesture that still means, among other things, "in your face."

When is it incorrect to formally address a person as Mr., Mrs., Miss, or Ms.?

Mr., *Mrs.*, *Miss*, and *Ms.* are courtesy titles for people without legitimate social titles or letters of accomplishment or any other individual means of identification such as a doctorate or other letters of scholastic achievement within their official recognition. These include military and governmental honours or any other circumstance where letters are legally attached to the name. Included in these are "Jr." or a numerical identification such as "III" or "the third." When these are included in the introduction or address, it is improper to also use the less significant Mr., Mrs., Miss, or Ms.

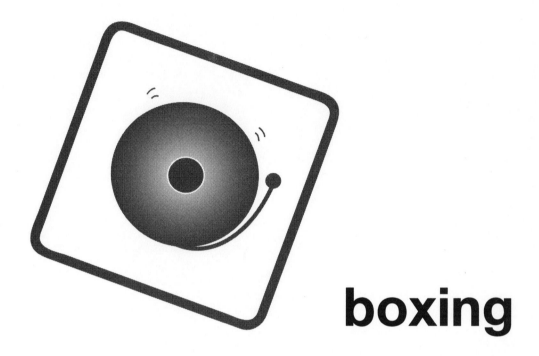

boxing

Why do we say a person isn't "up to scratch"?

During the early days of bare-knuckle boxing, a line was scratched across the centre of the ring, dividing it into two halves. This is where the fighters met to start the contest, or where they "toed the line" to begin each round. If, as the fight progressed, one of the boxers was unable to toe the line without help from his seconds, it was said he had failed to come "up to scratch."

Why is a boxing ring square?

In the days of bare-knuckle boxing, before modern rules, a circle was drawn in the dirt and prizefighters were ringed by the fans. When one of the men was knocked out of that circle, he was simply pushed back into the ring by the crowd. In 1867, the Marquess of Queensbury introduced a number of rules to boxing, including three-minute rounds and a roped-off square, which fans continued to call the "boxing ring."

Why do we call the genuine article "the real McCoy"?

In the 1890s, a great boxer known as Kid McCoy couldn't get the champion to fight him, and so to seem beatable, he began to throw the odd bout, and fans never knew if they'd see the "real McCoy." The plan worked, and he became the welterweight champion of the world. Once, while in a bar, McCoy was challenged by a drunken patron who didn't believe that he was the great boxer, and McCoy flattened him. When the man came around, he declared that the man who had knocked him out was indeed the "real McCoy."

Why is a fistfight called "duking it out"?

"Duking it out" and "Put up your dukes" are both expressions from the early 1800s when bare-knuckle boxing was considered a lower-class activity. When Frederick Augustus, the Duke of York, took up the sport, English high society was shocked. The Duke gained so much admiration from the other boxers, however, that they began referring to their fists as their "dukes of York" and eventually as their "dukes."

What's the origin of the expressions "rough and ready" and "rough and tumble"?

Both "rough and ready" and "rough and tumble" came from the sport of boxing. *Rough* still means "crude," so "rough and ready" meant a semi-pro or amateur who, although unpolished and perhaps not as well trained as he should be, was still considered good enough to enter the ring. If a contest was "rough and tumble," both fighters had agreed to throw away the rules, which led to a lot of tumbling.

Why when asking for a loan might you say you need a "stake" to carry you over?

Asking for a stake means you need to see money to continue with a project. The expression comes from the early days of bare-knuckle boxing, when promoters often stiffed the fighters by absconding with the gate money before the count of ten. To ensure that they'd be paid, boxers insisted that their share of the money be placed in a pouch on a stake near the ring, where they could see it during the bout. This was known as "stake money."

Poetic Origins of Classic Movie Titles

Chariots of Fire is from the hymn "Jerusalem," which uses William Blake's poem "And did those feet in ancient time," in turn inspired by the Bible, II Kings 6:17:

Bring me my bow of burning gold!
Bring me my arrow of desire!
Bring me my spear! O clouds unfold!
Bring me my Chariot of Fire!

Music to the hymn was written by Hubert Parry.

Inherit the Wind is from the Bible, Proverbs 11:29:

He that troubleth his own house shall inherit the wind;
And the fool shall be servant to the wise heart.

Gone With the Wind is taken from the third stanza of the poem "Cynara" by Ernest Dowson: "I have forgot much, Cynara! gone with the wind."

From Here To Eternity is a line from Yale's drinking chorus, "The Whiffenpoof Song": "Doomed from here to eternity ..."

One Flew Over The Cuckoo's Nest is from a nursery rhyme:

Wire, briar, limber, lock,
Three Geese in a flock,
One flew East, one flew West,
One flew over the cuckoo's nest.

show business

Why do actors say, "Break a leg" when wishing each other good luck?

"Break a leg" comes from the First World War, when, before flying, German airmen wished each other a "broken neck and a broken leg." Considering the dangers of combat with primitive aircraft, this was preferable to losing your life, which was all too common. After the war, the phrase was picked up by actors in the German theatre and eventually adopted by the British and American stages, where it was abbreviated to "break a leg."

Why are a vocal restraint and a joke both called a "gag"?

The original meaning of *gag* was to prevent someone from speaking, either by covering the mouth or through a legal restraint such as a gag order. The jocular use of *gag* originated in the theatre to describe times when an actor inserted an unscripted, and often humorous, line into a play. It was called a gag because the ad lib often caused fellow actors to lose their focus and become speechless.

Why is natural ability called "talent"?

In the ancient world a *talent* was a unit of weight used to value gold and silver. Today's use of the word comes from the Book of Matthew, wherein three servants are given equal amounts of money, or talent, by their master. Two invest wisely and profit while the third buries his and doesn't. That parable is how *talent* came to refer to the natural gifts we are all born with. The moral of the tale is that we must use our talents wisely or we will fail.

What's the purpose of a catchword?

Catchword is from the world of print. Two hundred years ago, the last word on a page to be turned began being routinely repeated at the top of the next page to smooth the transition. Newspapers followed by repeating the last word of an article when it was picked up deeper into the paper. In the theatre, a catchword is the cue for the next actor to start his lines. A catchphrase is a political or commercial slogan.

The first use of catchwords in a printed book was *Tacitus*, by John de Spira (1469).

Why when we memorize something do we say, "I know it by heart"?

Saying that we have learned something "by heart" means, of course, that we have committed it to memory, which more than likely involved a process of repetition, called learning by rote. *Rote* is from *rota*, the Latin word for wheel, meaning that to memorize something we turn it over in our minds many times before knowing it by heart. The ancient Greeks believed that it was the heart, and not the brain, where thoughts were held.

Why do we call a bad actor a "ham" and silly comedy "slapstick"?

In the late nineteenth century, second-rate actors couldn't afford cold cream to remove their stage makeup, so they used ham fat and were called "hamfatters" until early in the twentieth century, when these bad actors were simply called "hams." Physical comedy became known as "slapstick" because of its regular use of crude sound effects: two sticks were slapped together offstage to accentuate a comic's onstage pratfall (*prat* being an Old English term for "buttocks").

Why does *deadpan* mean an expressionless human face?

The word *deadpan* was first used in print by the *New York Times* in 1928 as a description of the great silent film comic Buster Keaton, who was also known as "The Great Stone Face." The theatrical slang use of *pan* for face dates to the fourteenth century. *Dead*, of course, means it's not moving, or it's expressionless.

Pancake makeup for an actor's pan was introduced in 1937 by Max Factor.

Why is a theatre ticket booth called a "box office"?

In early Elizabethan times, theatres admitted the general public into the ground-level "pit" without charge. Before the play began, a plate was passed through the mostly standing pit audience and, like a church collection, an established amount was expected for different seats and rows. For the wealthy patrons who bought private balcony boxes for the season, tickets were conveniently held near the entrance in what was called the box office.

Why is making it up as you go called "winging it"?

"Winging it" usually implies the same thing as having your first swimming lesson by being thrown into the deep end of a pool. It takes courage and sometimes ability you didn't know you had. It's an exercise familiar to good salespeople. The expression derives from an unprepared stage actor standing in the wings and cramming desperately before hearing a cue that will force him onstage.

Why is it bad luck to whistle backstage in a theatre?

Whistling backstage became bad luck during a time in England when stagehands were most often sailors without a ship. The curtain, flies, and props were moved manually by a system of ropes, so the sailors communicated as they did at sea: by whistling. If someone not involved in the intricate backstage manoeuvres were to whistle, a stagehand might take it as a cue, which could be disastrous for the production.

Why doesn't an "ovation" signify a "triumph"?

A triumph was a Roman celebration of a military victory over an enemy of the state. The victorious commander rode a chariot in a grand parade with his entire army and the booty and slaves he had won. An ovation was a less elaborate honour for a general who had won victory without bloodshed, perhaps by treaty or reason. He was denied a chariot and either walked or rode a horse during a less imposing ceremony.

Why does a good punchline make
a comedian "pleased as punch"?

Radio comedian Fred Allen once said that a good joke should have the same impact as a punch in the belly. The punchline is the twist that makes a joke funny, and the term was in use long before Fred Allen. It first appeared in *Variety* in 1921, but its use as the end of a skit goes back to the medieval husband and wife puppets Punch and Judy. Each skit ended with Punch getting the best of Judy, which gave us the expression "pleased as Punch."

Why are coming attractions called "movie trailers"?

Movies used to be shown continuously without a break between features. If someone arrived late for a show they would simply sit and watch for where they came in before leaving. To catch this crowd, and to signify an end to the film as well as chase as many people as possible from their seats for a new audience, coming attractions were spliced onto the end of the first showing as a "trailer," even though it preceded the next screening.

Why do we say we've been "upstaged"
when someone else grabs all the attention?

To be upstaged now means to lose due credit to a lesser person. In the theatre, "upstage" refers to the back of the stage, which at one time was built higher than the front. This was because the theatre floor was flat, and a slanted stage gave a better view of all the actors. Plays were crafted placing noble characters at the rear (where they appeared higher and more regal) even though they might have fewer lines than the others.

Why is a misleading sales pitch called a "song and dance"?

During the days of travelling vaudeville shows, there were featured stars and there were fillers. The fillers were the comics who were hired to keep the audience amused by telling jokes within a song and dance routine until the next headliner was ready to come on stage. Since then, any well-rehearsed routine that is intended to divert your attention from what you came to see has been called a "song and dance."

Why is someone deceptive said to be "blowing smoke"?

If someone's "blowing smoke," they're bragging or lying without anything tangible to back it up. The expression comes from magicians, who often use smoke to cover their slight of hand. Their trickery, like that of a dishonest tradesman, is concealed. "Smoke and mirrors" has the same origin.

What were the origins of vaudeville?

Tony Pastor introduced vaudeville in New York in 1861. The word *vaudeville* is an Americanization of *Vau de Vire*, the valley of the Vau River in Normandy, which became famous in the fifteenth century for the comedic songs of Olivier Basselin. An 1883 vaudeville bill from Boston's Gaiety Museum featured a midget named Baby Alice, a stuffed mermaid, two comedians, and a chicken with a human face. From these humble beginnings would emerge the great American theatre.

Why do we refer to a bad joke as being "corny"?

The reason a cheap joke is called "corny" comes from mail-order seed catalogues from the early twentieth century. In an effort to make reading about seeds interesting, the publishers mixed in cartoons, jokes, and riddles throughout the crop and garden book. These inserts were of desperately low quality and were known as corn catalogue jokes, and were eventually simply called corny, which came to mean any failed attempt at entertainment.

Why do we say we're "in stitches" when we laugh hard?

Like the stitches in sewing, those in the side from both running and laughing all come from the verb *stick*. The expression "to stick someone" is over a thousand years old and means "to stab" or "to prod." The stabbing or sticking of a needle through cloth in sewing is thus called a stitch, and because both the pain in the side from running and that from laughing feels like you've been stabbed or stuck with something, these too are called stitches.

Why is a theatrical flop called a "turkey"?

A "turkey" can describe any person or endeavour that doesn't live up to its promise, but is most commonly used to describe a bad play. In the late nineteenth century, the period between Thanksgiving and Christmas was the busiest season for the opening of new plays, just as it is now for movies. This hurried effort to catch the tourist trade served up disappointments with the same tedium as the turkey served for dinner between the two holidays, and so they were called turkeys.

Why do we say something perfect is right "on the nose"?

"On the nose" didn't come from horse racing; it came from radio. Several common hand gestures came from the early days of radio broadcasting, when elaborate productions required the director in the studio to be able to communicate without speech. Instead, they used hand signals. For "cut" a forefinger was slashed across the throat. Holding up the forefinger touching the thumb meant "good performance," and touching the nose signalled "perfect timing." It was right on the nose.

How did the Wizard Of Oz get that name?

The classic tale of Dorothy in the land of Oz came from the imagination of L. Frank Baum, who made up the story for his son and a group of children one evening in 1899. When a little girl asked him the name of this magical land with the Scarecrow, Tinman, and Cowardly Lion, he looked around the room for inspiration. He happened to be sitting next to a filing cabinet with the drawers labelled "A-G," "H-N," and finally "O-Z," which gave him a quick answer: "Oz."

Why is the evil adversary in a film or play called a "villain"?

The idea of a villain being the bad guy comes from feudal times when a class of serfs held the legal status of freemen in their affairs with everyone except their lords. These peasants were called "villeins" or "villains" from the word *villa*, the central dwelling of the landlord, who literally owned his tenants. Because they often stole to stay alive, the word *villain* came to mean someone who couldn't be trusted. The use of the word *villain* as the evil antagonist in a play or novel surfaced in 1822.

Why are celebrity photographers called "paparazzi"?

The word *paparazzi* as a tag for pushy celebrity photographers comes from Frederico Fellini's 1960 film *La Dolce Vita* and first appeared in its current use around 1968. In the movie, the character Signor Paparazzo (the singular of paparazzi) was an obnoxious, creepy little man who was despised by the stars. Before Fellini used it, *paparazzo* was a word in an Italian dialect for "buzzing insect."

Why is harassing a performer called "heckling"?

Heckling is an effort by a member of an audience to embarrass someone who is speaking publicly. This can be done with rude remarks or impertinent questions. Dealing with these is an art that politicians and public performers (especially comedians) had better become familiar with. The word *heckle* and its relationship to making someone uncomfortable dates back to the fifteenth century when a "heckle" was a steel brush with metal teeth used to comb flax or hemp to prepare its fibres for the manufacture of workable cloth. The use of a heckle on a human would have been (and still is) very uncomfortable.

Why do we say that something "fills" or "fits the bill"?

If something "fills" or "fits the bill," it's satisfying, whether it's a good meal or a job well done. The expression comes from the days when theatrical advertising was done through handbills or posters. "Filling the bill" meant adding acts to pad a weak program, but if a single star could pull in an audience through his or her individual fame and talent, their name was all that was needed, so it was enlarged to fit the bill.

Why are vain people said to be "looking for the limelight"?

In the early days of theatre, the players were lit by gas lamps hidden across the front of the stage. Early in the twentieth century, it was discovered that if a stick of lime was added to the gas, the light became more intense, and so they began to use the "limelight" to illuminate the spot on stage where the most important part of the play took place. Later called the "spotlight," the "limelight" was where all actors fought to be.

What exactly is an icon?

We often hear the word *icon* used to describe some outstanding character who is the subject of tremendous respect and even devotion, such as a pop star. An icon can also be a sacred picture of someone sanctified within the Eastern Orthodox Church. The reason that both are correct is that the word *icon* came from the Greek *eikon*, which means a likeness, an image, or a representation of the big picture, such as a generation or a religion. An icon is both an image and a copy. The pop icon is an important symbol or reflection of his or her own time, just as the religious icon mirrors the sanctity of its subject.

The computer icon was created in 1982 to symbolically represent a file, window option, or program.

music

What is the origin of the word *jazz*?

Jazz may be an American art form, but the word predates any application to music or sex. It first appeared in print in 1831 as *jazzing*, meaning the telling of fun stories. The first American use of *jazz* was in baseball as slang for enthusiasm in 1913. Its first musical use was a year later, to describe the vigor of West Coast bandleader Art Hickman. The word *jazz* wasn't used to describe black music until 1918.

Why do jazz musicians call a spontaneous collaboration a "jam"?

All musicians refer to an informal and exhilarating musical session as "jamming," but it first surfaced in the jazz world during the 1920s. *Jam* in jazz is a short, free, improvised passage performed by the whole band. It means pushing or jamming all the players and notes into a defined free-flowing session.

Preserved fruit was first called jam during the 1730s because it was crushed then "jammed" into a jar. To be "in a jam" has the same origin and means to be pressed into a tight or confining predicament. Jamming radio signals is a term from the First World War and means to force so much extra sound through a defined enemy channel that the original intended message is incoherent. All this is from *jam*, a little seventeenth-century word of unknown origin that meant to press tightly.

Why is anything pleasing said to be "cool"?

Cool, like *groovy*, was a very popular expression of satisfaction during the 1960s and early '70s, but only the former lives on. *Cool* surfaced in the early nineteenth century, and, like *groovy*, which meant "in the groove," as in a smoothly played vinyl record, it was popularized by bebop jazz musicians in the 1940s. *Cool* means unfazed and under control, like being on ice, which is real cool.

Why did Yankee Doodle stick a feather in his cap and call it macaroni?

The famous American patriotic song "Yankee Doodle" actually began as an English song of derision against the colonists. At the time, there was a Macaroni Club in London that catered to foppish, wealthy young men who copied everything Italian, including sticking a feather in their caps, which to many became the sign of a sissy. When the Americans began winning the war they took possession of the song "Yankee Doodle" as revenge.

Why was George M. Cohan forced to rewrite "It's a Grand Old Flag"?

In 1906, George M. Cohan was forced to change one word in his anthem to the American flag, which begins, "It's a grand old flag / it's a high flying flag …" Though today it's sung as a tribute to Old Glory, if Cohan hadn't made the change, the song probably would never be sung. Cohan's original lyrics started with, "It's a grand old *rag* …"

In the Scottish song "Loch Lomond," what's the difference between the high and the low roads?

In the song "Loch Lomond," two wounded Scottish soldiers are in a foreign prison. One will be set free, but the one speaking is to be executed. When he says, "You take the high road and I'll take the low road," he's referring to the Celtic belief that if a man dies in a foreign land, the fairies will guide his spirit home along the "low road," while the living man will travel an earthly or "high road" that will take longer.

Where did the Do, Re, Mi vocal music scale come from?

In the tenth century, Guido d' Arezzo was having trouble teaching monks their Gregorian chants, so he replaced the A, B, C music scale with sound symbols, which we now know as Do, Re, Mi. He could point to a spot where he had written them on his hand and the monks would know exactly which note to sing. These hand symbols evolved into the phonetic music scale and gave Maria a song to sing in *The Sound of Music*.

How old is the first known musical instrument?

In 1996, an excavation in northwest Slovenia uncovered a transverse flute made from the femur of a bear cub. It was perforated with four round holes, and its shape and structure strongly suggested a wind instrument. The amazing discovery was made in a Neanderthal cave, and the flute was dated to between 43,000 and 82,000 years old, making it the oldest musical instrument ever found.

Why is the entire range of a circumstance called "the full gamut"?

If you pass through the entire spectrum of emotional of other circumstances you've run "the full gamut." Since 1626, it has figuratively meant that you've run the full range of possibilities of anything; however, *gamut* literally means "the entire range of recognized notes on a musical scale."

Al Jolson sang about it and Stephen Foster and Ira Gershwin wrote popular songs about it ... so where is the Swanee River?

In the first draft of his 1851 song "The Old Folks at Home," Stephen Foster's river was the Pedee, but that didn't work so he searched an atlas and found the Suwannee River, which he shortened to Swanee. In 1919, Gershwin and Irving Caesar reused the name in the Jolson classic and made the Swanee the most famous river that never existed.

Who owns the song "Happy Birthday"?

"Happy Birthday" began as "Good Morning Dear Children" and was written by educators Mildred and Patty Hill in 1893. In 1924, a publisher changed the opening line to "Happy Birthday to You," and it became a ritual to sing the song to anyone celebrating his or her birthday. In 1934, after hearing the song in a Broadway musical, a third Hill sister, Jessica, sued the show and won. The Hill family was thereafter entitled to royalties whenever the melody was performed commercially.

Who was Matilda in the song "Waltzing Matilda"?

In the Australian song "Waltzing Matilda," a *billabong* is a pool of stagnant water. A *swagman* was someone who carried around everything he owned in a knapsack. *Waltzing* meant hiking, and *Matilda* wasn't a woman but rather an Australian word for a knapsack. So "Waltzing Matilda" means "walking with my knapsack."

Quickies
Did you know ...
- the average North American knows about 10,000 words?
- during one day, women on average speak 25,000 words; men average 12,000?
- the average four-year-old asks more than four hundred questions a day?
- that *diamond, silver, purple, month, skeleton, limited, ninth,* and *poem* do not rhyme with any other English word?
- that although there are more than 160 English words ending with the three letters "int," such as *point* and *faint,* "pint" doesn't rhyme with any of them?
- that *tremendous, stupendous, horrendous,* and *hazardous* are the only four English words to end in "dous"?

the world
of literature and
language

Why is an individual book from a set called a "volume"?

The word *volume* was first used in English to describe a manuscript or a large number of written words in the fourteenth century. At the time writing was done on parchments, which were then rolled up for storage. The Latin word for "a roll of writing" is *volumen*, from *volvere*, meaning "to roll."

Volume took the meaning "one book from a set" in 1523.

Voluminous, meaning a large mass of writing, first appeared in 1647. During the electronic age of the twentieth century, *voluminous* gave us the alternate meaning for volume as the degree of amplitude or loudness of a sound.

Why is a complete list of letters named the "alphabet," and why is a river mouth called a "delta"?

One of the first things we learn in school is our ABCs, a list of all letters used in the English language. The name comes from the first two letters in the original Greek alphabet: alpha and beta. The triangular mouth of the Nile River was called a "delta" because, like all rivers leading into the sea, it's shaped like the fourth Greek letter. Every delta in the world took its name from the Nile.

What are the most common words in the English language?

The most common word used in written English is *the*, followed in order of use by *of*, *and*, *to*, *a*, *in*, *that*, *is*, *I*, *it*, *for*, and *as*. The most common spoken English word is *I*. The most common word in the King James Bible is *the*.

Why do we say we're "boning up" when studying or preparing for an examination?

The phrase "boning up" comes from a British teacher of Greek and Latin who wanted to make life easier for his students. With that goal in mind he translated the Greek and Latin classics into English and then had them published and distributed within his classroom. His name was Mr. Bohn, and his grateful students called this new, speedier method of studying the classics "Bohning up."

Why is a spelling competition called a "bee"?

Entire communities used to gather in a festive mood to build churches or to help neighbours build a barn or a home. These events were called "bees" because the number of people swarming around the task was similar to a busy hive of bees. The spelling bee is the lone survivor from this era and was the name used in 1925 by a Louisville newspaper for a national competition that is still going strong.

Why is spring both a season and fresh water from the ground?

Spring is a season, but it's also part of a mattress, an underground water supply, and a surprise attack. *Spring* derives from *sprengh*, an ancient Indo-European word for "rapid movement." It was around A.D. 816 when *spring* was first used to mean "rising up," or the beginning of something. By the fourteenth century the first of the four seasons became the spring of the year.

What is the shortest English sentence ever created using all the letters of the alphabet?

Western Union developed the sentence "The quick brown fox jumps over the lazy dog" as a test for their telex operators, and it's thirty-five letters long. However, it isn't the shortest English sentence ever created using all the letters of the alphabet. That honour belongs to the sentence "Jackdaws love my big sphinx of quartz," which was authored by an anonymous scholar and is just thirty-one letters long.

Why do we call a critical instant the "moment of truth"?

The "moment of truth" is what the Spanish call that instant when a bullfighter chooses to make the final thrust of his sword and was introduced into English in Ernest Hemingway's 1932 novel *Death In the Afternoon*. The timing of that final move by the bullfighter is critical for both the matador and the animal, and so *el momento de la verdad*, or "the moment of truth," became synonymous with any critical decision.

What does it mean to say that you wouldn't give "one iota" for something?

If someone doesn't care "one iota," they don't care very much. Like the letter *I* in English, an iota is the ninth and smallest letter of the Greek alphabet, and because the English letters *I* and *J* were often confused, *iota* became *jot*, with both words meaning something very small. That's why to "jot something down"

means to condense information, while an iota is just a little bit more than a tittle, which is the dot over the lower-case *i*.

What's the origin of the expression "Put on your thinking cap"?

Teachers will often tell students to "put on their thinking caps" when they want them to take time to think things over. Caps have been associated with academics, jurists, scholars, and clerics for centuries. One of the most familiar of these caps is the mortarboard worn at graduation, so called for its similarity to the instrument used by bricklayers. In the seventeenth century, English judges wore a "considering cap" while pondering a sentence.

Why do we say, "Every cloud has a silver lining"?

"Every cloud has a silver lining" originated in a poem written in 1634 by John Milton. Milton tells of a young woman who becomes lost and alone in the woods after being separated from her two brothers. As night falls, her terror is lifted and her prayers answered when she sees a dark cloud turn its bright side down to guide her; the poem says, "There does a sable cloud turn forth her Silver Lining on the night."

What does the title refer to in the book *The Lord of the Flies*?

When William Golding published his classic novel in 1954, he chose a title suggesting a powerful, malevolent supernatural presence, which he called the Lord of the Flies. Translated into Hebrew, "Lord of the Flies" is *Ba'al zebhubh*, which since the twelfth century in English has been rendered as "Beelzebub," a Catholic reference to the Devil. Therefore, the Lord of the Flies is the Devil.

Why when abbreviating something do we say, "In a nutshell"?

"In a nutshell" indicates a drastically reduced summary. Long before modern electronics, a few scholars made attempts at condensing massive literary works so they could be more easily stored. It became an obsession to some to see just how small they could write. For example, a copy of the Koran was reduced on a parchment measuring four inches by half an inch. These copies were so small it was said they could be stored in a nutshell.

Why do the Scots refer to girls as "lassies" and boys as "laddies"?

Both *lassie* and *laddie* are reminders of the Viking raids and temporary conquest of parts of Britain in the Dark Ages and early Middle Ages. *Lass* began as the Scandinavian word *loskr* and meant someone light or slight. Around 1725 the word evolved into *lassie*, Scottish for an unmarried woman or girl. To the Vikings, *lad* was *ladde* and meant a boy or young man who was led, such as a foot soldier or a male servant. The word became *laddie* around 1546.

Extensions to pet and proper names, such as the *ie* in *laddie* or *lassie*, or the *y* in names like Robby or Donny, surfaced in Scotland around 1400 and became popularized as endearments by the poems of Robert Burns (1759–1796).

What are the longest words in the English language?

According to *The Guinness Book of Records*, the true longest English word is *floccinaucinihilipilification* (29 letters). It's defined as "the act of estimating [something] as worthless," and first appeared circa 1741. *Antidisestablishmentarianism* (28 letters) describes a nineteenth-century British movement opposed to the separation of church and state and is one of the longest English words. The longest word ever used by William Shakespeare appears in *Love's Labour's Lost* and is *honorificabilitudinitatibus* (27 letters). The longest word found in any major English language dictionary is *pneumonoultramicroscopicsilicovolcanokoniosis* (45 letters). It was used as a reference to a lung disease but has since been discovered to have been created as a hoax.

Lengthy words created by authors that never catch on outside of their transcripts are not considered a legitimate part of the English language. These include the nine lengthy words used by James Joyce in his novel *Finnegan's Wake*. The most famous appears only once on the first page as the symbolic thunderclap sounding the fall from Eden of Adam and Eve: Bababadalgharagh-takamminarronnkonnbronntonnerronntuonnthunntrovarrhounawnskawn-toohoohoordenenthurnuk.

Another long word that never made it into the real world because it has no defined meaning is *supercalifragilisticexpialidocious* (34 letters), the song title from the movie *Mary Poppins*.

Almost is the longest English word with all the letters in alphabetical order.

The longest words with the vowels in order (a, e, i, o, u) are *facetiously* and *abstemiously*.

Squirrelled (11 letters) is the longest one-syllable word in the English language.

The longest English word with a single vowel is *strengths*.

A popular joke among English schoolchildren is to ask, "What is the longest word"? The answer is *smiles*, because there is a mile between each *s*.

Why didn't Shakespeare ever use the word *penis*?

The word *penis* means "tail" in Latin and didn't enter English until fifty-two years after Shakespeare's death in 1616. However, the Bard of Avon used other references to the appendage several times; for example, in *Henry IV* parts one and two he named Prince Hal's sidekick "Falstaff" because he was rather portly and not attractive to women. Shakespeare was playing to his audience with the words *false* and *staff*, suggesting the character had a nonfunctional male appendage.

How did "one fell swoop" come to mean a single decisive action?

The expression "one fell swoop" was introduced by Shakespeare in *Macbeth*. When Macduff learns that his wife and children have been murdered he exclaims: "What, all my pretty chickens and their dam / At one fell swoop?" Metaphorically, Macduff compares his wife and children to chickens and their murderer to a bird of prey. During Shakespeare's time, *fell* meant "fierce," and survives today in the word *felon*.

What's the origin of the expression "Less is more"?

"Less is more" means "keep it simple, stupid"! It's the credo of every film actor and most other artists. Architects Mies van der Rohe and Buckminster Fuller considered it their personal motto, and they and everyone else who follows that advice got it from an 1855 Robert Browning poem titled "Andrea del Sarto." Del Sarto was a Florentine painter (1486–1531) who was considered a perfectionist. Browning introduced "less is more" within that poem, which ends the subject stanza with, "Ah, but a man's reach should exceed his grasp, or what is heaven for?"

Quickies

Did you know ...

- *varsity* is a short form of *university*?
- *valedictorian* simply means "farewell sayer" in Latin?
- *alumnus* in Latin means a male graduate or former student of a school? The plural is alumni.
- *alumna* in Latin is a female graduate or former student, with the plural being alumnae?
- *thesaurus* is from the Greek *thesauros*, meaning "storehouse" or "treasure"?
- *dictionary* is from the Latin *dictionarium*, a "collection of words and phrases"?
- *inaugurate*, or *inaugurere* in Latin, means to take office only when a flight of birds presents a favourable omen?

the language
of golf

Where do the golf terms *par* and *bogey* come from?

Until the introduction of the modern golf ball in 1898, an average score for any given hole was called a *bogey*, the Scottish word for ghost, meaning that the challenge was within the individual player against an unseen opponent. The modern ball took one less stroke to reach the hole, so the new standard was called *par*, a short form of *parity*, meaning "equal." Bogey was kept as meaning the original average with the old cloth-covered ball, or one shot over the new ball average of par.

How is par determined for each hole on a golf course?

Par is the number of strokes a good golfer should make on a particular hole, and it's based on distance. A par 3 hole is up to 250 yards for men and 210 yards for women. A par 4 is 250 to 470 yards for men and between 210 and 400 yards for women. Par 5 is for holes over 470 yards for men and over 400 for women.

Why does a golf "duffer" need a "handicap"?

The word *duffer* was once used to describe a counterfeit coin and was expanded to include a worthless person, who, like the counterfeit coin, was only taking up space — such as a duffer on a golf course. Because they are inferior, duffers need a *handicap*, or help, which is really a penalty against the superior players. The word *handicap* came from drawing of lots for positions in a horse race, which literally required putting a hand in a cap.

Why do golf courses have eighteen holes?

Golf courses might have had a dozen, sixteen, or even twenty holes if it hadn't been for a meeting of the club's membership board to standardize the number at St. Andrews, Scotland, in 1858. Those assembled at the game's birthplace decided that because it takes exactly eighteen shots to polish off a fifth of Scotch, and because players generally limited themselves to just one shot of Scotch per hole, they shouldn't have to play any further than when the whiskey ran out. So eighteen holes it is!

Why do golf balls have dimples?

Original golf balls were made of wood, and it wasn't until the nineteenth century that they evolved through a number of stages. They went from wet feathers stuffed into wet leather for shrinking to "gutties," balls made from a Malaysian form of rubber. At this point someone noticed that the new ball flew further when scuffed up after being hit a few times, and so dimples were added to encourage distance by imitating a well-used ball.

Why do golfers shout "Fore" as a warning to those ahead of them?

When early cannons fired a barrage into enemy lines, over the heads of their own charging infantry, the shots were often imprecise. British artillery officers would shout "Beware before" as a warning for their advancing troops to watch out for a misfired cannon ball. Over time, "beware before" was abbreviated to "before," then eventually shortened to "fore," which found its way into golf as a warning that a volley was on its way.

In golf, I know about eagles and birdies, but what is an albatross?

Albatross is the Spanish word for "pelican," and although to a mariner it may be bad luck, to a golfer it's an amazing accomplishment. More commonly known today as a double eagle, a three under par for an individual hole was originally called an albatross. Only one has ever been scored in the U.S. Open because the odds of making an albatross are 1 in 5.85 million. Gene Sarazen set the record in 1935.

Why are golfers' shortened pants called "plus fours"?

Knickerbockers or knee breeches are pants that only go down to the knee and were quite popular in the first half of the twentieth century. Bobby Jones, among other golfers, found knickerbockers and breeches too restrictive for a full swing. Tailors solved this by designing special golf knickers with an additional four inches below the knee seam, calling them "plus fours." The extra length allowed just enough slack to free up the golfer's swing. Some players wear them to this day.

Where did we get the phrase "Down to the short strokes"?

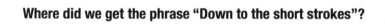

When a golfer begins at the tee, he hits the ball towards the green by driving, or using a long stroke. When the ball is on the green, he must get the ball in the hole by putting, or taking short strokes. Similarly, a painter (canvases, not houses) begins on a clean canvas using large and broad strokes of the brush. As the painting progresses the brush strokes become shorter and finer as detail is filled into the painting.

Why do we refer to golf courses as "links"?

The word *links* is a Scottish reference to the coastal strips of semi-barren land between the ocean beach and the inland farming areas. Links land was too sandy for crops so it was where the Scots put their first golf courses. There were no trees close to the beach and the sand traps were natural with tall, reedy grass as the only vegetation. Otherwise worthless, these narrow links of land became valuable as golf courses.

Why do we say we've been "stymied" when we are facing a difficult situation?

Stymied comes from the Scottish word *styme*, which means "unable to see," and its usage came from golf. A stymie was when a player's golf ball landed on the green directly between his opponent's ball and the hole, forcing the stymied player to either spin his ball around the other or hop over it with an iron. In 1951, a new rule allowed a golfer to mark the position and remove the obstructing ball for a putt.

Why are golf assistants called "caddies"?

In medieval France the first-born sons of nobility were known as the *caput*, or "head," of the family, while the younger, less valuable boys were called *capdets*, or "little heads," and were often sent to the military to train as officers. In English, *capdets* became *cadets*, which the Scots abbreviated to *cads* or *caddies*, meaning any useless street kid who could be hired for the day to carry around a bag of golf clubs.

Odds & Oddities
- The chance of hitting a hole in one in golf is 1 in 15,000.

between the lines of nursery rhymes

Who was Little Jack Horner?

At a time when Henry VIII was confiscating church property, one monk appeased the king with the gift of a special Christmas pie. Inside the crust were deeds to twelve manor houses secretly offered in exchange for his monastery. The steward who carried the pie to London was Jack Horner, who along the way extracted a plum deed for himself. It was for Mells Manor, where Horner's descendants still live to this day.

What is the origin of the children's rhyme "Eeney, meeney, miney, moe"?

"Eeney, meeney, miney, moe" is a children's rhyme where, with each word, the person counting or reciting points at one of a group of players to establish who will be "it." The ritual was handed down from the Druids, who used the same counting formula to choose human sacrifices. The precise meanings and origins of the words *eeney*, *meeney*, *miney* and *moe* are unknown. The theory that the rhyme is from an ancient Anglo-Saxon, Celtic, or Welsh numbering system can't be proven.

The rhyme was first written down in 1855 along with several other versions, for example, "Hanna, mana, mona, mike."

Have you ever wondered how Cinderella could have walked in a glass slipper?

The story of Cinderella was passed along orally for centuries before it was written down by Charles Perrault in 1697. While doing so he mistook the word *vair*, meaning ermine, for the word *verre*, meaning glass. By the time he realized his mistake, the story had become too popular to change, and so instead of an ermine slipper, Cinderella wore glass.

How did the poem "Mary Had a Little Lamb" become so famous?

"Mary Had a Little Lamb" was written in 1830 by Sarah Hale, the editor of *Godey's Ladies Magazine*. She was inspired after watching young Mary Tyler's pet lamb follow the girl to school, which, of course, was against the rules. The poem became immortal more than fifty years later when Thomas Edison used it as the first words ever spoken and then recorded on his new invention, the phonograph.

Who was Humpty Dumpty?

The nursery rhyme in which "Humpty Dumpty has a great fall" dates back to 1493 and refers to King Richard III of England. Richard had a hump on his back and had been dumped by his mount in the thick of battle, where he cried, "My kingdom for a horse" before being slain. The last line, "Couldn't put Humpty together again," was originally "Couldn't put Humpty up again," meaning back on his horse.

Why is rolling head over heels called a "somersault"?

A somersault is a stunt in which a person tumbles head over heels; it can be very difficult, as when performed by a circus acrobat, or very simple, as when performed by a child on a front lawn. The word has two Latin derivatives, *supra*, meaning "above," and *saltus*, meaning "leap." It entered England from France as *sombresault*. One of the word's alternate spellings was used to name the English county of Somerset.

The word *somersault* first appeared in English around 1530 as *sobersault*, and by the nineteenth century it was *sumersault*.

Who is Mary in the nursery rhyme "Mary, Mary, Quite Contrary"?

The children's nursery rhyme "Mary, Mary, Quite Contrary" is about Mary, Queen of Scots, and emerged during her struggle for power with Queen Elizabeth I. The "pretty maids all in a row" were her ladies in waiting (the Marys: Seaton, Fleming, Livingston, and Beaton). The cockleshells were decorations on an elaborate gown given to her by the French Dauphin. The rhyme was popular when Mary was beheaded in 1587.

"Twinkle, Twinkle Little Star" shares a melody with three other nursery rhymes, but which two classical composers also used the melody?

In 1806, Jane Taylor published "Twinkle, Twinkle Little Star" as simply "The Star." The tune was already in use for "Baa Baa Black Sheep" and the "Alphabet Song." The melody for all three came from a French rhyme called "Ah! Vous dirais-je Maman" (1765). Both Mozart and Haydn have incorporated the melody into two of their classical compositions: Haydn in "Surprise" Symphony No. 94 and Mozart in Theme and Variations K265.

Where did the game of hopscotch come from?

Hopscotch was brought to Britain by the Romans, who used it as a military training exercise. The courts were one hundred feet long, and the soldiers ran them in full battle gear to improve their footwork. Children copied the soldiers by scratching out small courses of their own and creating rules and a scoring system. The *scotch* in *hopscotch* refers to the markings scored onto the ground. As in butterscotch toffee, *scotch* means scored or notched into squares.

What is the origin of Mother Goose's nursery rhymes?

Most nursery rhymes were never intended for children. For centuries, these ballads came from bawdy folk songs or spoofs on social issues of the day, often sung or recited as limericks in local taverns. *Nursery* wasn't used to describe them until efforts were made in the nineteenth century to clean them up as children's lullabies. In 1697, a French writer, Charles Perrault, published *Tales of My Mother Goose*, a collection of fairy tales (including "Little Red Riding Hood" and "Puss in Boots").

Why when lifting a young child might you say, "Ups-a-daisy"?

Whether it's "Ups-a-daisy," "Whoops-a-daisy," or "Oops-a-daisy," you are speaking loving nonsense, usually to a child. "Up-a-dazy" dates back to 1711, and by 1862 it had mutated into "Up-a-daisy," spelled the same as the flower. The original meaning was an encouragement for a child to get up, and *dazy* was an endearing reference to *lazy*, an or *lackadaisical*.

What's the hidden meaning within "Pop Goes the Weasel"?

The old song, with every verse ending in "Pop goes the weasel," is a tale of Victorian London working-class poverty. The Eagle of the lyrics was a famous pub. The City Road still exists. *Pop* means to pawn something for cash, while a *weasel* in cockney rhyming slang is a coat. After spending his money on rice and treacle, followed by a visit to the pub, the man in the song is forced to visit the pawnshop for more money — thus selling his belongings, or "Pop goes the weasel."

Where does the Sandman come from?

The Sandman is an elf who sprinkles sand in children's eyes to make them sleepy. The character is derived from the remarkable mind of Hans Christian Andersen (1805–1875), the Danish writer famous for his fairy tales. Andersen's Sandman was a device to explain to children the reason for the grit or "sleep" in their eyes when they woke up in the morning. The Sandman is found in Andersen's 1850 story "Ole Lukoie," which means "Olaf Shuteye." Olaf carried two umbrellas. Over good children he held an umbrella with pictures that inspired beautiful dreams. Over bad children he held the other umbrella, which had no pictures and caused frightful dreams.

Andersen was born in the slums of Odense, Denmark, and his incredible life story is well worth reading for inspiration.

Why are the Sesame Street characters called Muppets?

The Muppets, who've had their own television show as well as a series of movies, are best known for their roles on *Sesame Street*, which first appeared in 1969. After 4,100 episodes, *Sesame Street* is the longest running television show in history and has received more Emmy Awards than any other show. The Muppets were Jim Henson's idea, and he named them by combining the words *marionette* and *puppet*.

Who or what were the inspirations for naming the Baby Ruth chocolate bar, the Tootsie Roll, and Hershey's Kisses?

Confectioner Leo Hirschfield created the Tootsie Roll. He named his chewy chocolate treat after his daughter Clara, whose nickname was Tootsie. The Baby Ruth chocolate bar was named in honour of President Grover Cleveland's baby daughter, Ruth. Hershey's named their chocolate treats Kisses because in the factory the machine that dispenses them kisses the conveyor belt.

Quickies

Did you know ...

- 90 percent of all the scientists in history are alive today?
- only 13 percent of all scientists are women?
- bulletproof vests, fire escapes, windshield wipers, and laser printers were all invented by women?
- women blink nearly twice as much as men?
- 90 percent of women who walk into a department store immediately turn to the right?
- by a statistic of four to one, women shoplift more than men?

money, gold, and finance

What is the origin of the dollar sign?

Thomas Jefferson used the letter *S* with two lines through it to symbolize a dollar in a 1784 document in which he suggested the dollar as the primary unit of American currency. Prior to this the symbol was in use for the peso throughout Latin America. Consequently, the most widely accepted explanation is that the dollar sign ($) is a depiction of the twin pillars of Hercules wrapped with a scroll, as found on early Spanish pieces of eight.

Where did the word *dollar* come from?

In 1516, a silver mine opened in the German town of Sankt Joachimsthal in what today is the Czech Republic (St. Joachim was the husband of St. Anne and the father of the Virgin Mary). The German word *thal* means "valley," and the town soon became known simply as Thaler. The silver coins minted from the silver mine were called *thalers*, which by 1600 had translated to English as "dollars" to describe the German coin or any foreign currency.

The Spanish peso was the first foreign currency to be known as a dollar.

Thomas Jefferson resolved that "the money unit of the United States be one dollar" in 1785.

The first American dollar was minted in Philadelphia in 1792.

Why do we call a dollar a "buck"?

The Indians taught the first European settlers the value of a buck. Like gold, deerskin or buckskin was used in trading as a unit of value against which everything else was assessed. "The buck stops here" is a different matter. That expression came from frontier poker, in which the buck was a knife made of buckhorn that was passed around the table to indicate who was dealing. When a hand was finished, the dealer "passed the buck" to the next player.

Why is a ten-dollar bill called a "sawbuck"?

Among the many slang expressions for denominations of money are *deuce*, originally a mild curse referring to the Devil when the number two showed up in dice or cards, and the Yiddish *fin* for a five. *Sawbuck* for a ten comes from the frame of a sawbuck, or sawhorse, on which farmers held logs to be cut into firewood. This frame rested on two *X*-shaped supports that resembled the two roman numerals for ten found on the early American ten-dollar bill.

Why is a British pound sterling called a "quid"?

When the people of Great Britain exchange money for goods or services, they will often refer to a pound note as a quid, even though centuries earlier a quid referred to a sovereign, the most important gold coin in history. One pound is equal to one hundred pence. When exchanged for something of equal value the deal in Latin is *quid pro quo* — something for something — which when abbreviated becomes simply *quid*.

Why do we call a quarter "two bits"?

European settlers brought their money with them to America, and coins made of precious metal were accepted everywhere at face value. The Spanish peso was divided into eight silver coins, which the English called bits, or pieces of eight. Two bits was one-quarter of a Spanish dollar. When money was printed and minted in the new world, although a dollar's coinage was divided by ten, the expression "two bits" continued to mean one-quarter of a dollar.

Why is money called "cash"?

The history of money is fascinating. The word *money* is from the Latin *moneta*, which derives from the Hebrew word *mone*, meaning "weight" or "coins"; it is referred to in the Bible as *maneh*. The word *cash* entered English in the late sixteenth century. It's from the French words *casse*, meaning "money box," and *cassier*, meaning "treasurer," which have given us the word *cashier* and its abbreviation *cash*.

The surname Cash is a variant of Case, and is an occupational name given to persons who made boxes or chests.

Why do we have piggy banks instead of bunny banks or kitty banks?

In medieval England, pots and dishes were made from a clay known as "pygg," and it was common practice to save spare change in a kitchen pot. Around 1600, an English potter who was unfamiliar with this custom was asked to make a pygg bank, which he misunderstood to be a clay vessel in the shape of the animal; so the end result was a clay pig with a slot in its back. The piggy bank had arrived.

Why is a differing opinion called "your two cents' worth"?

If someone speaks up out of turn or forcefully inserts their unsolicited opinion, we say he gave his "two cents' worth." The expression dates back to the late nineteenth century, when if you wanted to write an opinion to the editor of a newspaper or complain to a member of the legislature, the cost of mailing the letter was the price of a two-cent stamp. "Two cents' worth" became an Americanism for "of little value."

Why is a copper penny called a "red cent"?

In 1859, the United States Mint introduced a new one-cent coin. On its face was an Indian head, and because of its copper-nickel alloy, in time, the penny turned red. Combine this with the slang reference to Native Americans as "redskins" and the expression "red cent" was born. In 1864, the copper-nickel alloy was replaced by bronze, but the expression lived on.

Why were Native Americans called "red"?

The Beothuks (*Bee*-o-thucks) were the original natives of Newfoundland, Canada. They were outstanding to the first Europeans because they painted their entire bodies with red ochre, which they considered a sacred ritual. Neighbouring tribes called the Beothuks "Red People," while the Europeans tagged them "Red Indians" or "redskins." Other tribes occasionally used red ochre on their bodies as a seasonal insect repellant, but the Beothucks wore it year-round. Although it was considered a racial slur among most of the Native peoples on the mainland, the reference persists.

It's believed that Beothuk meant "good people." The arrival of the white settlers caused the extinction of the entire people through a terrible combination of brutal violence, starvation, forced isolation, and disease. The last member of the tribe was a childless woman named Shawnadithit. She died in 1829.

Why do we say that someone who inherited wealth was "born with a silver spoon in his mouth"?

If someone is "born with a silver spoon in his mouth," it means that he was born into wealth rather than having had to earn it. The expression comes from an old custom of godparents giving a spoon to a child at its christening to signify their responsibility for its nourishment and well-being. If they were wealthy, the spoon was usually silver, and if not, it would be pewter or tin.

Why is money called "dough"?

Dough is a mixture of dry ingredients kneaded in water then shaped and baked into such things as bread or pastry. Around 1851, while on their way home from classes, British schoolboys would very often spend their pocket money on sweets or baked dough from the pastry shop. When their allowance ran out, they would ask their parents for more "dough-money." Soon the two words became interchangeable and money became "dough."

Citizen soldiers were called "dough-boys" during the First World War because they were raw recruits requiring a lot of kneading and shaping to end up as fighting men.

If gold is so rare, why does there seem to be so much of it in circulation?

Gold is very rare, but it's also very malleable. If, since the beginning of time, all the gold ever mined were to be lumped together, it would make a cube about the size of a tennis court. A cube the size of a matchbox can be flattened into a sheet that would cover that same tennis court, and one tiny ounce of gold can be stretched into a wire fifty miles long. A little gold goes a long way.

What's the difference between yellow and white gold?

Pure or 24-karat gold is yellow and relatively soft. White gold includes an alloy of nickel and palladium. Zinc is added to harden the gold for gem settings. White gold can be more expensive than pure gold because it's harder to fabricate. 18-karat yellow gold is the most popular in Europe and is 75 percent pure gold. 18-karat white gold is 25 percent nickel. 24-karat gold is 99.9 percent pure gold, 22-karat gold is 91.67 percent, and 20-karat gold is 83.33 percent. 20-karat and above is yellow in colour.

In America 14-karat yellow gold is the most popular. 14-karat white gold is harder and yellowish and used in prong settings. It's often plated with rhodium (a form of platinum) to enhance the whiteness.

12-karat gold is 50 percent gold; it is commonly used in class rings and can be a number of colours depending on the added alloy. 10k gold is 41.67 percent gold and is the lowest alloy to be called gold.

Why is the discovery of riches called "the motherlode"?

The expression "finding the motherlode" is usually used figuratively for the discovery of an abundance of almost anything, but it comes from the mining camps of the late nineteenth century. A *lode* is a mining term for a vein of metal ore, the

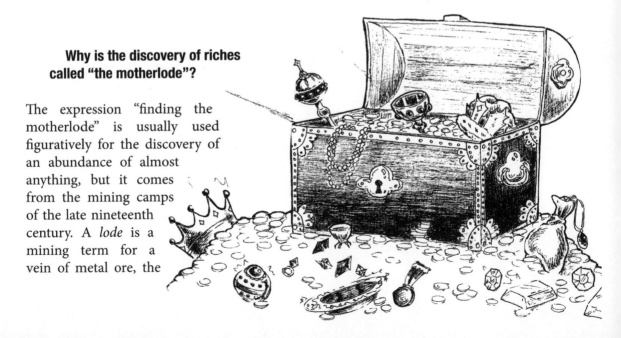

discovery of which would be exciting enough, but add *mother* and you've come across the origin of all the veins in the region. The motherlode is, literally, an abundant source of supply.

Why is a charge on imports and exports called a "tariff"?

When the Arab Moors invaded Spain in the eighth century they brought with them profound cultural and creative concepts that influence that country to this day. For example, when the matador skirts the bull in their life and death ballet, the Spanish crowd cries, "*Ole*," which evolved from the Arabic word *Allah*. Twenty miles from Gibraltar is the seaport of Tarifa, where the Moors introduced bounties on ships entering the Mediterranean, leaving us the word *tariff*.

Why do we say that someone with money is "well-heeled"?

Before cockfighting was banned in 1849, individual birds were often fitted with sharp steel spurs, giving them an advantage in mortal combat. They were "well-heeled." In the nineteenth century, the expression became slang for anyone armed with a weapon. Then, around 1880, the term began to mean anyone who was well off financially and who could overcome any obstacle with money instead of a weapon.

If you're short of cash why might you ask for a loan to "tide you over"?

If you ask for money to "tide you over," you are using a nautical term to reassure the lender that repayment is inevitable. When a boat or ship wants to enter a river from the ocean at low tide, its way will be blocked by the accumulation of mud or sand that has been swept downstream and collected at the mouth of the river. When the predictable tide rises and the obstacle is "tided over" the boat, like a borrower, can continue its progress.

Why was a prospector's credit line called a "grub stake"?

The first thing most poor gold prospectors needed to keep going was food and supplies. They would make a deal to share their future success with a general store or a wealthy acquaintance in exchange for credit to buy food, shovels, picks, and a pan to sift the gravel of a stream for nuggets. This credit was called a "grub stake." *Grub*, in this case, is a reference to shallow digging, as in "grubbing around." *Grub* can also mean "food." *Stake* was the money.

Who issued the first credit cards?

There once was a time when people only used cash. Credit was a personal issue between the dealer and individual customers. In the 1920s, gas companies and hotel chains started issuing cards for credit exclusively for use in their own establishments. By the late 1930s, some of these firms began recognizing each other's cards, but it wasn't until 1950 that the Diners Club came out with a fee-based card to use with a large number of unrelated businesses. Soon after, American Express took a similar approach. BankAmericard, which became Visa, issued the first bank credit card in 1959. MasterCard appeared in 1966.

Why are shares in a company called "stock"?

The modern concept of sharing capital ownership was initiated by the Dutch East India Company in 1612, which raised money by selling pieces of the business to the public. This process gave the Dutch East India Company the ability to grow and share its profits with its "shareholders." The original meaning of the word *stock* was the trunk of a tree. Like that trunk, stock in a corporation supplies the necessities of life to the branches. This nourishment to any size company is cash.

Stocks and *shares* are the same thing. *Stock* refers to an overall ownership in one or more companies within a portfolio. *Shares* signify ownership of one specific individual company.

Today a "stock market" is a place where securities are bought and sold, but the first one in London, England, was a fourteenth-century fish-and-meat market and was so called because it had been built on a site formerly occupied by the stocks used for corporal punishment.

Why is a middleman called a "broker"?

There are real estate brokers, wedding brokers, pawnbrokers, and, of course, stockbrokers. A broker is someone who arranges or negotiates things. It comes to English from the French wine industry, where *brocour* described the person who bought wine in bulk from the winery and then sold it from the tap. The accepted meaning became anyone who bought something in order to sell it again. In English, the word *brocour* became *broker*, meaning "the middleman."

Brocour first appeared in English in 1377 in Piers Plowman: "I haue lent lordes and ladyes my chaffare And ben her brocour after, and boughte it myself."

How did the centre of world commerce, Wall Street, get its name?

In September 1653, the settlers in what is now New York City felt threatened by the local Natives and by the possibility of an invasion by Oliver Cromwell's army from England. For protection, they built a large protective wall that stretched a half-mile across Manhattan Island. That wall was situated on the exact spot that we now know as the financial centre of the world: Wall Street.

Why are there "bulls" and "bears" in the stock market?

An eighteenth-century proverb mocks the man who "sells the bearskin before catching the bear." A "bearskin speculator," like the man in the proverb, sold what he didn't yet own, hoping that the price would drop by the time he had to pay for it. "Bulls" speculate, hoping the price will rise, and the struggle between the two comes from staged fights in which a bear needed to pull the bull down while the bull fought by lifting the bear with its horns.

If someone lacks confidence, why do we say that he's "selling himself short"?

If someone "sells himself short," he's probably nervous about the future, and for good reason. The expression comes from the stock market. "Selling short" means that you're selling shares you don't yet own. If an investor believes a stock is on the decline, he might gamble by selling it before purchasing it in the future at a lower price. The difference is his profit; unless the stock goes down, he pays the consequences of selling short.

Why is it said that something with proven quality has passed the "acid test"?

If someone has passed the "acid test," it usually means that he has proven his value through experience or trial. When gold was in wide circulation, jewellers and assayers needed a method of testing golden objects and nuggets that were brought to them for cash. Because nitric acid dissolves base metals but not gold, a drop was applied to the suspect object, and if the metal didn't dissolve, it had passed the acid text and was confirmed to be gold.

What is the "grey market"?

Grey market goods are legally sold through channels other than those authorized by the manufacturer. Unlike black market products, which may be counterfeits, grey market goods are the real thing. Entrepreneurs simply buy a product in one country where the item is significantly cheaper than another, then import it to the target market and legally sell the merchandise at a higher price. This situation commonly occurs with cigarettes and electronics, though importing legally restricted items leaves the grey and enters the black market. By avoiding the normal distribution fees or licences, consumers usually share in the profits of grey marketers through lower prices but are likely to discover that products acquired this way aren't supported or warranted by the manufacturer.

The existence of the grey market is an example of the economic practice called arbitrage. Grey market has a different meaning on securities markets. where the term refers to the buying and selling of securities to be issued in the future and, therefore, not yet circulating.

Quickies

Did you know ...

- that the speed of light is 186,272 miles per second? Sound travels at 1,088 feet per second, or roughly 742 miles per hour. This means that sound is about 900,000 times slower than light.
- that sound travels faster through water than air?
- a radio listener hears an announcer's voice before a person standing in the back of the average broadcast studio?
- if you have to slam on the brakes while driving at 55 miles per hour, your car will continue 56 feet between the time you decide to put on the brakes and the time you get your foot on the brake pedal?

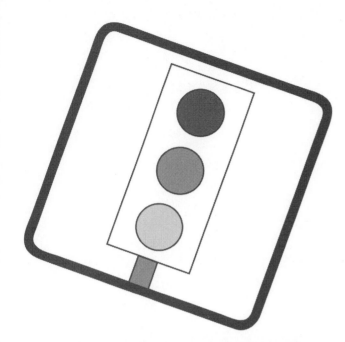

transportation and automobiles

Why do the British drive on the left side of the road while North Americans use the right?

The British custom of driving on the left was passed down from the Romans. The chariot driver stayed to the left in order to meet an approaching enemy with his right sword hand. Americans switched to driving on the right because on covered wagons, the brakes were built on the left, forcing the driver to sit on that same side and, consequently, to drive on the right so they could have a clear view of the road.

Why is a car's instrument panel called a "dashboard"?

The word *dashboard* came to the automobile directly from the horse and buggy. In the mid-nineteenth century, an apron, or board, was placed on the front of the vehicle to keep mud from the horses' hooves from splashing onto the passengers, especially when they were moving fast, or "dashing." Another carry-over term to cars from horse-drawn carriages is *axel*. The first wooden carriages used slender tree trunks to run under the wagon to hold the wheels in place. *Axel* is an early Scandinavian word for "tree."

Why is the energy from a car's engine referred to as "horsepower"?

When Scottish inventor James Watt received a patent on his steam engine in 1755, horses were being used to draw coal to a mine's surface. After calculating that one horse had the power to haul 330 pounds 100 feet in one minute, he proved that one steam engine could replace an entire herd of horses. This made Watt wealthy and gave us a formula to interpret engine capacity in horsepower.

Why do we park on a driveway and drive on a parkway?

The words *parkway* and *driveway* come from the days when only the well off could afford an automobile. The long, winding roads from the highway to the manor were, and still are, called "driveways." On the other hand, to ensure the pleasure of driving, highways were built carefully, with planted trees and groomed medians to imitate the natural beauty of a park, so they were called "parkways," meaning left in an enhanced natural state.

How did the Mercedes automobile get its name?

In 1900, the Daimler Corporation was commissioned to design and build a special racing car to add to the fleet of a wealthy Austrian named Emil Jellinek. Jellinek gave the special car the nickname "Mercedes," which was his daughter's name. Jellinek was so impressed with the car that he bought into Daimler, and when the company merged with Benz in 1926, company officials decided to keep the name and market a commercial car as the Mercedes Benz.

Why when wanting full speed and power do we say, "Gun it" or "Pull out all the stops"?

"Gun it" comes from early aviation and auto mechanics, who coined the phrase as an instruction to get more speed by pulling out the full throttle. This sudden injection of fuel caused a minor explosion in the combustible engine, which sounded like the firing of a gun. Stops on a pipe organ control volume, so to "pull out all the stops" refers to accessing the organ's maximum power.

Why are traffic lights red, green, and yellow?

Red, green, and yellow traffic lights developed directly from the trial and error of controlling railways during the nineteenth century. Trains needed advance warning to prevent fatal accidents and collisions. The first choice was red for stop, which was logical because red had symbolized danger for thousands of years. During the 1830s, engineers tried using green for caution and clear for go, but sunlight reflecting off clear lights gave false signals. So engineers solved the problem by introducing yellow for caution and making green stand for go. The very first traffic light using this system was introduced in Cleveland, Ohio, in 1914.

Where in the world were highways designed to be emergency landing strips during war?

Some highway systems are designed for use as landing strips, but they aren't in North America. There is a legend that the Eisenhower Interstate System in the United States requires one mile in every five to be straight so that it can be used as an airstrip during wartime, but no such law exists either in the United States or Canada. However, the highway systems of South Korea and Sweden have been designed with air war in mind.

Why do we say someone diverted from a goal has been "sidetracked"?

Early railroads had only a single track between destinations. Problems arose when a train was met by another going in the opposite direction or was overtaken by a faster one. This dilemma was solved with the creation of sidings, short lengths of track built parallel to the main line where one train could pull over while the other went by. The train had been "sidetracked," meaning that, for a time at least, it wasn't going anywhere.

Why is the last car on a freight rain called a "caboose"?

Up until the 1980s, laws required freight trains to have a caboose. It was a little shack on wheels and served as an office, a kitchen, and a bedroom for the crew. The caboose was also an observation deck from which brakemen could watch the train for shifting loads, overheating wheels, and other problems. The first such shanties were set up as tents on flatcars as early as 1830. *Caboose* is from the ancient German sailing term *kabhuse*, a temporary kitchen set up on the deck of a ship. Some of

> **Quickies**
>
> *Did you know ...*
> - you will spend about two weeks of your lifetime waiting for traffic lights to change?
> - you will walk roughly 65,000 miles in your lifetime?
> - that Carl C. Magee, of the Oklahoma City, Oklahoma, chamber of commerce, received a patent for the first "coin controlled parking meter" on May 24, 1938?

the nicknames used by rail crews for the caboose were "clown wagon," "hack," "brain-box," and "palace."

Why is top speed referred to as "full tilt"?

"Full tilt" means full speed. The word *tilt* began as *tealt*, an early English word for being unsteady. It was used as a reference to medieval jousting (also called tilting), where men on horseback leaned or tilted forward in their saddles and charged each other at top speed with lances, causing the contestant knocked from his horse to be more than a little unsteady. A letter written in 1511 makes reference to jousting as tilting: "Knightes shall present themselves … in harneys for the Tylte." "The History of Tom Thumb," circa 1600, contains the first written reference to "full tilt": "The cook was running on full tilt, when Tom fell from the air."

Why is "thumbing a ride" called "hitchhiking"?

Hitchhiking is a combination of two words. The term has two origins that collided in 1923 to describe an inexpensive way of travelling. *Hiking* means "to walk vigorously" and has been around forever. In 1578, the word *hitch* surfaced as a nautical description meaning "fastening with a hook," but it eventually gained broader use and was used in terms like "hitching a team of horses to a wagon" or "hitching a trailer to a car." *Hitchhike* was first employed in 1880 to describe hitching a sled to a moving car. The use of the thumb by someone looking for a ride is a symbolic hook to signal the hitchhiker's wish to become attached to a passing car.

What happened to the station wagon?

A station wagon was originally a horse-drawn carriage. The name transferred to cars in 1904, and in 1929 the first modern station wagon was manufactured. It referred to a car big enough to haul people and luggage to and from railway stations. Prior to the 1930s, most automobile makers used hardwoods to frame the passenger compartments of their vehicles, but when steel took over, designers extended a wood-panel finish to the exterior of multipurpose passenger-and-cargo cars. These became the classic station wagons that grew in popularity with suburban families after the Second World War. Station wagons were replaced by minivans or sport-utility vehicles (SUVs) during the 1980s and 1990s and have all but disappeared from the world's roads.

Where did the term *drag racing* originate?

Drag racing is a quarter-mile race between two cars starting side by side from a standing start. It began in the 1950s and was usually held on the main street of a small town. In the nineteenth century, because they were being dragged down the street by a horse, wagons and buggies were called "drags," and in the 1850s the name transferred to the main street; it became known as the "main drag," which gave drag racing a venue — and its name.

Why is something incredibly impressive called a "real doozy"?

A "real doozy" may be an old-fashioned expression, but it still means something remarkable. It was used to describe one of the most impressive cars ever made. Built between 1920 and 1937, the Duesenberg was the best and most expensive American car ever built. During the Great Depression, and at a time when a Ford sold for $500, a top-of-the-line Doozy retailed for $25,000. With a custom-built body and a high-horsepower engine, the Duesenberg quickly became a favourite vehicle of the rich and famous. It still is! As one of the most collectible cars in the world, Duesenbergs in mint condition have sold for millions of dollars. Now that's a doozy!

Why do we say we're "stumped" if we can't proceed?

We have all been stumped at one time or another, whether by a private or professional circumstance or perhaps by a mathematical or legal problem. *Stumped*, as in unable to proceed, comes from the first crude highways built by the early settlers in North America. It was the law that when trees were felled the stumps had to be at least fifteen inches high. That was fine until it rained and the ground turned muddy. The wheels on the wagons using the road would often sink until the axles got caught on tree stumps. The wagons couldn't move forward because they had been "stumped."

Why is a dead-end street called a "cul-de-sac"?

A cul-de-sac is any lane or street closed at one end so that the only way out is the same as the way in. The compound word *cul-de-sac* began as an anatomical term in 1738 for a very sensitive area behind the female cervix. It refers to a sack-like cavity or tube, open only at one end, and literally means "bottom of the sack." *Cul* is from the Latin word *culus*, meaning "bottom," while *sac* simply means "a bag." Although derived from French, the word *cul-de-sac* originated in England during a time when French was spoken by the ruling classes. It began meaning a dead-end street around 1800.

Cul is also a French vulgarity meaning "ass."

Why is a road called a "highway" and the ocean the "high seas"?

When the Romans built public roads between towns, they were raised higher and built better than other local private roads, and so they were called "highways." The implied sense of "for public use" also applies to the "high seas," which defines that part of the ocean beyond any countries' three-mile limit of sovereignty. In both cases the *high* means "for general or public use."

Odds & Oddities

- The odds of being killed during the course of a year in any sort of transportation accident are 77 to 1.
- The chance that one's next car ride will be one's last is 1 in 4,000,000, while the odds of being killed on a five-mile bus trip are 500,000,000 to 1. The odds of being killed while riding a horse are six times greater than the odds of meeting one's demise on a bus trip.
- The chance of dying from a car accident during one's lifetime is 1 in 18,585. Walking is safer. The one-year chance of dying while a pedestrian is about 1 in 50,000.
- The chance of dying in an airplane accident is 1 in 354,319.
- The odds of being killed in any sort of non-transportation accident are 69 to 1.
- The chance of being killed in a terrorist attack while visiting a foreign country is 1 in 650,000.
- The chance of dying from parts falling off an airplane is 1 in 10,000,000.

sailing on the
high seas

Why when abandoning ship do we say, "Women and children first"?

In 1852, the HMS *Birkenhead* was off to war in South Africa when she ran aground and sank off the coast of the Cape. The only useable lifeboats were quickly filled by the 20 women and children on board, while the 476 soldiers lined up on deck to go down with the ship. This is where the tradition of "women and children first" was born, and in naval circles is still called "the Birkenhead Drill."

What do the distress letters *SOS* stand for?

Morse code is a series of electrical impulses that signify the letters of a structured message. SOS doesn't stand for "save our ship" or "save our souls," as has been commonly believed. In fact, it stands for nothing. It was chosen as a distress signal at an international conference in 1906 because, at nine keystrokes — three dots, three dashes, three dots — it was thought to be the easiest combination to transmit.

Why are new ships christened with champagne?

Beginning around the tenth century with the idea that the departed spirits would guide seamen on the ocean, ships throughout the world were christened, or blessed, with the blood of sacrificial victims, which was splashed throughout the vessel. Eventually those who thought this too barbaric began using red wine, but the Christian church complained that this was an affront to its sacraments, and so ships were christened with white wine, the best of which is champagne.

Why are the sides of a boat called "starboard" and "port"?

In the primitive days of navigation, the helmsman stood at the stern of the ship, controlling the vessel's direction by hand with a rudder, which was on the right side and called a steer board, or, as the Anglo-Saxons called it, a "starboard." The left side of the ship is called "port" because with the steering mechanism on the right it was the only side that could be brought to rest against a harbour or port.

Why when we want someone to hurry do we say, "On the double"?

In civilian life, "on the double" means to do something in a hurry. In the military, where the expression originated, it is usually a clear command most commonly barked by a drill sergeant ordering his men to do a task "on the double," meaning to stop walking and start running. Just as bugles were used to relay drills to soldiers in the field, drums were utilized on ships to summon sailors to their battle stations. *Double* was an early reference to increase the drumbeat appropriately to convey urgency to all hands.

Why when someone we trusted turns against us do we say he's "shown his true colours"?

Sailing under false colours means to sail under an enemy flag, and it was once a legitimate naval manoeuvre used to get close enough to the enemy for a surprise attack. At the last moment, just before opening fire, the false colours were lowered and replaced by the ship's true colours. Although such deception is now considered dishonourable, we still say when someone we trusted reveals himself as the enemy that he is showing his "true colours."

Why is a quick exit described as "cut and run"?

If you make a rapid departure, especially under challenging circumstances, it could be said you've "cut and run." The reason is that the anchors of large sailing ships used to be attached to rope cables, so if the crew came under a sudden or surprise attack and there was no time to haul in the anchor, they would simply cut the rope, raise their sails, and run with the wind. They would "cut and run."

Who first said, "Damn the torpedoes, full speed ahead!"?

A torpedo can be a number of things, but it's best known as a self-propelled armed tube fired from a submarine. The word was first recorded as an explosive device for blowing up ships in 1776 and was referred to as a "floating mine." The word *torpedo* means "to numb." During the American Civil War, while he was attacking the Confederates at Mobile Bay, Alabama, in 1864, Admiral David G. Farragut (1801–1879) had his lead ship sunk by a mine. During the ensuing confusion, he uttered the famous words: "Damn the torpedoes, full speed ahead!"

Why when someone ignores the rules do we say he "turned a blind eye"?

In 1801, while second-in-command of a British fleet near Copenhagen, Horatio Nelson was told that his commander had sent up flags ordering a retreat. Nelson lifted his spyglass to his previously blinded eye and said he couldn't see the order, and then he ordered and led a successful attack. Nelson's insubordination became legend and gave us the expression "to turn a blind eye."

What was the original meaning of "stem the tide"?

The general (yet incorrect) use of "stem the tide" is to deflect a serious problem, but tides can't be deflected. A *stem* is the upright beam at the fore of the ship where the hull timbers form the prow. The nautical manoeuvre against a surging tide is the same as against an angry sea. The ship is turned to stem the onslaught. To "stem the tide" means that to overcome serious problems, you must face them head-on.

When someone is facing disaster, why do we say he or she is "between the Devil and the deep blue sea"?

To be "between the Devil and the deep blue sea" has largely been replaced by being "between a rock and a hard place," which came out of Arizona and originally meant to be bankrupt. The "devil" is the seam of a sailing ship's hull, which was reinforced to support cannons and which was where a board was fastened for those forced to walk the plank. The condemned sailor couldn't turn back, so his only option was the deep blue sea.

If you're abandoned and alone, why do we say you've been "stranded"?

If you've been stranded, you're abandoned and powerless. *Strand* came to English from the Scandinavians as meaning "beach" or "shore," and it now refers specifically to the beach area between the high and low tide. In the seventeenth century, a stranded ship had been beached or left aground on the strand after the tide went out. The general use of the word to describe helplessness dates to 1837.

If you want someone to stop "harping" on something, why might you say, "Pipe down"?

The use of *harping*, as in repeating the same annoying statement or sound, comes from the repetitive and irritating noise made from tuning each string of a harp. If you tell the person harping on one string to "pipe down," you are using a naval term. On early naval vessels, the boatswain's final function for the day was to whistle or pipe down a signal for the crew to settle in and be quiet for the night.

Where do we get the expression "batten down the hatches"?

"Batten down the hatches" is a traditional naval order to securely cover the openings or hatches to the hold on the deck of a sailing ship. *Batten* is the key word and comes from the same root as the French word *baton*, like the one used by an orchestra conductor or in a relay race. A batten is a strip of wood, which in this case was used to nail down a tarpaulin over the ship's hatches during a storm.

Why is gossip called "scuttlebutt"?

The word *scuttlebutt* comes from sailors of the British Navy. Nineteenth-century warships had large wooden casks with holes cut in the lid for drinking water. The word *scuttle* means a hole, like the one created to scuttle a ship, or in this case, the one in the cask. The water cask itself was called a *butt*. And just as is done by the water coolers of today's offices, sailors exchanged the latest gossip while getting a drink at the scuttlebutt.

Why is a pirate ship's flag called a "Jolly Roger"?

The purpose of a pirate ship's flag was to signal a merchant vessel that if it didn't surrender, it would be boarded and plundered by force. Pirates used a variety of flags. One was an hourglass that signalled time was running out. The skull and crossbones is of course the most famous flag, and it got its name, Jolly Roger, from the English pronunciation of "*Ali Rajah*," which is Arabic for "king of the sea."

Why did pirates wear earrings?

Earrings were used by seamen, especially warriors such as pirates, for very practical reasons and not for decoration. They were given to young sailors as a symbol of their first crossing of the equator, and their purpose was to protect the eardrums during battle. The pirates, especially those who fired the ships' cannons during close combat with the enemy, dangled wads of wax from their earrings to use as earplugs.

Why would you give a "swashbuckler" a "wide berth"?

Swashbuckler, a word we use for a pirate, was created from the archaic words *swash*, meaning "to make noise by striking," and *buckler*, meaning "shield." A swaggering brute yelling and banging his sword on his shield was called a swashbuckler. These bullies were given a "wide berth," which in nautical lingo means to anchor or berth a ship a safe distance away from another that might cause trouble.

Where does the disciplinary order "toe the line" come from?

"Toe the line" is the same as "toe the mark" and means "follow the rules or pay the consequences." In many sports, such as foot racing, the athletes were required to stand with their toes against a scratched line to ensure a fair start. As punishment in the navy, no matter what the weather, nineteenth-century trainees were forced to stand for hours with their toes touching a seam on the ship's deck, and this too was toeing the line.

Why when waking up do we say, "Rise and shine" or "Shake a leg"?

"Rise and shine" comes from a 1916 United States Marine Corps manual that instructed noncommissioned officers to enter the privates' barracks in the early morning and use the phrase to wake the men. While *rise* means "get up," *shine* means "make sure your boots and brass are ready for inspection." The Royal Navy used "shake a leg" to warn any women who might be sleeping in a hammock to show a leg or suffer the embarrassment of being rousted with the men.

What's the origin of the expression "son of a gun"?

Early in the eighteenth century, wives and girlfriends (as well as the occasional prostitute) were allowed to go to sea with the sailors during long voyages. When one of them became pregnant and was about to give birth at sea, a canvas curtain was placed near the midship gun where the birth would take place. If the newborn's father was in doubt, and it often was, the birth was registered in the log as the "son of a gun."

Why do we call the conclusion of anything unpleasant "the bitter end"?

"The bitter end" has been used to describe the conclusion of something distasteful since the mid-nineteenth century. It's a play on the word *bitter*, as in "sour," and the nautical *bitters*, the posts on a ships deck where cables and ropes are wound and tied. When securing the ship to the dock, or while at anchor, the very end of the rope or cable holding the vessel secure is called the bitter end.

Why is the telling of a tall tale said to be "spinning a yarn"?

If someone is "spinning a yarn" they are exaggerating the truth. First printed about 1812, the expression is nautical and has nothing to do with domestic spinning. Sailors were required to spend long tedious shifts working in pairs, spinning fibers into the endless miles of rope needed to keep their sailing ship sound. To pass the time, they entertained themselves by telling tall tales, or "spinning yarns."

Why is the speed of a ship measured in knots?

In the 1600s, sailors measured the speed of their sailing ships by tying knots in a rope at sixty-foot intervals, then further dividing and marking the space between the knots into ten equal parts that would each be one fathom in length. Then a heavy floating log was tied to the rope's end and thrown into the ocean. The rope was let out through a reel, and speed was measured by the number of knots that passed through the reel in thirty seconds of an hourglass.

Why is a limited space called "close quarters"?

Being at "close quarters," meaning to be overwhelmed within a small space, is a naval term from the 1700s. Merchant sailing ships laden with valuable cargo had their decks outfitted with four strong wooden barriers with musket holes to which they could retreat and continue to fight if they were boarded by pirates or privateers. They referred to these desperate circumstances as fighting at "close quarters."

Why when it appears that we can proceed with no danger do we say, "The coast is clear"?

The person who says, "The coast is clear" sounds as though he or she is being cautious about avoiding legal detection, and so it should be. It originated as the standard cry from the man in the crow's nest of every pirate ship before it chanced a landing. When the captain verified with his telescope that there was no danger in going ashore, he would repeat the cry, "The coast is clear!" And so it became an order for his fellow smugglers to prepare to land.

Why does "jury-rigged" mean a temporary repair with whatever is at hand?

In the seventeenth century, when a ship's mast was damaged at sea, a "jury mast" was rigged to hold the sail until the replacement could be found. Because this was a critical situation the repairs had to be done within a day, or in French *un jour*, which in this case is the origin of *jury*. Jury-rigged is a temporary repair and has nothing to do with "jerry-built," which means permanent bad work.

Why do we say that someone arrogant needs to be "taken down a peg"?

A ship's colours are raised or lowered to signal the ship's status. "All flags flying" signals great pride, but flags could also indicate degrees between failure and conquest. These flags were once held in place by a system of pegs, so lowering them was done by taking down a peg. This was a shame to the ship and its crew and gave us the expression for humiliation "to be taken down a peg."

Why do we say that someone who has overcome an obstacle with ease has passed with "flying colours"?

Since the eighteenth century, ships of the navy have used flags to communicate their status or well-being. The most prominent flag, of course, is that of the ship's country, but there are dozens of other banners, which are called "colours." The most elaborate use of this bunting is after a victory at sea, when a triumphant ship returns to its home port with a proud and full display of flying colours.

Why do we describe something approximate as "by and large"?

In early sailing jargon, *by* was "by the wind," and when a helmsman was ordered to fill the sails he was told to steer "full and by." This required great skill and was called steering small. A less experienced helmsman might have been told to steer large with the order "by and large," which meant use the wind but don't fill the sails. This is how "by and large" came to mean not quite, but close enough.

Why do we say that something lost has "gone by the board"?

During the time of wooden ships, sailors often referred to their sailing vessel as "the boards." We still use their language when we board a ship or are on board as part of a crew. *Outboard* is outside the boat, while *inboard* is inside. When a sailing ship's mast was broken by enemy cannon or in a storm and couldn't be salvaged, the captain would order the ropes holding it to be cut, letting it drift away or "go by the board."

Why is a severe labour dispute called a "strike"?

Conditions on board commercial sailing ships were miserable. On long voyages, food and water went bad and hygienic conditions were lower than for animals in a stable. If they suspected that a ship was poorly prepared, it wasn't uncommon for the crew to strike the main sail, making it impossible to go to sea until conditions improved. This gave us the word *strike* to describe any extreme action by labour against management.

Why is someone standing apart said to be "aloof"?

If someone is emotionally or physically reserved, we say they are "aloof." This remoteness is sometimes interpreted as being regally snobbish or simply shy. *Aloof* is derived from the nautical word *loof*, which in early sixteenth-century English meant "windward direction" or "the weather side of the ship." The helmsman directed the ship into the wind to keep from being blown onto coastal rocks. He was ordered to keep his distance from the shore with the order "Hold a-loof," which is how *aloof* took on the general meaning of "keeping clear."

Why are windows in ships and planes called "portholes"?

Openings on the sides of a ship have been called "portholes" since 1243. The word *port* comes from the Latin *porta*, which means "door" or "gate." Because steering apparatus or the "steerboard" was on the right, ships of the time docked on their left, which was originally known as the "larboard" side because it was the loading side. In the sixteenth century, "larboard" gave way to "portside" to avoid confusion with the similar-sounding "starboard" or right side. The term *porthole* is most commonly used to describe windows on both sides of airplanes and ships, but the it comes from the openings on the portside to load cargo onto ancient ships.

What does it mean when someone suffers a "sea change"?

Sea change is a term often used in politics that refers to a surprising and significant change from a previous position. Because early sailors were familiar with the sudden and unpredictable temperament of the sea, one minute calm and the next minute life-threatening and dangerous, they introduced the expression "sea change" into everyday English as meaning any sudden transformation.

Why do we say that somebody who is being treated badly has been "hung out to dry"?

Discipline on early British sailing ships was necessary but often extreme. The lash or cat-o'-nine-tails left sailors scarred for life, but the act of keelhauling — tying a victim with rope and pulling him under the ship, sometimes more than once — was the discipline feared most. If the prisoner survived drowning, he was suspended from the yardarm, where he was left hanging or "hung out to dry" for a predetermined period of time, then cut down to contemplate his misdemeanours.

Why do we say that something likely to happen soon is "in the offing"?

Something "in the offing" isn't about to happen in the present, or even soon, but it will certainly happen before too long. *Offing* (originally *offen* or *offin*) is an early nautical term that describes the part of the ocean most distant from the shore but still visible. So someone who was watching for a ship would first see it in the "offing" and realize that its arrival was imminent. The phrase "in the offing" was first used during the sixteenth century.

What is the origin of the word *squeegee*?

A squeegee brings to mind either spring cleaning or an annoying panhandler at a traffic light. The word probably had an equally unpleasant effect on the sailors who gave the scraping instrument its name. *Squeege* was an eighteenth-century alteration of *squeeze* or *press* and was the inspiration for the name of a tool used for scraping the decks of ships. In *Moby Dick*, American author Herman Melville (1819–1891) called the tool a squilgee, but other sources indicate that *squeegee* was a nautical term for the instrument as early as 1844.

Why is a person facing serious trouble said to be in "dire straits"?

Strait is a Middle English word that was used by sailors to describe a narrow or tight and difficult-to-manoeuvre channel of water such as the Straits of Gibraltar or the Bering Strait. The word comes from the Latin *strictus*, meaning "to bind tightly." *Dire* also has a Latin root and means "terrible" or "fearsome." Although "dire straits" now signifies any serious day-to-day problem, it originally meant facing an obstacle so difficult to overcome that the odds against navigating through it successfully were overwhelming.

Why is the residue of a shipwreck called "flotsam and jetsam"?

"Flotsam and jetsam" is sometimes used broadly as "odds and ends," but its origin dates back to the late sixteenth century as a description of debris left after a shipwreck. *Flotsam* is whatever is left of the cargo or ship that is found floating on water. *Jetsam* is cargo or parts of the ship thrown overboard to lighten the ship in an emergency, and which subsequently sinks or is washed ashore. Today the expression might also be used to describe debris from a plane wreck.

Flotsam came to English through the Old French verb *floter*, meaning "to float." *Jetsam* is an alteration of *jettison*.

Valuable items thrown into the sea but attached to a buoy so they can be recovered after the ship goes down are called *lagan*.

Why do sailors call the bottom of the sea "Davy Jones's locker"?

"Davy Jones" seems like such a nice normal name, but this mythical creature struck terror into the hearts of ancient mariners. Going to his locker meant you were a man overboard and destined to die, because the locker was at the bottom of the sea where Biblical images of Jonah and the whale came into play. Davy Jones presided over all evil spirits in the sea and could shape-shift into hideous forms, often perching on the riggings during hurricanes or shipwrecks.

Davy Jones first appeared in literature in 1751 in *The Adventures of Peregrine Pickle* by British novelist Tobias Smollett.

There is a colourful legend that Davy Jones was a pub owner who would get young men drunk and then confine them in the locker where he stored his beer until he could sell them to a ship short of hands.

Why did sailors sing "shanties"?

Sea shanties are the songs sung by sailors working on the great sailing ships of a more romantic time. A shanty man leads the songs. He chants a line, and the sailors respond within the rhythm of their work. Shanties take different forms, depending on the labour being done. There are short-haul shanties and long-haul shanties for operating the sails. There are shanties used to raise and lower the anchor, and there are shanties whalers used to sing.

Sea songs became known as *chanties* or *shanties*, from the French *chantez*, meaning "to sing," in around 1867. The word *shanty*, "a small, crude cabin," is French-Canadian and has a different root. The term *shanty town* was first recorded in Canada in 1876. The designation "Shanty Irish" was inspired by the title of a 1928 book by hard-boiled American writer Jim Tully (1886–1947).

Why did sailors begin wearing bell-bottom trousers?

British sailors started wearing bell-bottom trousers near the end of the eighteenth century. Before then they wore "slops," a loose-fitting mid-calf-length pant. "Bells" were only worn by "swabs," or regular seamen, and not by officers. Regulation dictated that the bells be made of wide cuffs large enough to roll up to the thigh during wading or deck swabbing. Although most eighteenth-century sailors couldn't swim, they were taught to pull up and tie the bells of their pants, creating air-filled life preservers, if they fell overboard.

American sailors stopped wearing bell-bottoms in around 1998 when they became part of the dress uniform only. However, when the supply ran out in 2000, bell-bottoms in the U.S. Navy disappeared altogether.

Why is someone lost in boredom said to be at "loose ends"?

The origin of this phrase is nautical and refers to the ends of the countless number of ropes on early sailing ships. These ends needed to be bound tightly to prevent unravelling, which could cause disaster at sea. Whenever a captain noticed that his men had too much time on their hands, which could lead to trouble, he would order them to check the ropes and repair any "loose ends."

Quickies

Did you know ...
- that blue blazers originated as military jackets worn by British sailors on the nineteenth-century ship HMS *Blazer*?

Is a flag flown upside down a signal of distress?

The use of flags to signal distress is a very old naval tradition, but flying the national flag upside down isn't one of them. From a distance it's hard to read whether a flag is or isn't upside down. The rule was that when you needed help, you drew attention to your ship by doing something unusual, such as arranging the sails in an un-seaman-like manner or by flying the ensign upright but in an unusual place. The most commonly agreed-upon distress signal in Britain's Royal Navy was to tie an ensign into a "wheft" or a "knot" and fly it from the foretop-gallant masthead. The word *wheft* is a variant of *waif*, which literally means "unclaimed property."

An ensign is a national flag displayed on ships and aircraft, while an insignia is a badge or emblem indicating rank, unit membership, or nationality. A flag is a cloth ensign and derives from *flagstone* because it is square and flat. On land an ensign tied in a wheft and flown upside down over a fort was sometimes a signal of distress, but the knot was still the key. Today there are sixteen standardized international naval distress signals.

More Lofty Origins of Overused Phrases

- "Where there's life there's hope."
  — Marcus Tullius Cicero (106 B.C.–43 B.C.)
- "Time is more valuable than money." — Theophrastus (*c.* 372–*c.* 287)
- "A man's home is his castle." — Sir Edward Coke (1552–1634)
- "Thirty days hath September, April, June, and November ..."
  — Richard Grafton (d. *c.* 1572)
- "Cleanliness is next to Godliness." — Charles Wesley (1707–1788)
- "The good die young." — William Wordsworth (1770–1850)
- "Hell is paved with good intentions." — Samuel Johnson (1709–1784)

the dope on
horse racing

What designates a colt, a filly, a mare, and a gelding in the world of Thoroughbred horses?

The official birth date of all Thoroughbred racehorses is January 1 of the year they were born, regardless of the actual birth date. All horses are foals until they are a year old. Between the ages of two and five, males are called colts while females are fillies. Beyond the age of five, male horses are simply called horses while females are mares. A male horse that has been neutered is referred to as a gelding, while one preserved for breeding purposes is a stallion. These designations are important because Thoroughbred racing uses age to determine equitable divisions for competition. *Gelding* is from the Viking word *geldr*, which means "barren."

Why is the ancestry of a Thoroughbred called its "pedigree"?

A pedigree for any animal is a lineage of heredity. For instance, pedigree must be traced to determine if a horse is a Thoroughbred, which is a breed of horse descended from three Arabian stallions brought to Britain and Ireland in the seventeenth and eighteenth centuries and bred with local mares. *Pedigree* came from the French *pie de grue*, meaning "the foot of a crane," which the forked lines of a family tree resemble.

Why do we ask for "the real dope" when we want the truth?

Dope is from the Dutch word *doop*, meaning "a thick sauce," and became a drug term from the semi-liquid form of opium smoked by drug addicts. The use of *dope* meaning "stupid" came from the ridiculous behaviour of someone under the influence of the drug. The use of "the real dope" as meaning information arrived in around 1900 when gamblers checking on racehorses needed to know whether or not any of the horses were drugged or doped.

Why is a sure winner called a "shoo-in"?

The confusion around a "shoo-in" is in the spelling, which is often written "shoe-in." The shoe isn't footwear. Instead, it's spelled as in *shooing* something to make it move quickly. The term comes from dishonest horse racing when, after conspiring to bet on a probable loser, the jockeys hold back their mounts and urge or "shoo in" a chosen horse through the pack, where it will cross the finish line first and pay off at great odds.

Why when someone has won without question do we say that he did it "hands down"?

To win hands down has nothing to do with placing a winning hand of cards face down. Instead, the expression comes from the earliest days of horse racing. If a horse had proven its superiority and was approaching the finish line well ahead of the pack, the jockey would release the reins, giving the animal free rein to the finish. He therefore would win the race "hands down."

Why is a horse race sometimes called a "derby"?

In England it's properly pronounced "darby," but everywhere else, including here, it's known as a "derby." In 1780, the twelfth Earl of Derby was having dinner with his friend Sir Charles Bunbury when they decided to sponsor a horse race for three-year-olds in Surrey, England. They tossed a coin to decide after which of them the race would be named and Derby won — otherwise the most exciting two minutes in sports would be the Kentucky Bunbury.

Why is an obstacle-filled horse race called a "steeplechase"?

In early England, the church was the centre of a town's existence and was usually the largest and most prominent structure. For travellers on horseback, the first sign of their destination was the lofty church steeple rising above the trees. To the tired traveller, the sight was exhilarating and inspired the horsemen to quicken their paces, very often racing to see who could arrive at the steeple first. From this, a horse race became known as a "steeplechase."

Why is an underdog victory called an "upset"?

The word *upset* means to be unhappy or tipped over. It had nothing to do with sports until August 13, 1919, when, in his seventh race, the great horse Man o' War, who had defeated all of the other greats of his day by fifteen lengths or more, fell victim to an inexperienced starter and lost the race to an unknown competitor named Upset. From then on, *upset* became synonymous with a victorious underdog.

Man o' War retired with a record of twenty wins and only that one loss to Upset. He retired as a three-year-old, lived to be thirty, and became one of the greatest sires in the history of horse racing.

How long is a furlong?

The furlong is an ancient British unit of measurement, literally meaning the length of a furrow. It's the distance a horse can pull a plow without resting, which was calculated at exactly 220 yards, or 201.168 metres. When the Romans introduced the mile to Britain, it was changed in length to accommodate a tidy eight furlongs. This was done because all property and other precise distances such as that of a horse race were measured locally in furlongs.

When a person is upset, why do we say someone's "got his goat"?

When someone "gets your goat," it usually means you've lost your temper or become angry enough to be distracted. It's a term that came from a horse trainer's practice of putting a goat in a stall with a skittish racehorse to keep him calm before a big race. An opponent or gambler might arrange for the goat to be removed by a stable boy, which would upset the horse and its owner and so reduce their chances of winning.

Why do we say that someone who has an advantage has "a leg up"?

If you have "a leg up" on your competition then you're ahead of the game because you've received a boost. The expression comes from the equestrian world. When a rider needs help mounting a large horse, he might ask someone for a leg up. That someone will then create a foothold by cupping both hands so that the rider can use this to step up and get into a position to get his leg up and over the horse's back.

Why does coming in "under the wire" mean you've just made it?

To make it "under the wire" means another instant and you'd have been too late. Before modern electronics, stewards posted at the finish line determined the winners of horse races. A reference wire was strung across the track above the finish line to help them see the order of finish — or which nose crossed the line first. The result of a horse race was determined by the order in which the horses passed under the wire.

Why do we call a person who competes on horseback an "equestrian"?

Equestrian is a word used to describe a competitive horseback rider and entered English in 1656 as meaning a "knight on horseback." The horse has evolved over 50 million years to become the majestic animal exhibited at various competitions today. *Equestrian* is from the Latin word for *horse*, which is *equus*.

Why are candies on sticks called "lollypops"?

At the end of the nineteenth century, most candies were too large and dangerous for a child's mouth, and because they were sold unwrapped, they inevitably caused a sticky mess on clothes, faces, and fingers. That was enough to make many parents keep their children from buying them. In a stroke of marketing genius, George Smith of Connecticut solved the problem by putting the candy on a stick. He named his invention after a famous racehorse of the time, Lolly Pop.

Why is an unknown contestant called a "dark horse"?

Sam Flynn, a travelling Tennessee horse trader, often found a horse race planned in the same town as an auction. So he mixed a coal black racing stallion named Dusky Pete in with his work horses, then quietly entered him in the local races and wagered heavily on Dusky Pete, who would invariably win. As word spread of Sam's deception, so did the caution: "Beware the dark horse."

Why is a determined person said to be "hell bent for leather"?

It is a good idea to stay out of the way of anyone "hell bent for leather." The word *bent* has meant a mental inclination other than straight since 1586 and resurfaced as "bent out of shape," meaning "extremely upset or weird," during the 1960s. "Hell bent" means the disturbed subject is in a big hurry and extremely determined to achieve a goal. The "for leather" part derives from an 1889 reference to horseback riding, with the leather being the bridal and saddle. The expression then meant "riding very fast" and began as "hell for leather."

Hell is often used in association with speed, for example "go like hell" or "run like hell."

holidays and special occasions

How was the date of Christmas established?

Early scholars believed that prophets died on an anniversary of their birth. Once they established Good Friday as either March 25 or April 6, they reasoned that Christ's incarnation was nine months later, which would be either December 25 or January 6. The choice was not solely to comply with pagan superstitions; in A.D. 386, when the date was established, any date would have collided with pagan rituals because they filled the calendar year.

Neither the date of Christ's birthday nor that of his crucifixion is given in the Gospels.

How did holly become associated with Christmas?

No one knows the exact date of Christ's birth, although May 30 is the most popular scholastic guess. December 25 was chosen early in the fourth century partly in an effort to convert those of other religions who celebrated the winter solstice. Holly was a prominent part of pre-Christian winter celebrations and was used to bring these others into the fold by having its leaves symbolize a crown of thorns and its red berries symbolize Christ's blood at the crucifixion.

Why are Christmas songs called "carols"?

A Christmas carol is a song of religious joy, but the musical form of a carol doesn't have to include Christmas. Its main feature is the repetition, either musically or chorally, of a theme, as in a circle. The word *carole* entered English from the French at the end of the thirteenth century, but it's much older than that. Originally, a carole was a ring dance where men and women held hands while dancing and singing in a circle.

How did the poinsettia, a Mexican weed, become associated with Christmas?

One hundred years ago, Dr. Joel Poinsett, the American ambassador to Mexico, introduced the plant to the rest of North America. A Mexican legend has it that two poor children had nothing to offer the baby Jesus during the Christmas festival, so on their way to church they picked some green weeds from the road side. When they placed them at the nativity the green petals turned a bright red in the shape of a star.

Is *Xmas* a disrespectful commercial abbreviation of *Christmas*?

Xmas has its roots legitimately grounded in the Greek word for "Christ," which is *Xristos*. In the sixteenth century, Europeans adopted the first letter from Xristos as an initial for Christ's name, and even though the practice had been common among the early Christians, some North Americans, not understanding the Greek language, mistakenly took the *X* as a commercial insult.

How did Christmas cake become a tradition?

A dish of porridge that once ended the fast on Christmas Eve evolved into a pudding with dried fruits and spices as a tribute to the Wise Men. By the sixteenth century, the pudding had become a fruitcake, served during the parish priest's home blessings on Twelfth Night. In 1870, after the Protestant Queen Victoria banned Twelfth Night celebrations because they were "unchristian," clever confectioners began selling their fruitcakes as "Christmas cake."

When exactly are the twelve days of Christmas?

The twelve days of Christmas are the days separating December 25 and the Epiphany, or the date of Christ's baptism, which is January 6 — the legendary date that the three Wise Men visited the stable with their gifts. It was once the custom to pile up gifts on December 25 and then distribute them over the days leading to January 6. In North America, the tradition is now only a memory through the carol "The Twelve Days of Christmas."

What is the meaning of the carol "The Twelve Days of Christmas"?

Between 1558 until 1829, Roman Catholics were restricted in practising their faith openly in England. During this time a Christmas song was written as a catechism for teaching young Catholics the scriptures. Each element in the carol has a code word for a religious reality, which the children could remember.

The partridge in a pear tree was Jesus Christ.

Two turtledoves were the Old and New Testaments.

Three French hens stood for faith, hope, and love.

The four calling birds were the four gospels of Matthew, Mark, Luke, and John.

The five golden rings recalled the Torah or Law, the first five books of the Old Testament.

The six geese a-laying stood for the six days of creation.

Seven swans a-swimming represented the sevenfold gifts of the Holy Spirit: prophesy, serving, teaching, exhortation, contribution, leadership, and mercy.

The eight maids a-milking were the eight beatitudes.

Nine ladies dancing were the nine fruits of the Holy Spirit: love, joy, peace, patience, kindness, goodness, faithfulness, gentleness, and self-control.

The ten lords a-leaping were the Ten Commandments.

The eleven pipers piping stood for the eleven faithful disciples.

The twelve drummers drumming symbolized the twelve points of belief in the Apostles' Creed.

At the end of the "Twelve Days of Christmas" your true love will have delivered 364 gifts.

Why are fruits and nuts offered over Christmas?

December 21 is the day of the winter solstice: the year's shortest day and longest night. It's known as St. Thomas Day, commemorating the last apostle to be convinced of Christ's resurrection. On this day a bowl of nuts and fruits is put on display to ensure prosperity in the new year, and by sharing these, the wish is extended to friends and neighbours. Failure to share this providence could mean a lean crop in the following seasons.

Why do we hang stockings at Christmas?

According to legend, the very first gifts St. Nicholas gave were to three very poor girls who needed money for their wedding dowries. On Christmas Eve they hung their stockings to dry by the fireplace. St. Nicholas slipped in at night and left gold coins in each of their stockings so they could marry the men they loved. Until recently, Christmas stockings were filled with nuts and fruit. The Italians introduced giving a lump of coal to naughty children.

What's the story behind "O Little Town of Bethlehem"?

In 1865, inspired by a horseback trip from Jerusalem to Bethlehem, Reverend Philip Brooks of Philadelphia composed a poem, which he eventually showed to Lewis Redner, the organist at the Church of the Holy Trinity, wondering if he could put the words to music. Redner was stumped — that is, until Christmas Eve, when it came to him in a dream. The next morning, the carol we know as "O Little Town of Bethlehem" was born.

What's the story behind "Silent Night"?

On Christmas Eve in 1817, when Father Joseph Mohr of St. Nicholas Church in Arnsdorf, Austria, found that a mouse had chewed through the bellows of his church pipe organ, he rushed to the home of music teacher Franz Gruber. The two men quickly wrote a musical piece, hoping it would save the Christmas Mass. With Father Mohr playing guitar, they sang their song in harmony to a small Austrian congregation who became the first to hear the most beloved carol of them all — "Silent Night."

"Silent Night" was performed by troupes of Tyrolean Folk Singers, but by 1848, when Father Mohr died penniless at fifty-five, "Silent Night" had fallen into obscurity. In 1854, King Frederick William IV of Prussia heard the song and was so moved, he became responsible for its revival.

How did "Greensleeves" become a Christmas song?

The ballad "Greensleeves" was first published in 1580, but no doubt had been known long before that. One early lyric ("Lady Greensleeves") was a love song to a well-dressed woman, possibly a prostitute. The music's first application to Christmas appeared in *New Christmas Carols of 1642* and was entitled "The Old Year Now Is Fled." William Dix, a British insurance agent, wrote a poem in 1865 entitled "The Manger Throne." In 1872 a publisher took three of the poem's many verses, set them to the "Greensleeves" melody, and published the resulting song as "What Child Is This?"

Contrary to a popular legend, England's King Henry VIII (1491–1547) did not write the music for "Greensleeves."

What are we saying when we sing, "Deck the halls with boughs of holly"?

The Middle Dutch word *decken* meant "to cover or adorn" and came from *dec*, which originally meant any cover, such as a tarpaulin or a roof, and was borrowed into English as a nautical term in the fifteenth century. Although today a backyard deck might mean a wooden patio, a ship's deck was not a floor but a roof to cover cannons. The Christmas carol "Deck the Halls" is saying simply "cover the walls" with boughs of holly.

Why is Christmas referred to as "the Yuletide"?

The ancient Germanic peoples celebrated the winter solstice with a feast day for the pagan sun god Jul, which is still the preferred Scandinavian reference to Christmas and survives in our Yule log. Fearing the sun god had disappeared during the year's longest night, a vigil was held from dusk to dawn and the Yule log was lit to encourage the sun's return and to discourage evil spirits returning to the Earth's surface.

It was Pope Gregory I who suggested that missionaries not challenge the Northern pagan practices and traditions, but rather transfer their meaning to Christianity.

The Yuletide covers all December feast days, including Chanukah.

Why do we kiss under the mistletoe?

Two centuries before Christ's birth, the Druids celebrated the winter solstice with mistletoe because it enhanced fertility and was a favourite of the gods. The Romans hung it prominently during orgies, which is how it became associated with kissing and also why the church banned it in the fourth century. The name *mistletoe* is from the Germanic word *mista*, meaning "manure" or "dung," because the plant grows out of oak trees well-fertilized by bird droppings.

Why do we light the Christmas tree?

In the sixteenth century, Germans began decorating fir trees with ribbons, flowers, apples, and coloured paper. Inspired by the reflection of stars off branches in the forest, Martin Luther placed lit candles on his indoor tree. After three hundred years of candles, Edward Johnson introduced electric Christmas lights outside his Fifth Avenue home in New York in 1882. Johnson also worked on the invention of the light bulb with Thomas Edison.

Considering his workload, how much time does Santa spend at each child's home?

Travelling at about a thousand miles a second, or 3.6 million miles an hour, Santa covers 111 million miles in 31 hours. Within one second he must visit 500,000 homes, which is why we seldom see him. Of course he does have help, and in some cases he delivers presents before Christmas or even works on Boxing Day, but it's still very hard work.

When is the proper time to take down the Christmas tree?

From the very beginning of Christmas traditions, January 6 — the day of the Epiphany — was the official end of gift giving, and the most popular day of the celebration. Some people still celebrate the Epiphany as being more important than Christmas Day. Regardless, January 6 is the last day of the festival, and that is the day to take down the tree and decorations. To do otherwise is bad luck.

Which Jewish tradition still influences Christmas celebrations?

The celebration of Christmas begins with Midnight Mass, and the calendar date is December 25, but every Christian knows that the reverence begins on Christmas Eve. Christmas Eve comes directly from the Jewish custom of beginning religious rituals with ceremonies starting at sundown the evening before the holy day with candles and prayers lasting until the following sundown — in this case, Christmas Day.

What's the story behind Chanukah?

The word *Chanukah* means "rededication." Over 2,300 years ago, the Syrians occupying Judea were overthrown after years of fighting by a Jewish army led by Judas Maccabaeus and his four brothers. The Syrians, led by King Antiochus, had ordered the Jewish people to reject their God and customs and replace them with Greek symbols and deities. The Syrians had desecrated the Jerusalem Temple with their own gods; while cleaning and reclaiming the temple, the Israelites found enough oil to light the eternal lamp for only one day, but incredibly the flame flickered for eight days, a miracle celebrated to this day as the "Festival of Lights."

The rededication of the temple was on the twenty-fifth day of the ancient month of Kislev (scholars are uncertain whether this was in the new calendar months of November or December).

Maccabaeus means "hammer."

Judea was, in part, what is now Israel.

Which culture began celebrating the new year with a feast of food and alcohol?

The earliest recorded New Year's festival was in ancient Babylon in what is now Iraq. Before the introduction of a calendar year, the celebration took place in spring during the planting season. The Babylonian feast was elaborate, lasting eleven days, and included copious drinking and eating in a tribute to the gods of fertility and agriculture. Celebrating the new year was both a thanksgiving and a plea for a successful new harvest.

Why is New Year's Eve celebrated with noisemakers and kissing strangers?

New Year's Eve is the night of Holy Sylvester, the Pope who converted the Roman Emperor Constantine to Christianity. With the Emperor's conversion, pagan gods fell from favour but fought back through the souls of the living. To combat their return, during the darkness of New Year's Eve, people wandered the streets shouting to strangers, frolicking with noisemakers, and generally acting foolish — a custom that resurfaces every New Year's Eve.

Pope Sylvester I (A.D. 314–335) cured the Emperor Constantine of leprosy.

Some New Year's Eve revellers disguised themselves as mummers so that the demoted gods couldn't identify and punish them as they wandered the streets.

What is the origin of New Year's resolutions?

In medieval times, during the last feast of the Christmas week, knights of the realm were required to place their hands on a peacock and vow to continue living up to their pledge of chivalry. This was known as the knight's "peacock vow." The New Year's custom of resolving to live a better life originated with the Babylonians, who promised the gods that they would return all borrowed farm and cooking tools and pay off personal debts.

What is the origin of the New Year's song "Auld Lang Syne"?

The tone and lyrics of "Auld Lang Syne" seem to capture perfectly the emotions involved in the passing of the fleeting accomplishments and losses of one calendar year coinciding with the rise of hope in a new one. *Auld lang syne* is Scottish and literally means "old long since," or, in modern language, simply "long ago." The song was written down by the poet Robert Burns, but he wasn't the composer. Burns heard the folk song being sung by an anonymous old man and copied it down before passing it on to become a ceremonial fixture of New Year's Eve.

What is the religious significance of Groundhog Day?

February 2 is an ancient Christian holiday celebrating Mary's purification and is known as Candlemas Day. Christians believed that if the day dawned sunny, crop planting would have to wait because winter would last six more weeks. During the 1880s, a few friends in Punxsutawney, Pennsylvania, went groundhog hunting every Candlemas Day. They became known as the Punxsutawney Groundhog Club, with a mascot named Phil.

Who receives the most Valentine's cards?

Valentine's Day is second only to Christmas as the largest annual card-sending holiday. One billion cards are sent each year! Women purchase 85 percent of all Valentine's cards, so men receive more, but then 15 percent of women send *themselves* flowers on February 14. In order of popularity, the cards are sent to teachers, children, mothers, wives, and sweethearts. As well, 3 percent of all Valentine's cards are sent to pets.

How did March 17 become St. Patrick's Day?

When the time came to honour the patron saint of Ireland's birthday, church officials gathered solemnly to choose a day, then realized that most of St. Patrick's life was a mystery. They finally narrowed his birthdate down to either March 8 or 9, but because they couldn't agree which was correct, they decided to add the two together and declared March 17 to be St. Patrick's Day.

How did the shamrock become a symbol of St. Patrick?

In the fifth century, Patrick, the patron saint of Ireland, transformed that country from its pagan roots to Christianity. During an outdoor sermon, Patrick was struggling to explain the Holy Trinity when he spotted a shamrock. He used its three leaves to illustrate how the Father, Son, and Holy Ghost grew from a single stem, symbolizing one God sustaining the trinity, and ever since, the shamrock reminds the faithful of that lesson.

Did St. Patrick rid Ireland of snakes?

There were never any snakes in Ireland. The story of St. Patrick banishing snakes from Ireland is a metaphor for the eradication of paganism during the fifth century. St. Patrick did, however, superimpose a circle representing the sun, a powerful pagan symbol, on what is known as the Celtic cross.

Why is the season of pre-Easter fasting called "Lent"?

Lent begins on Ash Wednesday and is the forty-day fast that precedes Easter. The forty days are an imitation of Christ's preparation for his ministry, which reached its climax with the crucifixion and resurrection. The word *Lent* has no religious significance whatsoever. It comes from the Old English word *Lencten*, which was the Anglo-Saxon name for the season we now call spring, within which Easter is celebrated.

In all languages other than English, the season of Easter fasting has a name derived from the Latin term *Quadragesima*, or "the forty days."

What are the origins of Ash Wednesday?

At the beginning of Lent, which always falls on a Wednesday, Catholics mark their foreheads with a cross made of ashes to symbolize their commitment to Christ. The ashes are from burned palm fronds used in the previous year's celebration of Palm Sunday. In ancient times, when someone died, it was a mourning custom to sit inside and cover one's head and body with dust and ashes as a mortal reminder that we are all "from ashes to ashes and dust to dust."

How did the rabbit and eggs become symbols of Easter?

The word *Easter* comes from the ancient Norse word *Ostara*, which is what the Vikings called the festival of spring. The legend of a rabbit bringing Easter eggs is from German folklore, which tells of a poor woman who, during a famine, dyed some eggs then hid them in a chicken's nest as an Easter surprise for her children. Just as the children discovered the nest, a big rabbit leaped away, and the story spread that it had brought the eggs.

How did the white trumpet lily become the Easter lily?

During the 1880s, while in Bermuda, Mrs. Thomas Sargent became enamoured of the beautiful white Bermuda trumpet lily. She took its bulbs back to Philadelphia, where it caught on among local florists. Since it blooms in spring, the flower soon became known as the "Easter lily," and its popularity spread. The lily had been introduced to Bermuda from its native Japan and is now grown primarily on North America's Pacific coast.

What are the origins of April Fool's Day?

Up until 1564, the French celebrated New Year's between March 25 and April 1, but with the introduction of the new Gregorian Calendar the festival was moved to January 1. Those who resisted became the victims of pranks including invitations to nonexistent New Year's parties on April 1. Soon the April 1 celebration of a non-occasion became an annual festival of hoaxes.

How did we start celebrating Mother's Day?

In 1907, Miss Anna Jarvis of West Virginia gave the congregation a white carnation to wear at the church service on the second anniversary of her

254 • NOW YOU KNOW BIG BOOK OF ANSWERS

mother's death. But Mother's Day became increasingly commercial, and Miss Jarvis spent the rest of her life trying to restore its simplicity. The strain of her efforts to stop Mother's Day and what it had become led her to the Marshall Square Sanitarium, where she died alone and penniless in 1948.

How did Father's Day get started?

During a Spokane, Washington, Mother's Day service in 1910, a Mrs. Sonora Dodd thought of how she and her five brothers had been raised on a small farm by her single father. She proposed a Father's Day celebration, and although it caught on locally, it was a political hot potato and didn't receive permanent recognition until an edict by President Richard Nixon in 1972. Father's Day is now the fifth-largest card-sending occasion in North America.

Where did the customs of Halloween come from?

The ancient Celts celebrated October 31 as New Year's Eve. They called it "All Hallows Eve." They believed that on that night, all those who had died in the previous twelve months gathered to choose the body of a living person or animal to inhabit for the next year before they could pass into the afterlife. The original Halloween festival included human sacrifices and scary costumes and was designed to protect the living from the dead.

Why do children ask us to shell out treats on Halloween?

As a challenge to Halloween, the Roman Catholic Church placed All Saints Day on November 1. On that day, Christians went from village to village begging for soul cakes, a mixture of bread and currants. One cake bought one prayer for the souls of the donor's departed relatives. The phrase "shell out" as a demand for payment comes from the shelling of dried peas or corn, once a currency of commercial exchange among the poor.

Why do children demand, "Trick or treat" during Halloween?

When the Irish introduced Halloween to America, children celebrated with a night of mild vandalism. Their bag of "tricks" included breaking or soaping windows or overturning outdoor toilets. Soon they realized that adults would offer candy or other "treats" to stop these tricks. They then offered the homeowner a choice of giving them goodies or suffering the consequences. This mild blackmail demand came as "Trick or treat?"

Why do we carve jack-o'-lanterns for Halloween?

In Irish folklore, a supreme con man named Jack, or Jack-o, once tricked the Devil himself. Upon his death, his sins barred him from heaven, and because he had once fooled the Devil he couldn't enter hell. After a lot of begging he finally persuaded Satan to give him one burning ember. Placed in a hollowed-out turnip it served as a lantern to light his way through the afterlife. Later in North America, the plentiful pumpkin replaced turnips for use as "Jack-o's lanterns."

How did bobbing for apples become a Halloween tradition?

Halloween was the Celts' most significant annual holiday. After the Romans invaded Britain, they respected and adopted a few of the Celtic practices, and during the first century A.D., the two cultures began integrating their late autumn rituals. In October, the Romans celebrated Pomona, the goddess of fruit and trees. Her symbol was an apple, which is how that fruit, whether bobbing for it or otherwise, became symbolic of Halloween.

religion and beyond

Why is a morality lecture called a "sermon"?

A sermon is generally thought of as a religious discourse delivered by a preacher from a pulpit, but it can also be any tedious lecture or exhortation on right and wrong from a pompous or self-righteous person. Its chief requirement is that it must be long, because the word *sermon* is from the Latin *sermonem*, meaning "the stringing together of words" within a speech or talk. It entered English from French in around 1200 as *sermun*. A *sermonette* is simply a short sermon and dates from 1814.

There is no mention of the word *sermon* in the Bible.

Why do Christians place their hands together in prayer?

The original gesture of Christian prayer was spreading the arms and hands heavenward. There is no mention anywhere in the Bible of joining hands in prayer, and that custom didn't surface in the church until the ninth century. In Roman times, a man would place his hands together as an offer of submission that meant "I surrender, here are my hands ready to be bound or shackled." Christianity accepted the gesture as a symbol of offering total obedience, or submission, to God.

Why do we refer to the celebrants of the first Thanksgiving as "Pilgrims"?

The New World settlers from the *Mayflower* weren't called Pilgrims until two hundred years after their 1620 arrival at Plymouth Rock. It was Daniel Webster, in a bicentennial celebration of their landing, who first described them as "Our Pilgrim Fathers." The word comes from the Latin for "traveller." *Perager* became *pelegrin*, then *pilegrim* in English, evolving into *pilgrim*. The term was first used to describe Christians who made a journey of religious devotion to the Holy Land.

How did the word *halo* come to mean divinity?

The word *halo* is Greek and literally means "threshing floor," because it described the circular track followed by a team of oxen while threshing golden-coloured grain. The idea of the halo has pagan roots and wasn't accepted by the Christian church until the seventh century. Its symbolism of heavenly authority is the reason monarchs wear crowns and Native chiefs wear bonnets of feathers. In religious paintings a halo suggests a sacred aura.

Why is happiness referred to as "seventh heaven" or "cloud nine"?

The ancient Jews believed that the highest heaven, or "heaven of heavens," the home of God and his chosen angels, was the seventh heaven. The Muslims agreed that the seventh heaven was the pinnacle of ecstasy. "Cloud nine" was coined by the American weather bureau and means "as high as clouds can get," or between thirty and forty thousand feet. Its meaning as a euphoric state came about in the 1950s.

How did astrology connect the lives of Winston Churchill, Franklin Roosevelt, and Charlie Chaplin with that of Adolf Hitler?

Chaplin and Hitler were associated astrologically from birth, because both men were born within the same hour in the same week of the same year. The date connecting Churchill and FDR with the German dictator is January 30. It's the date of President Roosevelt's birth, Winston Churchill's death, and Hitler's ascension to power in Germany.

Why is the head of the Roman Catholic Church called the "Pontiff" or "Pope," and where is the "Holy See"?

In Italian, the word *Pope* is an endearment meaning "father" or "papa." The responsibility of the leader of the Roman Catholic Church is to build bridges between God and mankind, and the title *Pontiff* is from the original Roman reference *pontifex*, meaning "bridge builder." "Holy See" is a corruption of "Holy seat," and refers to the place where this seat or throne is housed.

Why do we describe someone with
deeply held beliefs as "dyed in the wool"?

"Dyed in the wool" describes someone whose thoughts on politics or religion just can't be changed. The original meaning of the phrase was applied to the dying of raw wool, which, if done in bulk before being combed or woven, allows the wool to hold its colour much longer than wool dyed after processing. Today, "dyed in the wool" means that like the colour in the unprocessed yarn, convictions ingrained early, during childhood, will last the longest.

Why do we say that a bad deal will only "rob Peter to pay Paul"?

In the mid-1700s the ancient Cathedral of St. Paul's in London was falling apart, and the strain on the treasury was so great that it was decided that it would merge with the diocese of the newer St. Peter's Cathedral in order to absorb and use their funds to repair the crumbling St. Paul's. The parishioners of St. Peter's resented this and came up with the rallying cry, they're "robbing Peter to pay Paul."

Why is something tasteless said to be "tawdry"?

In A.D. 672, the eventual St. Audrey entered a convent for a life of penance and prayer. As a young woman she had worn fine necklaces, a habit she now considered the cause of her terminal neck tumour, which she covered with a scarf. After her death, women honoured her by wearing fine silk St. Audrey scarves, which through time were followed by cheap imitations for the English lower classes, who pronounced "St. Audrey" as "tawdry."

When someone we are discussing
shows up, why do we say, "Speak of the Devil"?

When someone recently mentioned in a conversation suddenly turns up we might say, "Speak of the Devil," as though our conversation has brought the subject into our midst. This is precisely what the expression means, because in the Middle Ages it was believed that any mention of the Devil would be an invitation for the evil one to appear either in spirit or in action, and so other than within ecclesiastical circles, his name was avoided at all costs.

Why do we describe an upset person as being "beside himself"?

If someone is "beside himself," he is extremely distraught. You might even say he is out of his mind, because the ancients believed that under extreme distress the soul left a man's body and stood beside the human form, which left the subject literally beside himself. This absence of the soul gave the Devil an opportunity to fill the void. Extreme pleasure could also cause this condition. The Greek word *ecstasy* means "to stand out of the body."

Why do we say that something dwindling is "petering out"?

Supplies that are gradually diminishing are said to be "petering out," and someone exhausted is "all petered out." The expression was used by both Abraham Lincoln and Mark Twain and is derived from a very old mining term used to describe a vein of ore that splits into branches and then gradually runs out, leaving the miners and investors high and dry. The image is of Saint Peter, who left Jesus when he was needed most.

Why is something we consider untrue called a "cock and bull" story?

In the sixteenth century a papal *bull* or *bulla* was a decree from the Roman Catholic Pope and was sealed with a stamp bearing the likeness of St. Peter accompanied by the cock that crowed three times before the crucifixion. After the reformation, Martin Luther issued bulls of his own that contradicted the Vatican. His followers considered papal decrees as lies and referred to them from their seals as "cock and bull."

Why was grace originally a prayer said after a meal?

Today, we say grace before a meal in thanksgiving for an abundance of food, but in ancient times, food spoiled quickly, often causing illness or even death. Nomadic tribes experimenting with unfamiliar plants were very often poisoned. Before a meal, these people made a plea to the gods to deliver them from poisoning, but it wasn't until after the meal, if everyone was still standing, that they offered a prayer of thanksgiving, or "grace."

Why do most flags of Islamic countries have the same basic colours, and what is the symbolism of the crescent moon and star?

The Turkish city of Byzantium was dedicated to the goddess Diana, whose symbol was the crescent moon. In A.D. 330, Constantine rededicated the city to the Virgin Mary and added her symbol, the star. The symbol was common on the arm of Christian soldiers, including Richard I. When Muslims captured the city in 1453, they reconfigured the two symbols and added their own religious significance — the crescent moon and star of Islam represent a conjunction of the moon and Venus during the dawn of July 23, 610, when the Prophet Mohammed (peace be upon him) received his first revelation from God. Mohammed carried two flags into battle: one was green, while the other was black with a white outline, the same basic colours of Islam to this day.

Byzantium became Constantinople before becoming modern-day Istanbul.

The Star and Crescent was first hoisted as a Muslim symbol by Mohammed II in 1453.

Christians dropped the symbol when it became prominent among Muslims.

Who gets to be a martyr?

Martyrs are people who choose torture or death rather than renouncing their beliefs or principles. The English word derives through Latin from the Greek *martur*, meaning "witness." The first Christian martyr is said to have been St. Stephen, who was stoned to death after being convicted of blasphemy by a Jewish court around A.D. 33. Jewish martyrs include a group of forty who died during the Crusades when they refused to renounce their faith and accept Christianity. In Islam the first martyr is said to be an old female slave named Sumayyah bint Khabbab, who was tortured and killed in front of Mecca by polytheists, people who believed in many gods.

Why is a religious woman who lives in a convent and vows poverty, chastity, and obedience called a "nun"?

Women who are sisters within a strict religious order today are called nuns, a word that has evolved through time to mean compassion and kindness. In Sanskrit, *nana* meant "mother," and it is often still used today as an endearment for grandmothers. In Latin, *nonna* means "child's nurse," again still used in the form *nanny*. In Greek, *nane* simply meant "good." All of these gave us the word *nun* to describe the strength and good intentions of the religious vocation.

Why is an intolerant person called a "bigot"?

A bigot is someone who is intolerant of any religion, race, group, or politics other than his or her own. The word began as a curse and was first recorded in English in 1598 as meaning "a superstitious hypocrite." *Bigot* originated as *bi got* from a common Old French slur against the Normans that today would be translated as "By God!" with the intended meaning of "God damn it!"

Legend has it that when the first Duke of Normandy, Rollo, was ordered to kiss the foot of the French King Charles III (879–929), he refused by uttering the curse "*Bi got!*"

Why is someone who challenges what appears to be an obvious truth called a "Devil's advocate"?

During Roman Catholic proceedings leading to the assignment of sainthood, a specific individual is given the job of investigating the candidate and the validity of any associated miracles. He then argues vehemently against the canonization by denigrating the potential saint on behalf of the Devil. His official Vatican title is the "Devil's Advocate."

Why at the end of a profound statement do Christians, Muslims, and Jews all say "amen?"

The word *amen* appears 13 times in the Hebrew Bible and 119 times in the New Testament as well as in the earliest Muslim writings. The word originated in Egypt around 2500 B.C. as *Amun*, and meant the "Hidden One," the name of their highest deity. Hebrew scholars adopted the word as meaning "so it is" and passed it on to the Christians and Muslims.

What Biblical curiosities are within a deck of cards?

Some people have found religious significance in a deck of cards. To them, the thirteen cards in each suit represent Jesus and the twelve Apostles or Jacob and the twelve tribes of Israel. The jack, king, and queen suggest the Holy Trinity, and when these court cards are removed the remaining forty cards remind them of the numerous references to the number forty in the Bible, including the number of days Jesus fasted and the years the Israelites wandered in the desert. Moses was on Mount Sinai for forty days, Jesus preached for forty months and was in the tomb for forty hours, Jerusalem was destroyed forty years after the Ascension, Elijah traveled forty days before he reached the cave where he had his vision (1 Kings 19:8), and Nineveh was given forty days to repent (Jonah 3:4).

Why shouldn't you say, "Holy mackerel," "Holy smokes," or "Holy cow"?

As innocent as it seems today, "holy mackerel" began as a blasphemous Protestant oath against the Friday fish-eating habit of Catholics. The fish was an early symbol of Christianity. Likewise, "holy smokes" is a snide reference to religious incense burning, while "holy cow" is a shot at Hindus who consider cows sacred. "Holy moley" is an abbreviation of "holy Moses."

Euphemisms are used as curses without direct reference to a religious icon. Even though it is clear what they mean, it is a way of swearing without offending the pious.

How did Pat Robertson's television show *The 700 Club* get its name?

Today, Pat Robertson's Christian Broadcasting Network is a multi-million-dollar conglomerate, but when they first went on the air in 1961, Robertson's refusal to seek commercial revenue meant that only prayer and telethons kept them going. At the time, Robertson told his audience that a club of seven hundred viewers contributing ten dollars each per month would pay expenses. The success of Robertson's effort gave *The 700 Club* its name.

Why do we say that someone who's finished or fired has "had the biscuit"?

If someone has "had the biscuit," they're definitely done, regardless of the circumstances. The expression has its origins in a Protestant allusion to the Roman Catholic sacrament of Extreme Unction. *Biscuit* is a contemptuous reference to the host (the sacramental wafer used by Catholics during the issuing of the last rites to a dying person). If he's "had the biscuit," it's all over.

What are "guardian angels"?

A guardian angel is a heavenly spirit assigned by God to watch over each person during his or her individual life. The angel is part of the dogma of the Roman Catholic faith and is there to help guide people and keep them from evil or danger. The feast to honour guardian angels is on October 2.

Like unidentified flying objects (UFOs), angels come in a variety of forms, depending on whose vision is believed. Moses was visited by an angel in the guise of a burning bush, while Jacob said that he saw wingless angels climbing a ladder to heaven. Witnesses swore they saw angels in human form beside the tomb of Jesus. Ezekiel (of the wheel fame) boasted that he saw cherubim with four wings, while Isaiah outdid him by claiming to witness seraphim angels with six wings. After that the common image of an angel with two wings, as depicted by most artists to this day, was settled on.

The English word *angel* is from the Greek *angelos*, meaning "messenger." The Hebrew word for angel is *malak*, which also means "messenger." In the Koran, angels are said to have two, three, or four pairs of wings or forelimbs, depending on how the Arabic word *ajnihah* is interpreted.

What is a "patron saint"?

Patron saints are chosen as guardians or protectors over specific areas of life. These can be chosen by people or groups without papal consent simply because the saint's interest or life experience relates to a group or individual. The church has, however, chosen many patron saints such as the writer Francis de Sales, who was picked to be the patron saint of writers and journalists. Angels can also be named as patron saints.

What does the *H* in "Jesus H. Christ" stand for?

The exclamation "Jesus H. Christ!" is often used as an attempt to avoid a blasphemous curse. Of course, even though it still takes the Christian Lord's name in vain, it is usually accepted as a joke. The epithet is based on "HIS" or "IHC," which is an abbreviation of Jesus' name in ancient Greek and is common in the earliest versions of the New Testament. It is still found on Catholic and Anglican vestments. The exclamation came from the misconception that these were Jesus' initials.

Why is the book of Christian scriptures called a "Bible"?

The Christian book of scriptures was first called the "Bible" by the Greeks. The ancient Phoenicians had found a way to make a form of paper from the papyrus plant, which gave us the word *paper*. They had done this in the city of Byblos, which is why the Greeks called the new paper *biblios*, and a collection of related writings or a book was soon called a *biblion*. By A.D. 400, the word *Bible* emerged to exclusively describe the Christian collection of scriptures.

Byblos is now called Jubayl in modern Lebanon. The lowercase word *bible* now means any book of authority.

Why is someone displaying absolute loyalty said to be "true blue"?

With the slogan "a true covenantor wears true blue," the Scottish Presbyterians adopted blue as their colour in the seventeenth century during their defence of their faith against Charles I. The instruction came from Numbers 15:38 in the scriptures, which tells the children of Israel to fringe the borders of their garments in ribbons of blue. Blue is a powerful symbol of Judaism and the national colour of Israel.

Why when someone receives an unfair judgment do we say they've been given a "short shrift"?

Shrift is an ancient word and comes from the act of shriving, which is the confessional process conducted by a priest. In his pursuit of forgiveness, a confessor seeks absolution for the sins of his soul through a process of penance administered by the priest. A short shrift refers to the brief time allowed with a priest to a condemned convict just before his execution.

Why do witches fear the expression "By bell, book, and candle"?

The expression "By bell, book, and candle" is often associated with witchcraft because those who practice the dark arts are in danger of being excommunicated by the Catholic Church. After pronouncing a sentence of excommunication, a bell is rung, a book (the Bible) is closed, and a candle is extinguished.

Why do we say that someone going nowhere is "in limbo"?

To be in limbo means nothing is happening, neither good nor bad. Because the Christian Church believed that only those "born again" could enter heaven they needed an afterlife destination for the other good souls. Limbo is the rim of hell and the destination for the righteous who died before the coming of Christ as well as infants, unbelievers, and the unbaptized. Limbo is a place without glory or pain.

Why are ministers of the gospel called "Reverend," "Pastor," or "Parson"?

Reverend first appeared in seventeenth-century England and is derived from the Latin *reverendus*, meaning "worthy of respect." *Pastor* is from the Latin word for shepherd, which is how Christ referred to himself. On the other hand, *parson* comes from New England, where because the minister was one of the few who could read or write they called him "the town person," which in the local accent became "the town parson."

What is a "sphinx?

Although the statue at Giza in Egypt is the most famous sphinx, there is another. According to Greek mythology, the original Sphinx was a female winged creature with the body of a lion that attacked travellers near Thebes and then strangled and devoured those who couldn't answer her riddle: "What creature has one voice yet becomes four-footed, then two-footed, then three-footed?" Eventually, Oedipus defeated the Sphinx with the answer to the riddle: "A human crawls on all fours when a baby, walks on two feet when grown, and uses a staff when old."

In Egyptian mythology, the Sphinx is just as nasty but is wingless and male with the body of a lion. *Sphinx* is the Greek word for "strangler."

Quickies

Did you know ...

- *jeepers* (1929), *jeez* (1923), *gee* (1895), and *gee whiz* (1885) are all euphemistic alterations of *Jesus*?
- *heck* (1865) is an alteration of *hell*?
- *dickens*, as in "It hurt like the dickens," is a euphemism for the Devil (from *devilkins*)?
- the fish is a powerful symbol of Christianity and was once a required meal on holy days? Halibut is from the Nordic word *hali*, meaning "holy," and *butte*, meaning "flat."

the many faces of
politics

Why do we call someone seeking political office a "candidate"?

In ancient Rome, someone seeking election would appear in public wearing a white robe to symbolize his pure character. *Candidate* comes from *candidatus*, meaning a man wearing pure white. Not fooled by the white toga, the Romans said that politicians needed to make three fortunes while in office: the first to pay back the money borrowed to buy votes, the second to bribe officials when eventually tried for misconduct, and the third for retirement.

Why when someone tells a secret do we say they've "spilled the beans"?

As a system of voting, the ancient Greeks placed beans in a jar. They called these small beans or balls were called *ballota*, which gives us the word *ballot*. A white bean was a "yes" and a brown bean was a "no." The beans were then counted in secret so the candidates wouldn't know who voted for or against them. If the container was knocked over, and the beans were spilled, the secret was out of the jar.

Why are governmental and legal delays called "red tape"?

English monarchs used to write legal decrees on rolls of parchment and then bind them up with red silk ribbons. To give their work an important appearance, government bureaucrats copied the "red tape" practice. Not to be outdone, lawyers followed with ribbons of their own. The expression took hold after Charles Dickens described the frustration of dealing with governmental and legal bungling as "cutting through red tape."

Where did the sarcastic phrase "Bob's your uncle" come from?

"Bob's your uncle" is a common British phrase and now means that you've accomplished something without much effort. It originated in 1887 when Prime Minister Robert Cecil appointed his nephew, Arthur Balfour, chief secretary for Ireland. The public was outraged at this blatant act of nepotism and began using "Bob's your uncle" to describe any situation where favouritism influenced the outcome.

Why is the use of behind the scenes influence called "pulling strings"?

Marionettes are puppets controlled by strings and were popular at the courts of the French monarchy. The puppet shows satirized gossip and could be embarrassing to anyone involved in scandal. When money was slipped to the puppeteer to keep him quiet or to influence him to embarrass someone else, it was said that the person offering the bribe — and not the puppeteer — was the one pulling the strings of the marionette.

Why is political favouritism called "pork barrel politics"?

Long before refrigeration, North American farmers kept supplies of salt pork stored in barrels, and the amount of meat on hand indicated the family's prosperity. If the barrel was low on pork, it meant the possibility of disaster through starvation. When a politician sought and gained favouritism for his constituents, he was said to have filled the pork barrels of those who had elected him, thereby assuring his re-election.

Why are political positions referred to as "left" and "right"?

Over two hundred years ago, King Louis XVI of France was forced to convene a form of parliament for the first time in more than a century. At the assembly, the more radical delegates took up seats on the left of the King, while their conservative counterparts sat on his right. Ever since, liberal views have been referred to as from the left, and conservative ideas as from the right.

How are the two Presidents Bush related to President Franklin Delano Roosevelt?

George Herbert Walker Bush became the second descendant of passengers on the *Mayflower* to become president; his son George W. Bush was the third. In 1620, Jane De La Noye was a small girl who arrived in America with her parents aboard the *Mayflower*. She was the first president Bush's grandmother eleven times removed. Her cousin, Phillip De La Noye, had his name become Americanized to Delano, and his grandson eleven times removed was Franklin Delano Roosevelt, making Roosevelt and the two George Bushes cousins.

Why do Conservatives call Liberals "bleeding hearts"?

The ultra-conservative view of those who propose extending the welfare state is that they are "bleeding hearts." That expression entered politics in the 1930s, and by the 1990s "my heart bleeds for you" had become a general put-down. It comes from the Middle Ages, when a socially conscious group known as the Order of the Bleeding Heart was formed to honour the Virgin Mary, whose "heart was pierced with many sorrows."

Why is a false promise called "pie in the sky"?

In the early 1900s, a radical workers union used a song called "The Preacher and the Slave" to blame the church for suppressing the poor with promises of rewards in heaven. The song included these lines (and from them, "pie in the sky" took the meaning of a false promise):

> You will eat, bye and bye,
> In that glorious land above the sky.
> Work and pray, live on hay,
> You'll get pie in the sky when you die, bye and bye.

Why is someone you don't want to hear from told to "take a back seat"?

"To take a back seat" means that you have little or no influence in the decisions required to fulfill an objective, and has nothing to do with "back-seat driving."

It comes from the parliamentary system of government, where the leaders of all parties — those who make and debate the critical decisions — are seated on the front benches of the House, while those who follow the party line with no input in these matters, other than a vote, take a back seat.

Why is something useless called a "boondoggle"?

The word *boondoggle* was first used in 1935 to describe "make-work" projects during the New Deal of American President Franklin Delano Roosevelt (1882–1945). It meant any useless task created simply to give men employment during the Great Depression. Surprisingly, the word comes from the Boy Scouts whose braided leather lanyard is simply cosmetic with no real purpose. It was named a "boondoggle" by R.H. Link after the leather frills worn by American frontiersman Daniel Boone (1734–1820). The word survives with the contemptuous political meaning of money wasted on unimportant or meaningless projects.

Why when we know the outcome do we say, "It's all over but the shouting"?

If the outcome of a circumstance is known before a procedure is ended, we say, "It's all over but the shouting." The expression comes from a widespread practice in early England. For centuries, when a straightforward public issue was to be decided, an assembly of townspeople was called for an informal election that was settled by shouting out a verbal vote rather than handing in a ballot. These assemblies were called "shoutings." When there was no doubt about the result even before the vocal vote was called, it was considered to be "all over but the shouting."

Why does "Hail to the Chief" introduce the American president?

When the American president enters a room "Hail to the Chief" is preceded by a fanfare of four drum and bugle ruffles and flourishes. The number of ruffles and flourishes indicates the importance of the person being introduced — not "Hail to the Chief," which is from the English dramatization of Sir Walter Scott's poem "The Lady of the Lake" and which became a popular band number for introducing any important person around 1812.

As a fanfare, four ruffles and flourishes is the highest American honour.

President Carter did away with "Hail to the Chief" for a time during his term.

Because it was a popular melody commonly used for dignitaries, there is no record of when "Hail to the Chief" made the transition into a signature for the president. It just evolved.

In 1810, James Sanderson wrote to a friend that Scott's "The Lady of the Lake" was being made into a play in London. Soon after, Scott received a note from an army officer friend including the music for the Boat Song, now known as "Hail to the Chief."

Why are those seeking political favour from elected officials said to be "lobbying"?

The term *lobbying* originated from the earliest days of the British Parliament, where an extensive corridor runs between the Chamber of Lords and the House of Commons. Because the general public was allowed into this corridor, or lobby, it was where constituents waited to meet with their representatives in order to influence their votes on current legislation. This practice was called "lobbying" because it took place in the lobby.

Where did the bearded figure Uncle Sam come from?

Sam Wilson was a meat packer who supplied preserved beef to the U.S. Army in the nineteenth century. The barrels of meat were stamped "U.S." to indicate they were property of the United States, but the soldiers joked that the initials stood for "Uncle Sam" Wilson and that the supplies were from that man. The bearded figure of "Uncle Sam" was drawn and introduced by Thomas Nast, the same cartoonist who created the Republicans' elephant and the Democrats' donkey.

Why do we say that a political candidate on a speaking tour is "on the stump"?

When early European settlers were moving west and clearing the land, every farm had an abundance of tree stumps in their fields. "Barnstorming" politicians who looked for a place of prominence to be seen and heard by the gathered electorate would invariably find a large tree stump to stand on from which he would make his pitch. This gave us the expression "on the stump," which is still used to describe a politician seeking election.

Why do we say that healing a relationship is "mending fences"?

In 1880, the strong-willed senator John Sherman was testing the water for a presidential nomination. He slipped out of Washington but was followed to his Ohio farm by a reporter who found the senator talking with a high-ranking party official while standing near a fence. When the reporter asked what they were doing, the response, "We're mending fences," gave him his headline, and it became a new phrase for healing relationships.

Why are unelected advisers to government leaders called a "kitchen cabinet"?

Most government leaders have unofficial non-elected advisers outside their legitimate cabinet, and these people have been labelled a "kitchen cabinet." The expression was coined in 1832 when Andrew Jackson (1767–1845) was president of the United States. He used to hold frequent unofficial private meetings with three close friends, and in order to avoid scrutiny or criticism, they entered through the back door of the White House and then through the kitchen. From that time on the press referred to the president's inner circle as the "kitchen cabinet."

What's unusual about the music to the American national anthem?

In 1814, after a night in a pub, Francis Scott Key was taken prisoner during the war between Canada and the United States. When he saw the American flag still flying over Fort McHenry he was inspired to write his famous lyrics with one particular barroom song, "To Anacreon in Heaven," still in his mind. And so "The Star Spangled Banner" was written to the tune of a traditional old English drinking song.

Why are British, Australian, and Canadian heads of government, cabinet chiefs, and church leaders called "ministers"?

The notion of the "prime" or first minister as the leader of government was introduced to Great Britain in 1646. Cabinet members or departmental ministers have been selected from elected representatives within that parliamentary system since 1625, but the reference to those holders of high office of the state as "ministers" began in 1916. In this case, the word *minister* means "servant." They are servants to the crown, not their constituents. In the religious world, *minister* means a servant of the church hierarchy, not the congregation, and dates back to 1315.

Robert Walpole (1676–1745) is usually considered to be the first "prime minister" of Britain. However, he was not actually called that. In Britain the term did not become official until 1905.

When addressing a "prime" or "cabinet" minister, it is inappropriate to prefix the greeting with "mister" as in "Mister Prime Minister" or "Mister Minister," which is a common mistake in the American media and sometimes in Canada when used by uninformed reporters. The word *minister* is correct in itself, and adding *mister* is redundant. The prefix *mister*, as in "Mister President," is correct when greeting the American president or his cabinet because they head a republic and not a crown state.

Why is the organized obstruction of legislation called a "filibuster"?

When an American legislator delays or prevents the passage of a bill through tactics including long speeches his action is called a "filibuster." The word is from the Spanish *filibustero*, which is what they called the pirates of the West Indies. *Filibuster* was first used to describe obstructionist tactics in the U.S.

Senate in 1851 because those in the minority who were holding up the passage of a bill until their demands were met were likened to pirates.

Within a democracy, what are the fourth and fifth estates?

Within British history, the first three estates with influence over legislation were the Church, the House of Lords, and the House of Commons. The term *fourth estate* has meant different forces of influence over Parliament at different times, including the army. It was first used to describe the press during a debate in the House of Commons in 1828 and has retained that meaning ever since. The fifth estate was added to include radio and television.

What was the cost to our human heritage of the American invasion of Iraq?

After conquering Saddam Hussein's army, the American authorities had incredibly overlooked appropriate civil security in Iraq. This amazing flaw in their plans created a legal vacuum within which 170,000 priceless artifacts from Baghdad's National Museum of Antiquities were either stolen or destroyed. These included five-thousand-year-old clay tablets inscribed with history's first written words. These were recognized as the origin of all mankind's written communications. Other tablets now lost included some of the world's first examples of mathematics including calculations based on the number 6, which led directly to our modern system of time-keeping using hours, minutes, and seconds.

Quickies

Did you know ...

- that *caucus*, a closed meeting of a political party to decide on policy, comes from the Algonquin word *caucauasu*, which means "counsellor"?
- that *toboggan* is from the French Canadian *tabagane*, which is a translation of the Algonquin *tobakun*, meaning "sled"?
- that *winnebago* has the same aboriginal meaning as Winnipeg, the capital of Manitoba, and that both mean "dirty water?"
- that "down the hatch" is a sailor's expression and refers to freight disappearing in volume through the hatch leading to the storage area below a ship's deck?
- that *queue* is the only English word that is pronounced the same with or without its last four letters?

all about numbers

If you have a myriad of choices, exactly how many choices do you have?

Since the sixteenth century, writers have used the adjective *myriad* to describe a large, unspecified, or overwhelming number, such as, "The student had a myriad of excuses for not turning in his assignment" or "Steve had myriad reasons for his wrong decision." Neither of these uses is literally incorrect, but based on its Greek root, one myriad is exactly ten thousand.

Why do they count down backwards to a rocket launch?

After NASA rolls out a rocket they start the countdown at T – 43 (said as "T minus 43 hours"), and with critical holds, it takes three days before liftoff. The countdown was introduced by German film director Fritz Lang in his 1928 movie *By Rocket to the Moon* and then, much later, copied by real life rocket scientists. Lang introduced the backward count of 5-4-3-2-1 to increase suspense.

Understanding 1 million

To understand a million, visualize driving 189 miles. The trip will take about three hours. Now measure the 189 miles in feet, which is 1 million.

How did the numbers eleven, twelve, and thirteen get their names?

The reason the nine numbers after ten are known as eleven, twelve, and the teens is clarified by looking at Roman numerals and considering that they are all plus or minus units of ten and were interpreted into archaic English with this in mind. Eleven (XI) or "leave one" means ten is one less than eleven. Twelve (XII) means ten is two less than twelve. Thirteen is three plus ten (or "teen"), four plus ten is fourteen, and so on.

Why is the furthest we can go called the "Nth degree"?

To take something to the "Nth degree" means we have exhausted all possibilities. N is the mathematical symbol meaning "any number." If you say "Nth plus 1" you mean "to the utmost." The expression derives from the mathematical formula *N plus 1* meaning "one more than any number," which of course is beyond the outer limits. The "Nth degree" originated as university slang in the nineteenth century.

Be a mentalist

Secretly write down the number 1089 and then turn it over in front of but out of sight of any number of friends. Ask each one to privately write down any three-digit number with the largest digit first, then the second largest, then the third. For example, 765. Then ask them to reverse that number (567) and subtract it from the original. Take the difference; (765 – 567 = 198) and then reverse this (891) and add these two together (198 + 891). No matter what numbers chosen by those participating, they will always end up with the number you hid in the beginning (1089).

Quickies

Did you know ...

- a trillion has twelve zeros (1,000,000,000,000) but a zillion has none? A zillion is a non-specific reference to a huge amount.
- $1.19 consisting of three quarters, four dimes, and four pennies is the greatest amount of money in coins you can have without being able to make change for a dollar?

royalty and heraldry

Why do monarchs refer to themselves using the royal "we"?

When Roman consuls spoke of public issues they did so on behalf of all those with whom they shared power and so they used the plural pronoun (in English, *we*) instead of the singular (*I*). The first king to use the royal "we" was Richard I of England, implying that he was speaking for his subjects as well as himself. It's improper for non-royals to use the plural self-reference, so when Margaret Thatcher did it in 1989, we were not amused.

How did Edward VII make it fashionable to leave the bottom button of a man's vest undone?

King Edward VII had a large appetite and an even larger tummy. He began leaving the bottom button of his vest undone because after a meal he simply couldn't do it up. Those who didn't want to make the king uncomfortable did the same, and so it became the fashion of the day. Edward's bulging belly may in part have been a consequence of his favourite dish, which was, of course, chicken à la king.

Why are aristocrats of the ruling classes called "bluebloods"?

The name *bluebloods* refers to the pallor of the Spanish ruling classes after the conquest of the darker skinned Moors. After the blood in them loses oxygen while flowing back to the heart, the veins of fair or untanned people whose skin is never exposed to the sun appear blue, while the veins of those with darker complexions, like the Moors, are less obvious. Their blue blood distinguished true Spanish aristocracy from the conquering Moors.

Does every family have a coat of arms?

There is no such thing as a family coat of arms. They were granted only to individuals, and those individuals were exclusively men. A coat of arms can only be used by the uninterrupted line of male descendants of the person to whom it was granted and is a privilege of nobility. The heraldic symbol was emblazoned on a warrior's shield and was also added to the fabric coat worn on the outside of his armor, which is why it's known as a coat of arms.

Heraldry is the language of symbols or emblems and is the lone surviving custom from the romance and barbarism of feudal times.

Blazoning is the heraldic term to describe a coat of arms.

The unique colour, shape, and design emblazoned on the warrior's shield all distinguished him as friend or foe on the battlefield.

Why do we say, "Buckle down" when it's time to get serious?

If a teacher or a foreman tells someone it's "time to buckle down," they mean "Quit fooling around, this is serious business," and they're using an expression from the days of knighthood. When preparing for combat, knights required their squires to attend to their armour by oiling it, laying it out, and then buckling it onto their masters' bodies. How well this was done could be the difference between life and death for the knight, so buckling down was very serious business.

What does the title *esquire* mean?

The British title *esquire*, like the magazine, has very masculine roots. An esquire was a young man who was a manservant to an armoured knight and whose job included holding his master's shield. With the passing of the knights, *esquire* was applied to any young man of noble birth who hadn't yet earned a proper title. Eventually the word became a term of respect for any promising young man.

Why do we call someone who continually takes the fall for someone else a "whipping boy"?

In the mid-seventeenth century, young princes and aristocrats were sent off to school with a young servant who would attend classes and receive an education while also attending to his master's needs. If the master found himself in trouble, the servant would take the punishment for him, even if it were a whipping. He was his master's "whipping boy."

Why do you wish a pompous person would "get off his high horse"?

A person on a high horse is probably presuming to be more important than they truly are. In medieval times the height of your horse told of your rank in society and on the battlefield. Knights rode high on horses bred large and strong enough to bear the weight of the man and his armour. In ceremonial processions, kings and noblemen always rode the tallest horses, and anyone overstating his importance would be taken off his high horse.

What does it mean to be at someone's "beck and call"?

To be at someone's "beck and call" means to be standing by prepared to immediately respond to that person's needs. The expression comes from the rules of servitude, when a *beck* was a silent signal, such as a nod of the head or a hand gesture, used to summon a servant. If this subtlety didn't work, then the master or mistress would resort to a *call*. This meant they had used a beck and a call to get the domestic's attention.

Why do most spiral staircases ascend in a clockwise direction?

Spiral staircases originated as a defence mechanism in medieval castles because all knights were right-handed. Southpaws were considered under the Devil's influence and were automatically disqualified for knighthood. While ascending a clockwise spiral staircase with a sword in his right hand, the defending knight could freely swing his sword arm, while the attacker was neutralized by the wall blocking his own right arm.

What does the "post" mean in "post office," and what is the "mail"?

In medieval Europe, a system of roads was built to speed messages from the heads of state to all corners of the realm. These were called post roads because riders on horseback were "posted" at intervals in a relay system copied by the Pony Express to speed the delivery of the mail. *Mail* is what they called the pouch that carried the letters. Urgent messages were marked "post-haste."

Why does the audience stand during the Hallelujah Chorus?

In 1741, after Handel introduced his majestic *Messiah*, demand was so great that in order to increase seating gentlemen were asked to leave their swords at home and women were asked to not wear hoops. When England's King George II first heard the Hallelujah Chorus he rose to his feet in awe, and the entire audience followed. From that day on, it's been tradition to stand during the final movement of the *Messiah*.

George Frideric Handel was inspired to compose the entire *Messiah* in just twenty-three days.

Why are prestigious hotels and apartment buildings know as "Arms"?

Some buildings are titled manors or halls and some call themselves arms, like the Windsor Arms in Toronto. The use of the word *arms* is a practice dating back to old English inns, which proudly displayed the coat of arms or heraldic insignia of the local lord above the front entrance. In America, there were no dukes or earls. Instead, they used the word *arms* to convey prestige.

Why is the word *late* used to describe the recently deceased?

To prefix a person's name with "the late" certainly signifies that he or she is dead, although you would be correct in using it only with the name of someone who had died within the past twenty years. Its use began with medieval rulers, whose first name often had been passed down through generations of males. To avoid confusion with the living monarch, i.e., James II, his deceased father would be referred to as "the late King James."

Why is a blue ribbon a symbol of champions?

Blue was the favourite colour of King Edward III, who in 1348 created the Royal Order of the Knights of the Garter, the highest honour in Britain. Its membership was and is limited to the king and princes of England as well as a very few knights of distinguished service. The insignia of the Royal Order is a blue garter, and because of this, blue ribbons have come to be a reward for any supreme achievement.

What is the origin of the twenty-one-gun salute?

All salutes are a signal of voluntary submission. Early warriors simply placed their weapons on the ground, but when guns came along, the ritual of firing off or emptying their canons was done to illustrate to approaching foreign dignitaries that they had nothing to fear. In 1688, the Royal Navy regulated the number of guns to be used in saluting different ranks. For a prime minister, nineteen guns should be used, but for royalty or heads of state, the salute should be done with twenty-one guns.

Quickies
Did you know ...
- there are ten states named after British royalty and one, Louisiana, named after King Louis XIV of France?
- Georgia was named in honour of George II of England?
- Maine took its name from the province of Mayne in France, which was a compliment to Queen Henrietta Maria who owned the property while she was the wife of England's Charles I?
- Maryland was also named after Queen Henrietta Maria?
- New Hampshire took its name from the English county of Hampshire?
- New Jersey is named after the Channel Isle of Jersey?
- New York honours the Duke of York?
- North Carolina and South Caroline are named after England's Charles I?
- Virginia took its name from the "Virgin Queen," England's Elizabeth I?
- West Virginia also honours Elizabeth I?

art and science

Why is an artist's inspiration called a "muse"?

Many great artists have been influenced by a muse, a person whose very existence inspires them to reach beyond themselves. It literally means the inspiration a man receives from a special woman. The word *muse*, as it is used in this case, comes from any of the nine beautiful daughters of Mnemosyne and Zeus, each of whom in Greek mythology presided over a different art or science. *Muse* is the origin of such words as *music*, *museum*, and *mosaic*.

What orbital advantage did Cape Canaveral have to cause NASA to choose the Florida location for its first space launches?

Cape Canaveral was chosen as a launch site not only because NASA needed the booster rockets to fall harmlessly into the ocean but also, and more importantly, because the Earth moves from west to east at 910 miles an hour. This Florida location allowed them to fire a rocket to the east with an added velocity push of 17,300 miles an hour from the spinning of the Earth.

How much space junk is orbiting Earth?

The U.S. Air Force estimates that 9,000 pieces of space junk larger than ten centimetres across are currently orbiting the Earth along with thousands of smaller pieces. Space junk has only scored one confirmed hit on an active spacecraft. In 1996 a French military satellite was hit and knocked into a new orbit. The international space station has been forced to take evasive action on three occasions. *Vanguard 1*, an American satellite launched in 1958, is the oldest piece of space junk still up there.

Who is the Thinker in Auguste Rodin's famous statue?

The French sculptor Auguste Rodin's statue commonly called *The Thinker* (*Le penseur*) is one of the best-known pieces of art in the world. Yet when Rodin (1840–1917) first cast a small plaster version in 1880, he meant it as a depiction of the Italian poet Dante Alighieri (circa 1265–1321) pondering his great allegorical epic *The Divine Comedy* in front of the Gates of Hell. In fact, Rodin named the sculpture *The Poet*. It was an obscure critic, unfamiliar with Dante, who misnamed the masterpiece with the title we use today — *The Thinker*.

Rodin's statue is naked because the sculptor wanted a heroic classical figure to represent thought as poetry.

Why is *aluminum* also spelled *aluminium*?

Aluminum is the most abundant metal in the Earth's crust where it is principally found in combination with bauxite. In 1808 when the English scientist Sir Humphry Davy (1778–1829) was figuring out how to isolate aluminum, he first called it alumium. In 1812, though, he renamed the metal aluminum, which is how it is still known in North America. That same year, however, the British decided the metal should be called aluminium to conform to the ending of most other related elements that end in *ium* such as sodium, potassium, et cetera. In 1812, Britain's *Quarterly Review* stated: "Aluminium, for so we shall take the liberty of writing the word, in preference to aluminum, which has a less classical sound."

What caused synthetic fibres to replace silk?

Silk is a fine, lustrous natural fibre made from secretions by very small silkworms to produce cocoons. The cultivation of silk began more than five thousand years ago in China, and the process is very labour-intensive and expensive. In 1935, while China and Japan were at war and the silk supply to Western countries was interrupted, scientists at the chemical giant DuPont came up with the synthetic fibre nylon as a replacement. The first commercial nylon products were toothbrush bristles in 1938 and women's stockings in 1940. Uses for the material expanded dramatically during the Second World War when it was substituted for silk in parachutes and replaced organic fibres in ropes, tents, ponchos, and many other products.

The synthetic textile fibres Orlon and Dacron were introduced by DuPont in 1948 and 1951 respectively. The registered proprietary names of DuPont's synthetic fibres begin with a random generic sound (such as *nyl* in *nylon*) and end in *on* from *cotton*.

It took three years to come up with the name *nylon*. An early front-runner was "no-run," which was abandoned because it wasn't true. Some people think that the word *nylon* is a combination of the abbreviation for New York City (NY) and the first three letters in London, but DuPont denies that.

What was the original purpose of Rubik's Cube?

In 1980, Rubik's Cube became a worldwide craze. Its Hungarian inventor, Professor Erno Rubick, had created the cube as a math aid for his students. After realizing the cube's potential as a toy, he sold 2 million in Hungary alone before introducing it to the West, making him the Communist world's first self-made millionaire. The Rubik's Cube has more than 43 quintillion configurations (43,252,003,274,489,856,000).

Why is a black hole black?

Black holes in space seem to be a recent phenomenon, yet Albert Einstein (1879–1955) predicted them in his theory of relativity in 1915. They are the incredibly dense centres of dead stars. Black holes appear black because their gravitational fields are so huge that even light can't escape. We find and measure black holes by calculating the orbits and other behaviours of nearby stars or gas clouds. Black holes capture our imagination because we believe that should we fly a spacecraft anywhere near them they will capture us. The Hubble Space Telescope has taken pictures of many suspected black holes. One is the core of Galaxy NGC 4261.

Why can't you escape a black hole?

There is no known escape from a black hole. To escape Earth, we have to travel at 25,000 miles per hour. If we go any slower, we won't break the planet's gravitational pull. When we run out of fuel, we will fall back to the ground.

Black holes are even harder to escape. To get out of a black hole, you must go faster than the speed of light, and Albert Einstein's theory of relativity says that is impossible.

Why are the instruments used for sending and receiving sound called "radios"?

The device we call a radio took its name from radio telegraphy and was commonly referred to as the wireless up until the Second World War, when the military preference for the term *radio* caused that name to catch on to describe the revolutionary receptacle of sound. The word *radio* is derived from *radius*, Latin for "spoke of a wheel" or "ray of light," because transmitted sounds travel out in all directions from a centre hub like the spokes of a wheel.

Radio was first used to describe the sound-broadcasting medium as an industry in 1922.

Why are weather forecasters called "meteorologists"?

Meteorology became the science of forecasting weather during the fourth century B.C., when it was believed that dramatic heavenly events were the cause of everything, especially weather — and there was nothing more dramatic than the arrival of a meteor. In Greek, *meteorology* means "a discourse from high in the air." Studying meteors to predict weather ended in the late seventeenth century, but weather forecasters are still known as meteorologists.

Exactly what is a proverb?

A proverb is an ancient expression of practical truth or wisdom. Proverbs existed before books; they were the unwritten language of morality and are treasures of the oral tradition of all mankind. They offer a deep insight into the everyday domestic life of the culture of their origin and resonate as truth through all time.

Japan: "Learning without wisdom is a load of books on the back of a jackass."

Japan: "Unpolished pearls never shine."

England: "The difference is wide that the sheets cannot decide."
Italy: "Better alone than in bad company."

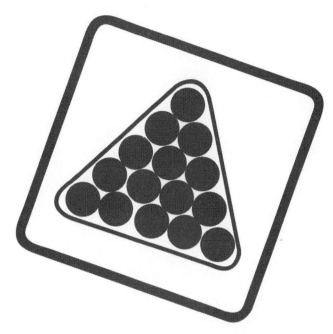

billiards and pool

Why are billiards played on a pool table?

During the nineteenth century, off-track gamblers would often play billiards while waiting to hear the results of a horse race. Sometimes, if they agreed on the merits of a particular horse, the gamblers would pool their money in an effort to win a greater amount on one bet or to soften the blow of a loss. The "pooled" money, both bet and won, was counted out on the playing surface of the billiard table, which the gamblers came to call their "pool table."

Why do we say that the person in charge "calls the shots"?

"Calling the shots" means being in control or taking responsibility for critical decisions. The expression comes from a form of billiards. In the game of straight pool the person shooting is required to specify both the ball he or she intends to strike and the specific pocket he or she plans to sink it into. In the mid-twentieth century, "calling the shots" moved out of the smoky pool hall and into everyday usage.

Why is spinning a ball called "putting English on it"?

The expression "putting English" on a ball is used in tennis, golf, soccer, and baseball and means you've spun and curved the ball to overcome a problem. The expression comes from English snooker, a pool game where one of the main strategies is to block an opponent from having a straight line shot at a ball he must hit. To do this, the shooter will create a spin on his shot to circumvent the obstruction. This spin is called "putting English on it."

"Body English" refers to the contortions made by a player as he physically transmits his intention for the ball while it's in motion.

What is a "masse" pool shot?

A "masse shot" in pool is required when a ball is between the cue ball and the one a player is required to hit. To strike the target ball, a spin on the cue ball is necessary to curve around the obstruction. This procedure is accomplished by hitting the cue ball with the cue stick held nearly vertically. The word *masse* derives from a description of a club used in medieval jousting tournaments.

Odds & Oddities

• Some Native Americans used this simple method to measure the height of a tree or other tall object: Walk away from the object, stopping periodically to view the object behind you by putting your head down between your legs. When you are at a distance that you can just barely see the top of the object, make a mark on the ground. Measure the distance from the mark to the base of the object and you will have a surprisingly accurate measurement of the object's height.

fashion and clothing

Why do we refer to a single item of clothing as a "pair of pants"?

Pants is short for *pantaloons*, and the item only became a single garment late in its history. Up until the seventeenth century, the legs were covered with two separate sleeves of fabric called "hose," which were tied to a belt with braces. The open crotch was covered with breeches and a long tunic. The plural reference to a single unit as a pair is extended to trousers, slacks, and shorts.

Pantaloons came from the comic wardrobe of a stock character in the Commedia dell'Arte.

Why do we say that someone well dressed wore his or her best "bib and tucker"?

In the seventeenth century, bibs were introduced to protect men's clothing from the consequences of their own bad table manners. Women did the same, but their bibs were fancier and were made of lace or muslin with frills to frame their faces. Because these bibs were tucked into the tops of low-cut dresses, they were called tuckers. On special occasions both men and women brought their own bibs and tuckers to the banquet and, just like their clothing, these made a fashion statement.

Why is something or someone of superior quality called "a cut above"?

"A cut above" dates from the eighteenth century and literally means the quality of the cutting or fashioning of a person's clothing. The superior appearance or station in life of someone with a good tailor or milliner is obvious when compared with a common man or woman, making them a "cut above" the ordinary. The phrase is related to the nautical phrase "the cut of her jib," meaning the style or cut of a ship's sails. You can also be a "cut below," as in "The girl herself is a cut below par" (A.B. Walford, 1891).

Why do we sometimes call women's underwear "bloomers"?

In the mid-nineteenth century, Mrs. Elizabeth Smith Miller (1822–1911) revolutionized women's wear by designing and wearing a clothing style that did away with voluminous dresses and tightly laced corsets. She suggested that women wear a jacket and knee-length skirt over a pair of trousers tucked into boots. The cause was taken up by magazine editor Amelia Jenks Bloomer (1818–1894) and was given a boost by the new pastime of bicycling. There was a lot of resistance before the new dress became acceptable and took the name of its most visible advocate, Amelia Bloomer.

The term *bloomers* soon became applied to just the trousers and eventually to any sort of long underwear.

Why is a formal suit for men called a "tuxedo"?

Up until an evening in 1886, the accepted formal dress for men was a suit with long swallowtails. But on that evening, young Griswald Lorillard, the heir to a tobacco fortune, shocked his country club by arriving in a dinner jacket without tails. This fashion statement caught on, and the suit took on the name the place Lorillard introduced it: Tuxedo Park, New Jersey.

What is the inspiration for argyle socks?

Argyle socks resemble a Scottish Tartan because that's what inspired them. In the eighteenth century, Archibald Campbell, the influential Scottish Duke of Argyle, created the pattern by having his socks woven to resemble his Campbell clan tartan, a style that's been with us ever since.

What is the origin of the polka dot?

The polka dot is a leftover from the polka dance craze that was introduced to America in 1835. *Polka* is the Polish word for "Polish woman," but the dance came from Czechoslovakia — just like the song "American Woman" came from Canada. The dance was in vogue up until the end of the nineteenth century, during which time dozens of by-products capitalized on its popularity, including one that still lingers: wearing apparel with the polka dot pattern.

Why does "lace" describe both an ornamental fabric and a string for tying shoes?

The word *lace* began its route into thirteenth-century English as the Latin word *lacere*, which means "to entice." On its way through Spanish and French, *lace* became a hunting term meaning "rope net," "snare," or "noose." In 1555, because fancy lace reminded someone of a hunting net, the word *lace* was employed to describe an ornamental netted fabric pattern and, shortly after, a cord for tying, such as a shoelace. As its use in hunting diminished, *lace* or *netting* took on the primary meaning of "ornamental trim."

The expression "to lace a drink" by adding a dash of liquor derived from the new habit of adding sugar to coffee or tea during the seventeenth century, and also meant "ornamental trim."

The Spanish word for a hunting lace or a rope was *lazo*, which gave cowboys the lasso.

"Laced mutton" was an old expression for a prostitute.

Why do men wear neckties?

Roman soldiers wore a strip of cloth around their necks to keep them warm in winter and to absorb sweat in the summer. Other armies followed suit, and during the French Revolution the Royalists and the Rebels used ties to display the colours of their allegiance. They borrowed the design and the name, *cravat*, from the Croatian Army.

Quickies

Did you know …
- Ellis Island is named after tavern owner Sam Ellis?
- between 1892 and 1954, more than 16 million people passed through Ellis Island, hoping to become Americans?
- in 1892 Annie Moore, a fifteen-year-old Irish girl, was the first person to be processed at Ellis Island?
- the last person processed through Ellis Island was a Norwegian named Arne Peterssen in 1954?

Later, ties became a French fashion statement, offering a splash of colour to an otherwise drab wardrobe.

How did the bobby pin get its name?

The bobby pin got its name in the 1930s, but the inexpensive little wire gadget had become popular with flappers during the Roaring Twenties. A short haircut for young women came in vogue for the first time in history, and the bobby pin helped keep its shape. The *bob* in "bobby pins," like the one in "bobby socks," means "to cut short," and was previously used to describe the cropped or bobbed tail of a horse.

Who qualifies as a "metrosexual," and where did the term originate?

The word *metrosexual* was coined in 1994 by writer Mark Simpson. However, it was Simpson's 2002 article in *Salon* concerning soccer star David Beckham that introduced *metrosexual* to everyday use. A metrosexual is a straight but fastidious and style-conscious urban male whose self-indulgence never keeps him far from his true love — himself.

Why is a light, short overcoat called a "jacket"?

A short coat is called a "jacket" for the same reason that *Jack* is used generically to mean any male stranger ("hit the road, Jack"). It was the French who began using Jacque this way as a reference to any common or unsophisticated male. The word took on the meaning of a peasant or ordinary man's outerwear in France and spread throughout Europe, arriving in England as *jacket* during the thirteenth century.

A nickname for John, Jack is also used as an endearment like "buddy" or "mate" and has been since the days of Middle English. During this same time, Dicken became popular as the original nickname for Richard until it evolved into Dick, while Robin was a nickname for Robert before it became Rob.

language of the
warriors

Why is a newcomer called a "rookie"?

A rookie is anyone new to an organization requiring teamwork, whose lack of experience may cause errors. The word originated in the American military during the Civil War when massive numbers of young and untrained soldiers were rushed into battle, causing major problems with discipline. The veterans called these incompetent recruits "reckies," which through time became "rookies."

Why when someone dies do we say, "He bought the farm"?

During the Second World War, airmen introduced the expression "He bought the farm" after a pilot was shot down. It caught on with all the armed services and meant that if you gave your life for your country, your impoverished family would receive insurance money for your death, which would help pay off the mortgage on the family farm. Death for your country meant you were buying the farm for your parents.

Why is someone who has been defeated forced to say "Uncle"?

Being forced to say "uncle" after losing a fight is a man thing and dates back to the late nineteenth century in the United States. In today's terms picture a chauvinistic Republican defeating a Libertarian in some form of physical combat. To the chauvinist, the highest order of submitting to decency is believing in the state, and so to stop the beating the defeated man must cry, "Uncle Sam," which in time became "uncle."

Why do we call a cowardly person "yellow"?

Yellow, meaning cowardly, is actually an abbreviation of "yellow dog," an American insult that first appeared in the nineteenth century to describe a cowardly or worthless person. In the early twentieth century, when employers were fighting trade unions, they insisted that new employees sign a pledge never to join a union. This pledge was called a "yellow dog" contract by union members, with the implication that anyone signing it was yellow.

Why are armoured battle vehicles called "tanks"?

In ancient India, large pits were dug to collect the monsoon rains and were called *tanken*. In the seventeenth century the concept was brought home to Britain and was introduced in English as "tank," a place to store water. In 1915, when the British designed a heavily armoured combat vehicle, they built them under the cover of building water tanks and shipped them to the front in crates marked "Tanks." They were introduced at the Battle of the Somme.

Why is a perfectionist called a "stickler"?

Stickler is from the Middle English word *stightlen* and means "to arrange." A stickler is a person who does everything by the book. Historically, the stickler was the title of a judge at a duel. Within life and death circumstances he was entrusted to see that the laws of gentlemanly combat were followed to the letter and that the outcome was fair.

What is the difference between bravery and courage?

Both bravery and courage are acts of valour and imply a certain strength and fearlessness. There is, however, a subtle difference in meaning between the two words. Courage comes from the French word *coeur*, meaning "heart." It is a quality of character that allows someone to carry through with a difficult premeditated plan of action. Bravery, on the other hand, comes from the Spanish word *bravado*, meaning a single or spontaneous act of valour. It is not planned, but rather a knee-jerk reaction that often occurs within a crisis.

Why do we describe a close contest as "nip and tuck"?

A closely fought contest where the outcome is in doubt is said to be "nip and tuck." It equates to the expression "blow for blow," when the advantage keeps changing from one competitor to another. The answer is in the original aggressive meanings of the two words. A *nip* was (and still is) a bite, while a *tuck* was a small, narrow dagger used by artillerymen when overrun and forced into hand-to-hand combat. "Nip and tuck" literally means a vicious, life-and-death struggle.

Why is an all-out fight called a "pitched battle"?

One of the meanings of the word *pitch* is "to set things in order." For example, when you pitch a tent, you are using a military expression for lining up the tents in rows. Unlike a skirmish or a surprise attack, a pitched battle was one in which the two sides lined up in formation facing each other until the order was given for the carnage to begin. The two disciplined sides held their ranks as they approached and then met each other in what was called a pitched battle.

Why is malicious destruction called "vandalism"?

A vandal mindlessly defaces public property. During the fifth and sixth centuries the Vandals, a Germanic warrior race, expanded south from their Baltic base. They would go beyond defeating their enemies by desecrating their cultural symbols in an effort to humiliate as well as conquer. When in 455 they overwhelmed and then sacked Rome, the Vandals continued to deliberately mutilate public and religious monuments, an act that to this day bears the name "vandalism."

Why were women warriors called "Amazons"?

Homer created the ancient Greek myth of fierce women warriors known as Amazons. *Amazon* is made up from *A*, meaning "without," and *mazos*, meaning "breast," because legend has it that they removed one breast to better throw a spear or use a bow and arrow. Amazons only visited men to become pregnant, and at birth only girl children were allowed to live to be raised by the Amazon warrior mothers.

Why were all Roman soldiers required to have a "vagina"?

The modern anatomical use of the word *vagina* didn't appear in a medical sense until 1908. Its original Latin meaning was a "sheath" or "scabbard", so in classical times Roman soldiers were required to carry their swords in a vagina, often made from a split piece of wood.

Vanilla is also derived from the Latin word *vagina* and got its name through Spanish soldiers' discovery of the plant in Mexico in 1521. The Spanish adopted the word as *vaina*, with *vainilla* as a diminutive, which meant "little sheath." It was because the shape of the plant's pods resembled a sheath or scabbard that Hernando Cortes' soldiers called it a vainilla plant.

How do statues of men on horses tell how the rider died?

Statues of horse and rider are exclusively of monarchs or great warriors and are usually found in places of honour. The tradition is that if the horse is depicted with all four hooves on the ground, the rider died of natural causes. If one hoof is raised, the rider's death came later from wounds incurred during battle, and if two hooves are in the air, the rider portrayed in the statue died on the battlefield.

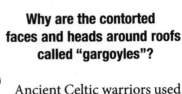

Why are the contorted faces and heads around roofs called "gargoyles"?

Ancient Celtic warriors used to place the severed heads of their enemies around the top of their fortresses as a warning. In time these inspired architects to add the twisted faces of gargoyles to prominent buildings. Gargoyles had the practical purpose of collecting rainwater and dropping it clear of the walls through their throats. In ancient French, *gargouille* means "throat."

Why do we call an unstable person a "basket case"?

A "basket case" is a derogatory reference to someone considered unstable and has a very sad origin. During the First World War, because some soldiers were so badly maimed or shell-shocked that a stretcher wouldn't hold them, they were carried off the field in wicker baskets. In 1919, after the war, the dark expression "basket case" began being cruelly applied to anyone with an impairment, either physical or mental.

What's the origin of the panic button?

The first panic buttons were installed in bombers during the Second World War. If his plane was hit by enemy fire, a pilot could push a button that set off an alarm throughout the aircraft. The crew responded with a drill, which, in severe cases and if a crash was imminent, could lead to the entire crew bailing out. When too many chose to parachute when hearing the alarm even though the situation wasn't critical, pilots were advised to think twice before "pushing the panic button."

What's the origin of the phrase "Don't shoot the messenger"?

"Don't kill the messenger" was first expressed as long ago as 442 B.C. by Sophocles. *Kill* became *shoot* in the American West during the nineteenth century. The expression arose during a time when messages between opposing armies, such as terms for surrender, were delivered by hand. The angry reply was often the symbolic return to his own side of the murdered messenger.

Why is a notable achievement said to be a "feather in your cap"?

Among tribal warriors, including those native to North America, a feather was awarded for each enemy killed in combat. These were worn as a headdress and eventually on armoured helmets; like wearers of today's campaign medals, the most decorated stood out as heroes. Women began wearing feathers in their caps as a signal of betrothal after it became customary for a warrior to give one of his hard-earned feathers to the woman he loved.

Why are foot soldiers called "infantry"?

The word *soldier* is from the Latin word *solidus*, meaning a gold coin, because it cost money to raise an army of mercenaries. The word *infantry* is from the Latin *infant*, meaning "non speaking," because, like children, well-disciplined soldiers never talk back or challenge orders. Curiously, another use of the word *soldier* is in reference to an army ant, due to the fact that other than humans, ants are the only creatures on Earth to go into battle in formation.

Why do we say that a guilty person must "face the music"?

To "face the music" comes from the military "drumming out" ceremony for disgraced soldiers. This ritual called for only drums to accompany the dishonoured as he was stripped of his rank and colours in front of his assembled unit. For cavalrymen, this humiliation was enhanced by having the offender sit backwards on his horse so that while leaving he could still see, as well as hear, the drums and the band. He was forced to face the music.

Why does "sally forth" mean to go forward with a new venture?

Today it implies less danger, but "to sally forth" was originally a military term meaning to suddenly rush forward. The Latin derivation of *sally* is *salire*, meaning "to leap." Castles and fortresses had closely guarded openings in the walls designed for mounting a quick counterattack against a siege. These were called sally ports, from which the defenders would vigorously rush, or sally forth, into battle.

What is the meaning of the battle cry "give no quarter"?

In battle, to give no quarter means to take no prisoners. In this case, the word *quarter* has no numerical value but rather refers to the antiquated use of the word for a dwelling place or area, such as the Latin Quarter or a soldier's living quarters or barracks. To grant or give quarter would mean to show mercy and provide prisoners with shelter. "No quarter asked and no quarter given" means this is a fight to the death.

During the American War of Independence, which country contributed the most soldiers to fight alongside the British?

The country that contributed the most soldiers to fight with the British against Washington was America itself. By 1779, there were more Americans fighting alongside the British than with the colonists. Washington had about thirty-five hundred troops, but because one-third of the American population opposed the revolution, up to eight thousand loyalists had joined the British Army.

Why when someone's humiliated do we say they were forced to "eat crow"?

The expression "to eat crow" came from an incident during the War of 1812 when the Americans invaded Canada. A hungry New England soldier who strayed across enemy lines had shot a crow for food when he was discovered by an unarmed British officer who managed to get hold of the American's rifle by pretending to admire it. He then turned the weapon on the young man and forced him to eat part of the crow raw before letting him go.

What are you doing when you "pillage and plunder" while "ransacking" a village?

The Vikings were good at ransacking during raids on Britain and other countries, so they gave us the word *ransack*, which started out meaning to search a house, legally or otherwise, for goods, stolen or otherwise. *Pillage* and *plunder* are almost interchangeable, with *pillage* strictly referring to searching a home for booty, while *plunder* denotes removing what you find.

Whether your home has been searched by the police or a burglar — or a Viking — it's bound to be a mess because it's been ransacked.

Why do we say, "Lock and load" when preparing for the inevitable?

The expression "lock and load" comes from American G.I.s during the Second World War and refers to loading the M1 rifle for imminent combat. The phrase means to insert a full ammunition clip into the rifle, then lock the bolt forward, forcing a round into the chamber ready to fire. The original order was "load and lock," but after John Wayne reversed the order to "lock and load" in *The Sands of Iwo Jima*, the expression stuck.

Why is someone who doesn't live up to expectations called a "flash in the pan"?

On a pioneer flintlock rifle the hammer struck a flint to create a spark that ignited a small amount of priming powder in what was called the pan. This ignition then set off the main charge of gunpowder, causing a small explosion that fired the bullet through the barrel. When the powder in the pan didn't ignite properly it created a flash, but the rifle wouldn't fire. It looked good, but it was only a "flash in the pan."

Why are military guards, some garden fences, and people on strike all called "pickets"?

A picket line, of course, is a group of union people exercising their right to protest, while a military picket is a guard on duty to protect the perimeter of an encampment. The word *picket* comes from the early French settlers, who made fortified stockades from sharpened tree trunks, which they called *piquet*, meaning "pointed sticks." It lives on in the pointed slats of picket fences and in the actions of union strikers.

Why is the control area of an aircraft called a "cockpit"?

When the hideous sport of cockfighting was legal, the birds were taken to a pit in the ground where they fought to the death. These fights were quick and bloody, and for this reason, the "cockpit" became the designated name of the room on a warship were surgeons attended the wounded and dying. During the First World War, pilots, like the roosters, were inserted into a confined space to do battle, and so they named that space the cockpit.

Why did First World War fighter pilots wear long silk scarves?

The dashing image of First World War fighter pilots wearing long silk scarves had nothing to do with fashion. The open-cockpit biplanes were very primitive with no rear-view mirror, so the pilot depended entirely on his own vision to avoid or mount an attack. The scarf was used to wipe grease from his goggles and to keep his neck from chafing against his collar as he constantly turned his head while watching for the enemy.

How did "die hard" come to mean resilient?

"Die hard" was coined on May 16, 1811, by a British man, Colonel Inglis, who had gathered the men of his 57th Foot Regiment just before the Battle of Albuera, against Napoleon. The colonel ended his address with, "Die hard my lads, die hard" — and that they did. They were victorious, but only 1 of the 24 officers and 168 of the 584 men survived.

What is a "Mexican standoff"?

The classical Mexican standoff occurs when three people level guns at one another in such a way that if one gunman shoots a member of the trio the person not being shot at will in all likelihood kill the first shooter. In other words, a stalemate ensues. It's a no-win situation. The expression's roots are in the American West where conflicts with the original Mexican settlers were often resolved with guns and even war, which is how Texas, New Mexico, and California became part of the United States. The term *Mexican standoff* came out of these struggles as an ethnic slur, just as *gringo* arose as an epithet for the other side.

Where did the expression "bite the dust" come from?

We probably all heard "bite the dust" for the first time while watching an old Western B movie when a cowboy hero does away with a pesky varmint to impress the schoolmarm. The phrase was first used in English literature in 1750 to imply wounding or killing by satirical novelist Tobias Smollett (1721–1771) in *Adventures of Gil Blas of Santillane*, his translation of the original French novel by Alain-René Lesage: "We made two of them bite the dust and the others betake themselves to flight." The inspiration for the expression can be traced back to the Bible in Psalm 72: "They that dwell in the wilderness shall bow before him and his enemies shall lick the dust."

What is the meaning of "cut to the quick"?

"Cut to the quick" is employed in two ways. Sometimes it means (a) "get to the point" or "cut to the chase," but more often it implies (b) "causing deep emotional pain." The *quick* in both cases is the flesh of the finger beneath the nail. Either way, the expression means cutting through the

inconsequential to the meaningful. An example of (a) would be a combatant cutting through an opponent's armour or clothing to get to the flesh (or point of consequence), while the meaning when used as (b) would be to cut deeply or stab through the superficial exterior to a vulnerable part.

"Cut to the quick" is related to the phrase "the quick and the dead." *Quick* here comes from an old English word, *cwicu*, which meant "living."

Why is some extreme behaviour called "beyond the pale"?

The expression dates back to the English Crown's first efforts to control the Irish by outlawing their language and customs. But the unruly Irish were just that, and by the fifteenth century the English still controlled only a small area around Dublin, protected by a fortification called "the Pale," meaning sharp sticks (i.e., impaled). To the British, to go "beyond the Pale" meant that you were entering the uncivilized realm of the wild Irish.

Why does "getting the drop on someone" mean you've taken the advantage?

When two men face each other in a duel or a gunfight, they used to lift the older heavy pistol toward the sky before dropping it level to take aim. The first one to lower his forearm and lock his elbow in place was said to have the drop on the other. Since then, anyone having an advantage over the other under any circumstance is said to "have the drop on" his opponent.

Where did we get the expression "down in the boondocks"?

"The boondocks" refers to an isolated, unsophisticated rural region. Although it's been used in England since 1909, American Marines stationed in the Philippines during the Second World War popularized the term. A *bundok*, in the primary language of the Philippines, is a mountain. The word became entrenched in our language when rediscovered during the 1960s by American soldiers in Vietnam.

Why is someone of little importance called a "pipsqueak"?

The Allied soldiers came up with the perfect synonym for "non-threatening" during the First World War. The Germans had brutal artillery, but they also had a smaller gun that stood out from the other incoming rounds by its unimpressive squeaking noise. It struck with a sound more like "pip" than "boom." The boys in the trenches called them "pipsqueaks," and after the war, they transferred the meaning as a description of someone of little significance.

What is the difference between the words *bickering* and *dickering*?

Even though they both involve a disagreement, there is a dramatic difference between *bickering* and *dickering*. *Bickering* now means to quarrel, but the word began as *bicken*, Dutch for "an attack involving a misunderstanding by slashing or stabbing." *Dickering* came from the Roman habit of packaging units of ten hides for bartering or haggling with barbarians. These packets were called *decuria* from *decem*, meaning "ten," and gave English the word *dicker*.

Why are deadly hidden devices called "booby traps"?

The English word *boob*, meaning "stupid" or "dunce," first appeared in 1599 and comes from the Spanish word *bobo*, also meaning "stupid," which came from the Latin *balbus*. While a booby prize is awarded to the supreme loser, it was during the First World War that the nineteenth-century booby trap changed from being a harmless practical joke to its deadly modern wartime meaning of laying explosive traps for enemy soldiers.

Why is a dismissive final remark called "a parting shot"?

In 247 B.C., the warriors of the Parthian Empire were such skilled archers on horseback that even Rome couldn't conquer them. They had developed a saddle with a stirrup, which enabled them to turn and fire arrows while riding away at full gallop. This incredible manoeuvre during a strategic retreat was known as the Parthian shot, which gave us the expression "a parting shot."

The Parthian Empire included, in part, what is now Afghanistan, Pakistan, and most of Iraq and Iran. They took over the region after conquering the Scythians, who had developed the magnificent breed of horse that was the key to the Parthians' success.

While firing arrows, a rider could steady himself with the newly invented stirrups and then guide his mount with his legs.

When something is over why do we say, "That's all she wrote"?

"That's all she wrote," meaning "that's the end of it," has a heartbreaking history. During the Second World War, it wasn't uncommon for an overseas serviceman to receive a brief, cutting letter from a girlfriend telling him that their romance was over and that she'd found someone else in his absence. When questioned by his buddies, the anguished soldier's response would be, "That's all she wrote," and it became so common it entered our language as meaning "it's over."

Why do yellow ribbons symbolize fidelity?

Yellow ribbons were first used during the Vietnam War. The inspiration came from a Civil War legend about a soldier returning home from the infamous Andersonville Prison. He had written his wife to hang a yellow handkerchief on the oak tree in the town square if she still loved him; otherwise he would stay on the stagecoach and move on. A modernized version became the hit song "Tie a Yellow Ribbon," and a new custom was born.

L. Russell Brown was inspired to write the song one late spring morning, and he drove thirty-three miles to Irwin Levine's house to tell him the story. Irwin changed the yellow handkerchief to a ribbon so as not to offend anyone with the reality of what makes handkerchiefs yellow. They also updated the story by changing the stagecoach to a bus.

The song was released in February 1973. It was the number one hit by April 1973. The song became a hit again in 1981 when the fifty-two Iran hostages were returned after 444 days of captivity.

Why is an elderly person sometimes called an "old fogey"?

We use the phrase "old fogey," perhaps cruelly, as an insult for someone whose advanced age has put them out of touch with modern fashion. The expression surfaced, however, as an honour when in 1811 it was used to describe any soldier disabled from battle wounds. *Fogey* is from the French word *fougeux*, meaning "fierce" or "feisty," so the original *fogey* was a courageous veteran disabled through heroic combat.

Why is an exact likeness called a "spitting image"?

A boy who looks like his dad is sometimes said to be a spitting image of his father. There is another similar expression — "spirit and image" — but it isn't related. At the apex of the glory that was the British Empire, just about every man was familiar with the spit and polish discipline of military life. When a man polished his boots, he used saliva to bring them to where he could see his own reflection, and that is the origin of "spitting image."

How did crossing a line in the sand become a military challenge?

The concept of a literal "line in the sand" was first created by a lone Roman senator who rode out to meet a Macedonian king at the head of an army poised to invade Egypt, a Roman protectorate. The king balked until the senator drew a circle around him in the sand and demanded that he order a withdrawal before stepping out of that circle or face the wrath of Rome. The king paused and then complied.

This account has been verified by contemporary historians. The senator was Popillius Laenas.

Why are some well-armed soldiers called "dragoons"?

A regiment of heavily armed European cavalrymen became known as "dragoons" after they began carrying muskets. When fired, the muskets breathed fire just like their fearsome namesake, the dragon. *Dragoon* is simply a variable pronunciation of *dragon*. Today, a dragoon is usually a member of a tank regiment.

Why are those for and against war called "hawks" and "doves"?

Those who side with war have been called "hawks" since 1798, when Thomas Jefferson coined the term *war hawk*. The description of those who favour peace as "doves" is from the Biblical book of Genesis. When Noah sent a dove over the water to see if it was receding, it returned with an olive leaf, indicating there was land nearby. The modern use began during the Cuban Missile Crisis and continues to the present.

Why do we call a traitor a "turncoat"?

Someone who changes sides during a war is called a "turncoat" because of the actions of a former duke of Saxony who found himself and his land uncomfortably situated directly in the middle of a war between the French and the Saxons. He quickly had a reversible coat made for himself, one side blue for the Saxons and the other side white for the French. Then, depending on who was occupying his land, he could wear the appropriate colour of allegiance.

Why is a military dining hall called a "mess"?

A mess hall is what military types call their dining halls. The term's origins go back to the Middle Ages, when British sailors began calling their meagre, often grub-infested meals a "mess," which they clearly were. *Mess* originally meant the food for one meal. It has since evolved to signify a specific area where sailors, soldiers, and aircrew gather to eat, drink, and socialize.

In order to maintain discipline, there are usually three levels of mess: officers, non-commissioned officers (sergeants), and rank-and-file soldiers.

Why does to "bear the brunt" mean "to take the heat"?

To "take the heat" is the literal translation of "to bear the brunt," because *brunt* and *burn* mean the same thing. From the Anglo-Saxon word *brenning*, or *burning*, *brunt* was a vivid reference to the hottest point of conflict during a battle. It took on a more general meaning to describe contentious domestic and business issues, but it always means the utmost pressure within a circumstance, or the point of greatest fury.

When did we begin numbering the world wars?

In 1887, the first use of the term *Great War* was in reference to the Napoleonic Wars. The description was applied to the 1914–18 war from the start — it had even begun being used in anticipation in 1909. The 1914–18 was also labelled a world war when it began. It wasn't called the First World War until 1931, when it became clear that it hadn't been the "war to end all wars." The first reference to a Second World War as a future possibility was in 1919. When it happened in September of 1939, it was immediately given the title of the Second World War.

"Only the dead have seen the end of war." — Plato

Why is a glaring error called a "snafu"?

During the Second World War, massive military operations were so huge they were usually fouled up by their sheer weight and size. The frustrated servicemen called them SNAFUs, an acronym for "Situation Normal: All Fouled Up." Some say that "fouled up" was a polite adaptation for family use, but regardless, the expression *snafu* lived on, and now, as it did then, means a glaring error.

Why is a restricted limit called a "deadline"?

A deadline is an absolute limit, usually a time limit, and was popularized by the newspaper business, in which getting stories written and printed on time is of ultimate importance. But the expression comes from American Civil War prisoners, who were kept within crude makeshift boundaries, often just a line scratched in the dirt or an easily breached rail fence. They were told, "If you cross this line, you are dead," and soon the guards and prisoners simply called it what it was: a deadline.

Why do we say, "I heard it through the grapevine"?

During the American Civil War, a Colonel Bee set up a crude telegraph line between Placerville and Virginia City by stringing wires from trees. The wires hung in loops like wild grapevines, and so the system was called the "Grapevine Telegraph," or simply "the grapevine." By the time war news came through the wires it was often outdated, misleading, or false, and the expression "I heard it through the grapevine" soon came to describe any information obtained through gossip or rumour that was likely unreliable.

What exactly is a last-ditch stand?

In the sixteenth century, when an army attacked a walled city or fortress, they would advance by digging a series of trenches for protection until they were close enough to storm the walls. If there was a successful counterattack, the invaders would retreat by attempting to hold each trench in the reverse order from which they had advanced until they might find themselves fighting from the "last ditch." If they failed to hold that one, the battle was lost.

Where did the expression "the whole nine yards" come from?

During the South Pacific action of the Second World War, American fighter planes' machine guns were armed on the ground with .50-calibre ammunition belts that measured exactly twenty-seven feet, or nine yards, in length before being loaded into the fuselage. If, during combat, a pilot gave everything he had by firing all his ammunition at a single target, it was said he'd given it "the whole nine yards."

In modern warfare, is it infantry or machines that determine the outcome?

Machines win modern wars. A 1947 study found that during the Second World War, only about 15 to 25 percent of the American infantry ever fired their rifles in combat. The rest, or three-quarters of them, simply carried their weapons, doing their best not to become casualties. The infantry's purpose is not to kill the enemy, but rather to advance on and then physically occupy his territory.

Why is an overly eager person or group said to be "gung-ho"?

The adjective *gung-ho* comes from the Chinese word *gonghe*, meaning "work together." It entered the English language through U.S. Marines who picked it up from the Communists while in China during the Second World War. Because the Marines admired the fervour of the Chinese leftists in fighting the Japanese, while the rightists under Chiang Kai-shek seldom fought, they adopted "gung-ho" as a slogan. They emulated the Communists with "gung-ho" meetings and eventually called themselves "the gung-ho battalion."

How did the poppy become a symbol of remembrance?

(a) Poppies have been associated with the war dead since the Napoleonic wars in the nineteenth century when it was noted how thickly the blood-red flowers grew over the graves of soldiers buried in the previously barren fields in the region of Flanders in France. The reason was that the sterile chalk soil had become enriched by lime from the residue left after the heavy gunfire and artillery bombardments, causing an explosion of poppies. When the fighting was over and the lime was absorbed, the poppies disappeared.
(b) In May 1915, a forty-three-year-old native of Guelph, Ontario, Canada, was serving as a brigade surgeon in the region of Flanders during the second battle of Ypres. The posting was a nightmare. During some of the fiercest fighting of the war he attended to the terribly wounded during wave after wave of relentless

enemy attacks. It was during this time that Lieutenant-Colonel John McCrae learned of the nearby death of his close friend Lieutenant Alexis Helmer of Ottawa. Overcome with emotion and during a calm in the battle, he reacted to the sights and sounds around him by taking a scrap of paper from his pocket. Staring out at the endless white wooden crosses marking makeshift Canadian graves, and amidst the mud and chaos, he heard and saw the incredible natural contradictions to the madness. There were birds in the sky and there were the wild poppies where none had been before.

Within twenty minutes he had written fifteen lines of what he saw and felt before stuffing it back in his pocket and returning to the wounded and dying.

What John McCrae wrote that day was eventually published on December 8 of that year. He unfortunately wouldn't live to see the influence of his poem. McCrae died of pneumonia at Wimereux, France, on January 28, 1918.

His impressions during that bleak day at Ypres would eventually inspire the use of the poppy as the symbol of remembrance of the mad human sacrifices of war.

"In Flanders Fields"

In Flanders fields the poppies blow
Between the crosses, row on row,
That mark our place; and in the sky
The larks, still bravely singing, fly
Scarce heard amid the guns below.
We are the Dead. Short days ago
We lived, felt dawn, saw sunset glow,
Loved and were loved, and now we lie
In Flanders fields.
Take up our quarrel with the foe:
To you from failing hands we throw
The torch; be yours to hold it high.
If ye break faith with us who die
We shall not sleep, though poppies grow
In Flanders fields.
— John McCrae

(c) In November 1918, after reading McCrae's poem, an American schoolteacher, Moina Michael, immediately made a personal pledge to always wear a red poppy as a symbol of keeping faith with those who died.

Two years later a French woman visiting New York, Madame Guerin, learned of the new custom and decided, after returning to France, to use handmade poppies to raise money for the destitute children in war-torn areas of her own country. This inspired the Great War Veterans Association of Canada to officially adopt the poppy as the flower of remembrance for their 117,000 comrades-in-arms who had died in battle during the First World War.

Today's lapel poppies first appeared in 1922 and were assembled by disabled veterans as a small source of income.

The poppy also stands internationally as a symbol of collective reminiscence, as other countries have also adopted its image to honour those who have paid the ultimate sacrifice.

business and the marketplace

Why are notes taken at a business meeting called "minutes"?

The reason the written records of a meeting are called the minutes is because, in order to keep up, the minute-taker wrote in a shorthand or abbreviation. The word used to describe this condensed writing was *minute* (pronounced "my-noot"), meaning "small," and because the spelling is the same, the minutes (my-noots) became "minutes." The same circumstances apply to Frederick Chopin's Minute Waltz: It's really his small or minute waltz.

Why are shopping centres called "malls"?

Shopping centres mushroomed in the 1950s but weren't called malls until 1967. *Mall* comes from the popular sixteenth-century Italian ball and mallet game *palamaglio*, which came to England as *pall-mall* (pronounced "pell mell"). By the eighteenth century the game had been forgotten, except on the name of a London street where it had been played and on a parallel ritzy avenue named the Mall, where fashionable aristocrats strolled and shopped.

Why do we say, "We're just gonna hang out"?

"Hanging out" usually means getting together for no particular reason other than to pass time and see what's happening. The expression comes from a time before commercial signs, when English shopkeepers set up poles in front of their stores from which they would hang flags describing their goods. These flags were called hangouts, and they became a place where people would stop to linger and gossip with their friends.

Why is the presiding officer over a committee called a "chairman"?

Whether it's a chairman or a chairwoman, that person is in the seat of authority and has been since the fourteenth century. At that time a *chair* was a throne (it came from the Greek word *kathedra*, leading to the word *cathedral* for the place housing the seat of the bishop). In business, the person in charge sat in a comfortable armed chair, while everyone else sat on stools, and so he took the esteemed title "chairman."

Why is something recently manufactured called "brand new"?

The original meaning of the word *brand* was a fire burning within a furnace or forge. To say an item, whether pottery or forged metal, was "brand new" meant it was fresh from the fires of its creation. This usage dates back to the sixteenth century. The verb *to brand* comes from the same source and means to mark ownership on something, from wine casks to livestock, using a hot iron from a fire.

Why is something unused sometimes said to be "brand spanking new"?

To exaggerate that a purchase is straight from the manufacturer without any previous owner, an item such as a new car might be called "brand spanking new." *Spanking* refers to the traditional slapping of a newborn baby to start them crying to ensure that they are breathing without obstruction.

Why is an honest conversation referred to as "talking turkey"?

"Talking turkey" comes from an encounter between a white settler and a Native American in 1848. After they had bagged a turkey and a buzzard, the fast-talking white man suggested, "You can have the buzzard and I will take the turkey, or I will take the turkey and you can have the buzzard" — or, in modern language, "Heads I win, tails you lose." The Native's response, "Why don't you talk turkey with me?" was passed on so often by those overhearing the argument that talking turkey became part of the language.

Why is a gullible shopper called a "mark"?

A "mark" is someone who can easily be taken advantage of and came to us from midway carnival operators (or "carnies") who run games of chance. The word *midway* was first used to describe the outdoor amusements at the 1893 World's Exposition in Chicago. After a carnie found a victim, and before sending him on his way with a cheap prize, the rogue would slap the rube on the back with a dust-covered hand, marking him as a sucker for operators down the line.

Why is a miserly person called a "cheapskate"?

The word *cheapskate*, meaning tight with money, surfaced in America during the 1890s as a reference to loan sharks. In this case, the word skate began as *skyte*, a Scottish slur for a low-life. "A skyte" (eventually "a skate") was also Scottish slang for a worn-out horse. With the evolving new lingo of the multicultural Americas, and exclusive to this expression, the pronunciation of *skyte* became "skate" (not the kind used on ice).

Ice skates were introduced to England from Holland in 1662 as *skeates*, from the Dutch word *schaats* from the Frank *skakkja*, meaning "stilts."

What is the chief difference between a limited company (Ltd.) and one that's incorporated (Inc.)?

A company name ending in "Ltd." means that the amount of risk or liability for its shareholders for any corporate failure or debt is limited to the amount of their personal investment in that company. In an incorporated company or corporation ("Inc."), the business is recognized as a single entity, and the personal assets of its principals are protected from creditors if the business fails. Only stockholders risk losing the amount of their investment.

Why is a "touchstone" the standard against which things are measured?

A "touchstone" is a figurative standard of value or quality against which something is measured. The word comes from ancient times when a special stone was used to guard against counterfeit money. The gold or silver content of coins wasn't well governed, so phony money was often mixed with other metals and passed off as authentic. Merchants tested the purity of coins by rubbing them on a hard black stone. The colour of the streak left on the touchstone disclosed the coins' true value.

Ultraviolet scanners provide a kind of touchstone for today's paper money. Passing a bill under the scanner gives an instant indication of its authenticity based on a number of security features built into the bill.

If something sounds honest, why do we say it "rings true"?

In the nineteenth century, before the mint started issuing coins with reeding or grooves on the edges to prevent it, some dishonest people would shave the precious metal just enough to go visually undetected. They would then have full value for the coin as well as that of the shavings. If suspicious, a merchant would bounce the coin on a hard surface to hear if it "rang true," thereby proving its authenticity.

The word *ring* is from the Anglo-Saxon *hringan*.

What does monger mean in words like *hate-monger* or *gossipmonger*?

There are gossipmongers, warmongers, scandal-mongers, hate-mongers, and many others to whom we show extreme disrespect by adding the perceived curse *monger* to their action; yet when the word stands alone it isn't that severe. From the Old English word *mangian*, *mong* simply means "to peddle, sell, or barter," so a fishmonger sells fish, while a hate-monger peddles hate.

Why is a stash of surplus money called a "slush fund"?

The term *slush* began as a sailor's reference to the grease from the cook's galley, which was used to lubricate the ships masts. When the voyage was over, the surplus grease was sold, and the money was put into a "slush fund" to be shared by the enlisted men. By 1839, when a ship returned to port, any battle-damaged equipment or surplus supplies were also sold and the money added to the profits from the grease in the slush fund.

What ends are we talking about when we say we are trying to "make ends meet"?

"Making ends meet" means to balance what you make with what is required to live, especially in difficult times, and comes to us from the sixteenth-century farmers of England. The saying refers to the beginning and the end of a year — or from the end of one year to the end of the next. If someone could overcome the unpredictable and seasonal problems throughout the year without losing money, they had survived by making ends meet.

Why are we warned not to take any wooden nickels?

During the nineteenth century, it was common practice at commercial exhibitions to promote the event through wooden coins that could be redeemed at face value only by exhibitors or participating merchants at and during the run of the fair. When the exhibition closed and moved on, patrons were often left with wooden nickels or other coins that were useless unless they could be pawned off to an unsuspecting local retailer.

Where did the expression "paying through the nose" come from?

In Northern Ireland during the ninth century, the British introduced a harsh poll tax of one ounce of gold per year on all Irish households. The tax was nicknamed the "Nose Tax" because if a person didn't or couldn't pay, he had his nose slit. This cruel but effective procedure gave rise to the expression "paying through the nose," meaning if unreasonable payments aren't made, there will be dire consequences.

Why do we say someone without money is both "broke" and "bankrupt"?

Bank comes from the Italian word *banca*, meaning "bench," over which medieval moneylenders did business in the streets of Venice. If he became insolvent, the law intervened and broke the lender's bench, which in Italian is *banca rotta*. *Rotta* referred to the broken bench, but another figurative word in use for a broken man was the Latin *ruptus*. With his bench broken, the banker's spirit was *banca ruptus*.

Odds & Oddities
- The odds of a person dying from smoking a pack of cigarettes a day are 1 in 3.
- dying from obesity — 1 in 4.
- dying from working twenty years in a coal mine — 1 in 23.
- dying from urban air pollution — 1 in 70.
- dying from living with a smoker — 1 in 4,200 (you have a greater lifetime chance of being struck by lightning — 1 in 3,000).
- dying from something — 100 percent.

medical
complications

Why do we say we are "under the weather" when we get sick?

When the weather turned bad at sea, the constant rolling of the rough water caused a rocking motion that brought on seasickness. Those passengers affected were taken below deck, because the sway diminishes the lower you get on the ship (especially down near the keel). Those taken below deck because of seasickness were brought "under the weather."

How did we start the ritual of kissing a wound to make it better?

Everyone with children has kissed a small bruise or cut to make it better. This comes from one of our earliest medical procedures for the treatment of snakebite. Noticing that a victim could be saved if the venom was sucked out through the point of entry, early doctors soon began treating all infectious abrasions by putting their lips to the wound and sucking out the poison. Medicine moved on, but the belief that a kiss can make it all better still lingers.

Why when we hurt our elbow do we say we've hit our "funny bone"?

When we strike our elbow, although it's no laughing matter we say that the tingling sensation is from our funny bone. In fact, the prickling discomfort comes from striking the ulnar nerve, and the word *funny* comes from some scholar with a sense of humour who turned the whole thing into a pun during the nineteenth century. The ulnar nerve passes over the end of the humerus, which inspired the term *funny bone*.

Why do we say that a timid person has "cold feet"?

To have "cold feet" means to lose your nerve when facing danger; it began meaning "cowardly" more than a hundred years ago. This is a bit harsh, because everyone's bodily extremities (including the hands and feet) become cold when terrified because under the circumstances, the body draws blood away from these areas to fuel vital organs for combat or flight. So cold feet don't make the coward … it's the running away.

Why are frenzied women referred to as "hysterical" but not equally frenetic men?

The physicians of ancient Greece considered hysteria to be an exclusively female problem caused by a disorder within the woman's distinctive internal organs. *Hystera* is the Greek word for womb and survives today in the medical procedure *hysterectomy*. Men suffer the anti-social symptoms of hysteria less frequently than women, but when they do, they are called sociopaths.

Why are subjects of human experiments called "guinea pigs"?

Experimental human guinea pigs are not named after the animal associated with medical testing. Human volunteers selected for observation under trial were usually desperate for money and would receive the nominal daily fee of one guinea for their trouble. A guinea was a forty-shilling piece first minted in 1664, so called because it was minted from West African (Guinea) gold.

The guinea pig animals are misnamed, because they are from Guyana in South America and not Guinea in West Africa.

What was the initial purpose of the chainsaw?

In unskilled hands, a chainsaw can be dangerous. It might even cut through an arm or a leg. Ironically, that was what the first chainsaw was invented for. A German named Bernard Heine (1800–1846) invented an early type of chainsaw in 1830. He called it an osteotome. In those days, before general anaesthetics, surgeons depended on speed to shorten the suffering of patients. The chainsaw was designed to speed up amputations by cutting through bone more quickly than was possible with conventional methods. The device was operated by turning a crank manually, much like you would if you were using a hand mixer. A Swiss German, Andreas Stihl (1896–1973), patented and developed an electric chainsaw for cutting wood in 1926. Three years later he patented a gas-powered model. Stihl is generally regarded as the father of the modern chainsaw.

Why after a routine medical checkup do we say we've received a "clean bill of health"?

If you say a doctor has given you a "clean bill of health," you're using a nautical expression from the days when sailing ships were required to obtain a document from local officials at every port of call declaring that they had not been exposed to any epidemic or infectious disease. If they didn't have this bill of health, the next port would quarantine the ship, crew, and cargo for forty days.

What are the differences between a "pandemic," an "epidemic," and an "endemic"?

In 1666, the year after Britain had been struck by the bubonic plague, Gideon Harvey used the words *endemic* and *pandemic* in "The Anatomy of Consumptions." *Demic* is in all cases from the Greek word *demos*, meaning "people."

Some diseases are specific to a certain people or place and are called "endemic," with the Greek prefix "en" from *endemos*, meaning "in" or "native to" a defined district.

Other diseases spread outside their original boundaries and are "epidemic." The Greek prefix "epi" is an abbreviation of *epimemia*, meaning "among," and suggests a disease or plague has jumped its original boundaries.

A "pandemic" uses the prefix "pan" from the Greek word *pandemos*, meaning "all people." The word is used to describe a disease spreading throughout an entire country, continent, or the whole world.

Where did the pharmacist's symbol of "Rx" come from?

To the Romans, the pursuit of the healing arts and the distribution of medicine was the highest professional calling possible and therefore could only be ordained by Jupiter. The *R* in "Rx" is from the Latin word *recipere*, meaning "to have been prescribed" or "to take," while the small *x* was the god king's symbol of approval. To the Romans, the "Rx" meant that the great god Jupiter himself had a hand in the prescription.

Why is the common winter viral infection called "the flu"?

In 1743, an outbreak of a deadly cold-like fever originated in Italy and swept through Europe. Because doctors believed that diseases and epidemics were ordained or influenced by the stars they called it (as the press reported it from Italy) an *influenza*. The English word for *influenza* is *influence*, which although abbreviated to *flu* still means the disease flows from the influence of the heavens.

Why is reconstructive surgery called "plastic"?

Plastic surgery was first practised in India around 600 B.C. when noses that had been amputated as punishment for criminals were reconstructed with skin from the forehead. The word *plastic* is from the ancient Greek word *plastikos*, which means "to mold into shape." The plastic arts include sculpting and ceramics. The modern term *plastic surgery* came from a surgical handbook published in 1838.

The word *plastique* for reconstructive surgery was introduced in 1798 by a French surgeon named Desault.

Why are the bundles of tissue fibres that move our bones called "muscles"?

In the average adult male body, there are forty-five pounds of bone compared to sixty-five pounds of muscle. The average female has 15 percent less. We call them muscles because when a Roman physician saw how they rippled under the skin when flexed, it reminded him of the skittering of a small mouse, or *musculus*, and so that's what he called them. En route to English, *musculus* became *muscle*.

Why is the lump in a man's throat called an "Adam's apple"?

The Adam's apple is found only in men, and it got its name from an ancient embellishment of the story of Adam and Eve. Folklore had it that when Adam swallowed the forbidden fruit, one large piece of the apple got stuck in his throat and remained there, forming a lump. This lump in every man's throat, his Adam's apple, is an eternal reminder of his humility in the eyes of God.

Why is a terrible or fake doctor called a "quack"?

The first reference to a healer as a quack goes back into the sixteenth century, when it was common for dubious medicine men to travel from town to town dispensing their miracle cures from the back of a horse-drawn wagon. The quack refers to the meaningless sound of a duck, which had the same validity as the claims made by the medicine men that their salves or ointments had healing powers. Today's quacks still dispense bad medicine.

Why is the word *quarantine* used to describe enforced isolation of contagious diseases?

Before the age of modern epidemiology, attempts to control the outbreak of a contagious disease included an arbitrary forty days of enforced confinement. New and strange diseases were often carried from abroad by ships, so a quarantine of crew and cargo helped discourage epidemics. Forty days was chosen because of its prominence in the Bible. *Quarante* is the French for forty, and *quarantine* literally translates to "forty-ish."

What are "patent medicines"?

All new inventions, including medicines, require a patent; that is, their components must be revealed. The word *patent* means an "open letter" and is a grant made by a government that confers upon the creator of an invention the sole right to make, use, and sell that invention for a set period of time. During the nineteenth and early twentieth centuries, travelling medicine shows sold what they called "patent" concoctions, claiming cures for all manner of illnesses. They got around the open-letter concept of a patent and kept their ingredients secret by taking a patent out on the shape of the bottle or its label instead of the formula inside. The patent medicine industry began a slow decline in 1906 after years of critical newspaper articles led to the passage of the U.S. Pure Food and Drug Act, which required ingredients to be listed on labels.

Patent is from the Latin *patentum*, meaning "lying open." Many brand names that started as patent medicines are still with us, including Absorbine Jr., Bromo-Seltzer, Pepsi-Cola, and Coca-Cola.

Why do we say a nervous person waits with "bated breath"?

The body has instinctive reactions to emotional circumstances, and one of these is how we breathe during times of apprehension. Our breathing becomes short and controlled when we are in crisis. *Bated* is a variation of the word *abated*, both meaning "restricted." Therefore, when someone is in a state of fear or suspense and his breathing becomes restricted, he is said to be waiting with "bated breath."

How are burn degrees assessed?

The seriousness of a burn is assessed in degrees depending on the number of layers of skin involved. A sunburn or a red mark on a finger touched to an iron is a first-degree burn. A second-degree burn blisters. Third-degree burns mean that all skin is destroyed right down to the layer of tissue under the skin. Burns on faces, hands, and feet can be more serious than a wound on the thigh, for example, because of the importance of these body parts. Burns to the genital area are also more dangerous because they are vulnerable to infection.

Why is rabies sometimes called "hydrophobia"?

It was once believed that dogs with rabies were afraid of water, which isn't the case, but in Greek, *phobia* means "fear" and *hydro* means "water," which is why the disease was called hydrophobia. To be made raving mad from rabies surfaced in 1804 as *rabid*. It's from the Latin word *rabere*, meaning "to be raving mad."

In the Welsh and Breton languages, the belief in the relationship between dogs and the rage of rabies and hydrophobia was so strong that their words for hydrophobia are compounds based on their words for *dog* (which in Welsh is *cynddaredd* and in Breton, *kounnar*). *Enrage*, on the other hand, is Old French for "to be made rabid."

Why is the vehicle that takes people to the hospital called an "ambulance"?

The French began treating wounded soldiers in the field in 1809 by bringing the hospital to the injured. Those who could walk or be carried on a stretcher were taken to a tent or field hospital and treated immediately. The French verb for "to walk" is *ambulare*, which gave us the English word *amble*. In 1242 the word *hospital*, like *hospitality*, first took the meaning of "a shelter for the needy." It began referring to an institution for sick people in 1549. So the literal translation of *ambulance* is "a place to which the needy can walk or be carried." During the Crimean War in the mid-nineteenth century, the word *ambulance* was transferred to horse-drawn vehicles that for the first time conveyed the wounded from the field to the hospital.

Canada's first hospital was a "sick bay" at Port Royal in Acadia between 1606 and 1613. It was run by two male attendants from the Order of St. Jean de Dieu.

Canadian doctor Norman Bethune (1890–1939) introduced delivering blood to the battlefield using a battered old station wagon during the Spanish Civil War in 1936 and then later improved his battlefield ambulance service while in China, where he died himself from septicemia contracted during the course of his work as a surgeon.

Why is dwelling on an error called "rubbing it in"?

If you continually remind someone of a shortcoming or mistake making them feel worse, they might complain that you're "rubbing it in." The expression refers to the pain or discomfort of having salt rubbed into their wounds, which in earlier times was both a torture and a means of killing bacteria in an open wound.

What causes "goosebumps" on our skin when we are frightened?

Fear not only causes goosebumps but also makes our hair stand on end, and both reactions are related. When we are frightened, our bodies draw blood away from our extremities (like skin) and redirect it to support our vital organs. As a defence against this tendency, our very hairy primitive ancestors developed an evolutionary response to keep the body warm. When blood is drawn away from the skin, it triggers tiny muscles that tighten the skin and force body hair to stand up to trap heat. This reaction causes stiffening where we once had a lot more body hair, and because the raised flesh looks like the skin of a plucked goose, we call the result goosebumps.

How do we avoid trouble by "keeping danger at bay"?

"Keeping danger at bay" obviously means taking action to protect your interests, but how does *bay* figure into it? The ancients believed the bay tree had mystical powers because it seemed never to be struck by lightning. The Greeks and Romans wore its leaves during thunderstorms as protection, and wreaths were made from bay leaves to symbolize invincibility for athletes and victory for warriors. During epidemics and plagues such as the bubonic horror in London, many people carried bay leaves, hoping to keep the sickness "at bay."

What is the history of Aspirin?

Aspirin is the most successful pharmaceutical drug ever produced. Its main ingredient is found in the bark of the willow tree and was known as a pain reliever in 1500 B.C. In 1828, the ingredient salicin was isolated. In 1897 chemist Felix Hoffman developed a synthetic form, known as acetylsalicylic acid, at the Bayer factory in Germany; it was referred to as "Aspirin" for the first time in 1899.

The word *salicin*, the compound in the willow bark that relieves pain, is derived from *salix*, the Latin for "willow tree." North American Indians used birch bark to make salicylate pain remedies.

137 million Aspirin tablets are taken every day. In 1915, Aspirin became available without prescription.

Bayer produces 50,000 tons of acetylsalicylic acid each year — enough to produce 100 billion tablets. If these tablets were laid side by side they would form a line stretching to the moon and back.

What are the statistical odds of getting AIDS?

Sexual practices vary on different continents and within different cultures, which affects the risk factor. These figures were reported by a major American medical association and relate only to North America. They should be used for general information only and not as a guide for sexual safety.

The odds of becoming infected with AIDS during a single episode of penile-vaginal intercourse with a non-risk straight partner without a condom are 1 in 5 million, while with a condom the odds are 1 in 50 million.

Having sexual intercourse or sharing needles with a gay or bisexual male, a hemophiliac, or an IV drug user from a major urban area is high-risk. The odds of becoming infected with AIDS during a single straight encounter with a high-risk partner using a condom are as minimal as 1 in 10,000, and they are 1 in 1,000 without protection.

Even if a person from the high-risk group has tested negative for the HIV virus, there is still a 1 in 50,000 chance of becoming infected with AIDS during straight sexual intercourse if no condom is used because there is a window between 45 and 180 days during which a newly infected person can infect others but still test negative.

If you have a one-night stand with an HIV-positive person without using a condom your risk of getting infected is 1 in 500; with a condom 1 in 5,000. Having sex five hundred times with an HIV-positive partner even with a condom will increase your chances of becoming infected to 1 in 11. Without a condom your risk of getting AIDS increases to 2 out of 3.

Odds & Oddities

- The chance of having a stroke is 1 in 6. The chance of dying from heart disease is 1 in 3.
- The chance of getting arthritis is 1 in 7.
- The chance of getting the flu in the course of a year is 1 in 10.
- The chance of contracting the human version of mad cow disease is 1 in 40,000,000.
- The chance of dying from any kind of fall is 1 in 20,666.

the modern and
ancient olympics

What do the five Olympic rings and their colours represent?

The five Olympic rings were formally introduced in 1920 and represent the union of the five continents or regions of the world that are linked by the Olympic spirit and credo during the Games. The six colours of the Olympic flag, including the rings and white background, are taken from all of the nations' flags. At least one Olympic colour appears on every flag in the world.

Why is a marathon exactly 26 miles, 385 yards long?

In 1908, the first modern Olympic marathon was designed to start at Windsor Castle and end in front of the royal box in the London stadium, and that became the official distance. The race honoured Pheidippedes, who in 490 B.C. had run 22 miles, 1,470 yards to carry news to Athens that the Greeks had defeated the Persians on the plain of Marathon.

Would ancient Greek athletes have had any chance against our well-trained modern Olympians?

At least two ancient Greek athletes would have done well in the modern games; their Olympic records stood until the twentieth century. Twenty-six hundred years ago, an athlete named Protiselaus threw a cumbersome primitive discus 152 feet from a standing position. No one exceeded that distance until Clarence Houser, an American, threw the discus 155 feet in 1928. In 656 B.C., a Greek Olympian named Chionis leapt 23 feet, 1.5 inches, a long jump record that stood until 1900, when an American named Alvis Kraenzlein surpassed it by 4.5 inches.

Why is a small sporting facility called a "gymnasium" while a larger one is a "stadium"?

The word *gymnasium* is from the Greek word *gymnos*, which means "nude."

Thus, *gymnasium* literally means "a school for naked exercise." The first Olympic event for the nude male athletes, or gymnasts, was a foot race known as a *stade*, which was a Greek unit of measurement for the distance of the race (which was six hundred feet), and that is why the facility was called a stadium.

What does it mean to "rest on your laurels"?

The practice of using laurels to symbolize victory came from the ancient Greeks. After winning on the battlefield, great warriors were crowned with a wreath of laurels, or bay leaves, to signify their supreme status during a victory parade. Because the first Olympics consisted largely of war games, the champions were honoured in the same manner, with a laurel: a crown of leaves. To "rest on your laurels" means to quit while you're ahead.

Why do we say that someone well conditioned has been "whipped into shape"?

During the ancient Olympics, athletes were expected to go into training ten months before the start of the games. The last month was spent at the site, where — regardless of the weather or bodily injuries, while on a strictly limited diet, and without shoes, shorts, or the right to complain — whenever they faltered, they were whipped by their trainers. These Olympians were literally whipped into shape.

What is the origin of the phrase, "It matters not whether you win or lose, but how you play the game"?

The noble expression about how you play the game is a Greek historian's fifth-century B.C. reference to the Olympians. He wrote, "Tis not for Money they contend, but for Glory." It resurfaced in 1927 when the great sportswriter Grantland Rice wrote, "For when the great scorer comes to write against your name, He marks not that you won or lost but how you played the game."

funeral traditions

Why do people in mourning wear black?

Today, mourners wear black as a symbol of sadness and respect for their lost loved ones, but it didn't start out that way. Many years ago it was believed that the spirit of the departed, fearing harsh judgment, would try to remain on Earth by inhabiting a familiar body. The mourners wore black and stayed indoors or in shadows to hide from the departed spirit who sought to possess them.

Why are cemeteries filled with tombstones?

Today, a tombstone is a tribute marking someone's final resting place, but the custom began within ancient fears that the departed spirit might rise from the grave to search out and inhabit the body of a living person. To prevent this, the coffin was nailed shut, a heavy stone was placed on its lid, and it was buried deep in the ground. For even greater security, another, heavier stone was placed over the grave, giving us the tombstone.

How did wakes become part of the funeral tradition?

The Irish are the most famous for their wakes, holding elaborate and festive celebrations with testimonials and toasts to the recently deceased. The custom began long before the advances of scientific undertaking and was a way of passing enough time to ensure that the subject wasn't about to be buried alive. The ritual was held to see if the subject would wake up, which sometimes happened, and so it was called a "wake."

Why do Jews place stones on a grave when they visit a cemetery?

At the end of the movie *Schindler's List*, the cast and some of the survivors visit the graves of those whom Schindler worked with and place a stone on the headstones, where Christians customarily place flowers. This ancient Jewish custom dates back to Biblical times, when stones adorned graves as markers. Today the stones reflect the importance of each soul and are a permanent record of all the people who come to pay their respects.

Why do funeral processions move so slowly?

The Romans introduced the lighting of candles and torches at funeral services to ward off evil spirits and guide the deceased to paradise. The word *funeral* itself is derived from the Latin word for "torch." By the fifteenth century, people were placing huge candelabras on the coffin even as it was carried to the burial ground. The funeral procession moved at a very slow pace so that the candles wouldn't blow out.

Why when challenging the unknown do we say, "Let her rip"?

"Let her rip" is an expression we use when we are apprehensive about the outcome of a new venture but determined to see what happens. Its origin is the tombstone inscription R.I.P for "rest in peace," and the phrase came into use as a pun for embarking on a new and unknown adventure, because to the religious people who coined it, although whatever comes after death isn't a certainty, we have no choice but to just do it.

Why are those who carry the coffin at a funeral called "pallbearers"?

The ancient Sumarians buried their dead in woven baskets that the Greeks called *kophinos*, giving us the word *coffin*. Because people feared that the departed soul was looking to posses a new body, or re-enter his own, the coffin bearers wore hoods and black clothes, then hid the coffin under a black cloth that the Romans called a *pallium*, which gave us the prefix "pall," as in *pallbearer*.

Why when someone's been dispatched do we say they've been "snuffed out"?

Snuff, of course, is a pulverized tobacco that is inhaled through the nostrils. During the eighteenth century in Ireland, it was a common custom to place a dish of snuff inside the coffin so that those at the wake could enjoy a pinch while they said their final farewell. One woman loved the tobacco smell so much that she had her coffin filled with snuff and two bushels distributed among the guests. This custom gave us the expression "snuffed out."

Quickies

Did you know ...
- the most hazardous season is summer?
- the safest age of life is ten years old?
- the most risky age is forty-five?
- people over seventy-five are twice as likely to be in fatal accidents as the rest of us?
- you are more likely to get attacked by a cow than a shark?
- you will die sooner if deprived of sleep than if deprived of food?
- you can't kill yourself by holding your breath?
- most people die of natural causes between 4:00 and 5:00 a.m., "the hour of the wolf"?

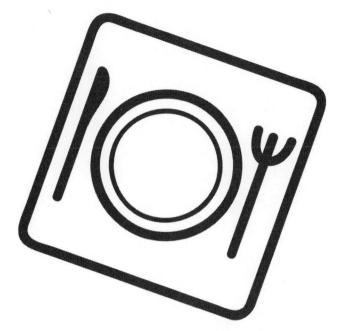

food and dining

Why are places we go to order food called "restaurants"?

Up until 1765, diners were offered only what innkeepers chose to serve. But then a Paris chef named Boulanger began offering a choice of nourishing soups to passersby, and on a board hanging over the door he painted the word *Restaurant*, meaning "to restore." Boulanger was so successful that throughout the world dining rooms still display his original sign, "Restaurant," a promise to restore energy.

Why do we drink a toast on special occasions?

By the sixth century B.C., Greeks had discovered that poisoning wine was an excellent way to get rid of their enemies, and so to reassure guests at a social function, it became necessary for the host to take the first drink. The Romans added a piece of burnt bread, or *tostus*, to the custom because it absorbed acid, making the wine more pleasant to drink. Flattering words were spoken during the toasting ceremony to reassure the guests of their safety.

Why does everyone touch wine glasses before drinking at a dinner party?

The custom of touching wine glasses comes from a medieval host's precaution against being poisoned by a guest, or vice versa. The original ritual was that while touching glasses, a little wine was exchanged, poured from one goblet into the other, around the table. Then everyone took their first drink at the same time. By mixing drinks this way, the host and everyone else could be assured that no assassin was in their midst.

What is the difference between "flavour" and "taste"?

"Taste" is the immediate sensation experienced when you insert something into your mouth. It's triggered by the taste buds on the tongue. "Flavour" is the mixed sensation of taste and smell. Each taste bud responds to the four sensations of sweet, sour, bitter, and salty before the aroma completes the flavour sensation. The senses of smell and taste can change the flavour as a person matures.

What do we mean by "the proof is in the pudding"?

"The proof is in the pudding" means that the outcome is uncertain until the task is completed. The expression began as, "The proof of the pudding is in the eating." Pudding wasn't always exclusively a dessert. When the expression was coined, a pudding was any food presented in a solid mass and was often a main course, such as Yorkshire pudding. Popularized in 1605 by Cervantes in *Don Quixote*, the saying has been traced back to 1300. Today, "the proof is in the pudding" means that you can't tell the value of something simply by its appearance.

Why do you "wet your whistle" to "whet your appetite"?

Although they aren't related, there is some confusion between the words *wet* and *whet*. For example, you wet your whistle by simply having a drink, because in the fourteenth century a whistle was a euphemistic reference to your voice or throat. "Whet your appetite" arrived two centuries later when whetstones (grindstones) were used to sharpen knives and farm implements. Water was used on the whetstones to prevent overheating. *Whet* is from the Old English word *hwettan*, meaning "to sharpen." Therefore, whetting your appetite means to sharpen your appetite, which can be done with certain aperitifs customarily drunk before a meal.

Why when two people share the cost of a date do we say they're "going Dutch"?

War has influenced the slurs in our language more than anything else. For example, when a soldier runs from battle the French say he's gone travelling "English style," while the English say he's on "French leave." During the Anglo-Dutch wars of the seventeenth century, British insults were that "Dutch courage" came from a bottle, while a "Dutch treat" meant that everyone paid their own way, which of course was no treat at all.

Why do we say they'll "foot the bill" when someone's paying all the costs?

To "foot the bill" dates back to a period when women had no means of financial support, so families offered dowries to entice eligible men to marry their daughters. The cost of the wedding and the dowry were "footed up," meaning itemized, then totalled at the bottom of the ledger. In the fifteenth century, the "foot" was the bottom line, so to foot the bill meant to pay the full amount at the bottom of the invoice

Why are sausages and mashed potatoes called "bangers and mash"?

"Bangers and mash'" is a traditional English meal of sausages, mashed potatoes, gravy, and very often pork and beans. Nothing could be more working-class or middle-class comforting than this dish. *Banger*, as slang for "sausage," dates from 1919 and refers to the noise made when the skin of a frying sausage explodes in the pan. It literally "bangs."

Why do we call wealthy members of society "the upper crust"?

In the days of feudalism, when noblemen gathered for a meal in the castle, those of higher rank sat at the head of a T-shaped table, and the rest sat in order of diminishing importance away from them. For such occasions a yard-long loaf of bread was baked, and the honour of cutting the upper crust belonged to the highest-ranking person at the head table, who would then pass the bread down in order of rank, but always keeping for himself the "upper crust."

Why is enhancing a food's taste called "seasoning"?

When the Gauls found that some food tastes could be improved through aging or the passing of the seasons, they called it *saisonner*. After being conquered by the Normans in 1066, the British called the new aging process "seasoning." With the introduction of Middle Eastern spices from returning Crusaders in the thirteenth century, seasoning took on the meaning of anything that embellishes the taste of food

Why do the Chinese use chopsticks instead of cutlery?

While Europeans were still cutting up carcasses on the dinner table, the Chinese had for centuries considered the practice barbaric. A Chinese proverb, "We sit at the dinner table to eat, not cut up carcasses," dictated that eating should be simplified, and so food was cut into bite-sized pieces in the kitchen before serving. The chopstick (from *kwai-tsze*, which means "quick ones") was the perfect instrument to convey this pre-cut food to the mouth.

How did the eggplant get that name?

An eggplant is actually a fruit, but it is eaten like a vegetable. Originally from Southeast Asia, the eggplant was taken to Africa by the Persians. In the eighth century A.D., the eggplant was introduced to Europe through Spain by the Arabs. It was given its name by Europeans in the middle of the eighteenth century because the plant they knew had white or yellowish fruit the same shape and size as goose eggs.

Why do we call a good meal a "square meal"?

In the eighteenth century, a British sailor's sparse diet consisted of a breakfast and lunch of little more than mouldy bread and water. If he were lucky, the third meal of the day included meat and was served on a square tin platter. Because of the shape of that platter, they called it their "square" meal: the only substantial meal of the day. "Three squares" now means three good meals a day.

Why do we say that someone well off is living "high on the hog"?

"High on the hog" is a recent expression that dates back only to the mid-1940s. It means you can afford to eat well. The best pork cuts (chops, hams, roasts, et cetera) are found higher on the pig than those traditionally prepared and eaten by the less affluent. Of course, being poor doesn't mean you can't eat well. Delicious meals have been made from those areas "low on the hog" (feet, belly, knuckles, and jowls). These meals were eaten by fieldhands and hard labourers who had worked up a hearty appetite, so being hungry might have made these dishes even more enjoyable to them than those eaten by the overfed upper classes.

Why when someone is snubbed do we say they're getting "the cold shoulder"?

In Europe during the Middle Ages, the "cold shoulder" had two purposes. If guests overstayed their welcome they were often served cooked but cold beef shoulder at every meal until they tired of the bland diet and left. The other "cold shoulder" was leftover mutton that was saved to give to the poor to discourage them from begging at the pantry.

How did marmalade get its name?

Legend has it that whenever the French-speaking Mary, Queen of Scots, wasn't feeling well, she would insist on a medicinal concoction made with boiled oranges. The orders the kitchen received were that Marie was *malade*, which is French for "sick," leading to "Marie malade," or marmalade. This, of course, is untrue. *Marmalade* is from the Portuguese word for the orange jam, which is *marmelada*, and it was popular long before the Scottish queen was born.

If it wasn't the French, then who invented french fries?

The Belgians are crazy about french fries; as a matter of fact, fries are their national dish, and they've been eating them with buckets of mussels since the mid-1800s. The French also claim inventing fries, because to "french" any food means to cut it very thin. The problem is that the Belgian claim predates the French technique by about fifty years. Usually this discussion ignores the fact that 40 percent of Belgians speak French, so they can take the credit.

The largest producer of french fries in the world is McCain Foods Limited, a Canadian company in Florenceville, New Brunswick. McCain has thirty potato processing plants on six continents around the world.

Why do we describe warm food as "piping hot"?

Today, piping hot usually means comfortably warm food straight from your own oven to the table, but it took a few centuries to evolve into that meaning. There was a time when everyone bought freshly baked bread every day from a neighbourhood or village baker. When the bread was ready, the baker would signal from his front door by blowing on a pipe or horn, which caused people to hurry to get bread before it ran out and gave us the expression "piping hot."

Why is cornbread sometimes called "Johnny cake"?

Cornbread, or "Johnny cake," is a country comfort food that was given to the first North American settlers by the Natives. The cake was and is made principally of maize or corn and was baked on a heated flat stone from an open fire. The white trappers who first tasted cornbread were guests of the Shawnee tribe and so they called it Shawnee cake, which soon became a staple with the settlers as the mispronounced Johnny cake.

Was the tomato ever considered poisonous?

The tomato is native to Mexico and Central America, where it was known in an Aztec (Nahuatl) dialect as *tomatl*. The Spanish introduced it to Europe in 1604 as *tomate*, which gave way to *tomato* in England in deference to the earlier New World native plant, the potato (1565). Because the tomato is a member of the nightshade family, which all contain poisonous alkaloids, and even though the Spanish and Italians found the fruit edible, the English considered it potentially poisonous and grew the plant only for ornamentation. It was only after its acceptance by the Americans, once tomatoes had been introduced through New Orleans by French chefs, that the English took to the tomato as an important element of their own everyday cuisine.

The tomato was also called a "love apple" and was believed to be an aphrodisiac. Its Aztec name, *tomatl*, literally means "the swelling plant."

Even though the tomato is botanically categorized as a fruit or a berry, for trade purposes the U.S. Supreme Court declared it to be a vegetable in 1893. The term *vegetable* is exclusively culinary and has no botanical meaning.

What's the origin of ketchup?

In the 1690s the Chinese mixed together a tasty concoction of pickled fish and spices and called it *ke-tsiap*. By the early 1700s, the table sauce had made it to Malaysia, where it was discovered by British explorers, and by 1740, it had become an English staple. Fifty years later, North Americans added tomatoes to the Chinese recipe, and ketchup as we now know it had arrived. Tomatoes were considered poisonous for most of the eighteenth century because they're a close relative to the toxic belladonna and nightshade plants.

Why do we call those tasty sweet treats "candy"?

The sweetness in candy and sugar was called *saccharon* by the Greeks and *saccharum* by the Romans, so it's clear where we get the word *saccharine*. After conquering most of the southern Mediterranean around 1000 A.D., the Arabs built the first sugar refinery on the Isle of Crete, which they had renamed *quandi*, meaning "crystallized sugar." In English, *quandi* became *candy*. Caramel was also invented by the Arabs. They called it *kurat al milh*, meaning, "ball of sweet salt."

Why is the word *straw* in *strawberry*?

The Germans call them *erdbeeren* ("earth berries") because they grow on the ground. The Romans called them *fragaria* ("fragrant berries") because of their sweet smell. So how did these delicious treats become known in English as *strawberries*? It's because the climate of both Britain and Ireland is very damp, and so to grow them, farmers needed to protect emerging berries from the muddy soil. They did this by spreading a layer of straw around each new plant.

Why are those tasty round pastries with holes in the centre called "doughnuts"?

In 1809, Washington Irving's *Knickerbockers History of New York* described small, tasty balls of fried dough that, because they resembled walnuts, were called Dough Nuts. The Dutch had introduced them as oil cakes and usually baked them as treats for holidays. After the introduction of baking powder and tin doughnut cutters, the hole was manufactured commercially around 1845.

How did the caramel-covered popcorn Crackerjack get its name?

Today a "cracker" is someone who breaks into your computer, but among other things, it also once meant something excellent or special. The *jack* in "Crackerjack" is the sailor, and the little dog on the package is named Bingo. Trademarked in 1896, Crackerjack got lucky when Jack Norworth included it in his 1908 song "Take Me out to the Ball Game," after which it became part of American culture.

Jack and Bingo didn't appear on the box until 1918, when returning First World War servicemen were very popular.

"Jack" was a nickname for all sailors.

Why do we call outdoor cooking a "barbeque"?

Barbeque is one of the first Native American words to enter our language. The Spanish borrowed *barbacoa* from the Arawak people of the Caribbean. The word described the large wooden frame that the Arawak used either to dry meat or to sleep on. Around 1661, this same framework was found to be excellent for supporting whole animals for cooking over a fire, and the barbecue was born.

How did an ice cream dish become known as a "sundae," and why is it spelled that way?

In pious New England during the 1880s, the church convinced local councils to ban ice cream sodas on Sunday, because enjoyment of the flavoured treat overshadowed the reverence of the day. The soda fountains' response was to simply hold back the carbonated soda from the syrup, fruit, nuts, and ice cream and change the name to sundae. The spelling was a clever way to legally promote the dish without referring to the Lord's day.

Why is a cup of coffee sometimes called a "cup of joe"?

Up until 1913, the United States Navy practised the British tradition of each sailor receiving a daily ration of rum. But that year, Secretary Joseph (or Joe) Daniels, a non-drinker, prohibited any alcohol on board any American vessel. This made coffee the strongest drink available to the disgruntled sailors, who began referring to their mugs of coffee as a "cup of Joe."

Who invented the Caesar salad?

In the beginning, a Caesar salad was made with whole leaves of romaine lettuce, tossed at the table and eaten with the fingers. It was intended as an entrée. Today, served at restaurants of every type, it is a salad of convenience and often includes chicken or beef. When the salad was first introduced, though, the non-vegetable ingredients were strictly seafood such as anchovies and shrimp. The salad was created in 1924 by Caesar Cardini (1896–1956) at his Italian restaurant in Tijuana, Mexico.

How did allspice get its name?

Allspice is not a combination of spices; it is one spice with a flavour that hints at several others. Europeans discovered allspice in Jamaica, where, because its berry looks like a peppercorn, it is called Jamaica pepper. The other spices its flavour emulates are cinnamon, cloves, and nutmeg.

Why is mealtime sometimes called "chow time"?

Chow is a Mandarin Chinese word meaning "to cook" or "to fry," while in Cantonese, *chow* means "food." The chow chow is a breed of dog that was in fact originally bred by the Chinese to be eaten. In the early days of North American settlement, Chinese immigrants, because of their culinary talents, were often put to work cooking for the labour gangs who then picked up the phrase "chow time" as meaning "it's time to eat."

Why is chocolate-flavoured coffee called "mocha"?

Mocha coffee got its name around 1773 when Ethiopian beans shipped from the Yemeni port city of Mocha became the most popular coffee in Europe. In the mid-nineteenth century, Americans began adding chocolate to mocha coffee as a flavouring, but it wasn't until recently, when boutique coffee shops began using the term, that mocha coffee took on the meaning of "chocolate-flavoured." Mocha coffee's primary definition is still officially "a pungent, rich Arabian coffee."

What is the origin of beef jerky?

Beef jerky is dried beef cut into long, thick edible strips. It was a mainstay during the settlement of the Old West. The beef was dried in the sun and carried without need of preservatives in a saddlebag or backpack. *Jerky* is from the Spanish word *charqui*, meaning "dried meat."

Where did the expression "have your cake and eat it too" come from?

"Having your cake and eating it too" is an idiom meaning that you want to do the impossible by disposing of or consuming something that you want to enjoy, while at the same time keeping it intact. It's an attempt to overcome an either/or situation. It was first written down in 1562 as "Would you both eat your cake and have your cake?" and somewhere along the line it became, "Have your cake and eat it too."

"Wolde ye bothe eate your cake, and haue your cake?" — *A Dialogue Conteynyng Prouerbes and Epigrammes of 1562* by John Heywood.

"Eat your cake and have it" — 1816 poem "On Fame" by John Keats.

Why are dishes served with spinach called "Florentine"?

When cooked with spinach, eggs Benedict become eggs Florentine. When Catherine de Medici of Florence married Henry II of France, she brought with her several master cooks. Soon they were introducing France to new foods such as artichoke hearts, truffles, sweetbreads, and ice cream. When Catherine's cooks served up dishes with the unfamiliar spinach, they were referred to as *à la Florentine*, after the queen's birthplace.

What is the origin of mayonnaise?

Mayonnaise is a creamy thick sauce made from oil, egg yolks, lemon juice or vinegar, and a chef's selected seasonings. In 1756, after the Duc de Richelieu defeated the British at Port Mahon on the island of Minorca, his chef created a victory feast that was supposed to include a sauce made of cream and eggs, but because there was no cream available the creative chef substituted olive oil, and since then tomato and club sandwiches have never been the same. Mayonnaise is a mixture of liquids that normally can't be combined. This is called an emulsion.

What is hollandaise sauce?

Hollandaise sauce is another emulsion and is different from mayonnaise only in that butter is used instead of oil and lemon juice cannot be interchanged with vinegar. It's usually seasoned with salt and black or cayenne pepper. Although it's a French creation, it was believed to have been copied from an existing Dutch sauce and so was named "hollandaise." It's the principal ingredient of eggs Benedict.

What is the origin of eggs Benedict?

During the late 1880s, financier Le Grand Benedick complained to the chef of New York's Delmonico restaurant that the restaurant breakfast menu was stale. The chef, Charles Ranhofer, claimed that he was then inspired to create what he called "Eggs à la Benedick."

A second claim to the dishes origin comes from stockbroker Lemuel Benedict, who wandered into the Waldorf Restaurant with a hangover in 1894 and claims to have ordered dry toast, crisp bacon, poached eggs, and a side of hollandaise sauce. The chef, Oscar Tschirky, eventually substituted English muffins and Canadian bacon and added truffles and came up with eggs Benedict in honour of the hung-over stockbroker.

Eggs Benedict is not named after Benedict Arnold, even though he was "English [like the muffin] underneath."

What is the origin of the word *tip*, as in "tipping a waiter"?

Tip is not an acronym for "To Insure Promptness." In the 1800s a tip was understood to be a bribe. As insider information, *tip* first appeared in the seventeenth century and derives from the Low German word *tippen*, which means "to touch discreetly." A tip is something confidential, whether given or received — either from a stockbroker or to a waiter.

Eggs Benedict variations
- Eggs Florentine replaces bacon with spinach.
- Eggs Pacifica replaces bacon with smoked salmon.
- Eggs Blackstone uses back bacon, while adding a tomato slice.
- Artichokes Benedict uses cooked fresh artichokes instead of muffins.
- Eggs Benedict XVI honours the German background of the current pope. Sauerbraten or sausage and rye bread are served with eggs and sauce.
- American Southern-style substitutes gravy for hollandaise sauce, and is served with biscuits instead of English muffins. Any kind of bacon is used along with eggs fried sunny side up.

Eggs Benedict trivia
- The American actor Dirk Benedict adopted the stage name after searching for something more suitable for Hollywood than his family name, "Niewoehner."

Why is not eating called "fasting"?

The original meaning of *fast* was "hold firmly," as in "she held fast to her principles." As a practice of not eating, fasting is all about maintaining firm self-control. Today fasting can take many forms and is practised by both the religious and non-religious. As a protest, prisoners use it to demonstrate that their captors don't control their will or bodies. As a religious exercise, it is a demonstration of a person's steadfast allegiance to God. Some people fast simply to purge their bodies of toxins.

The word *fast* began in Old English as *faest*, meaning "firmly steadfast" or "mentally strong," and has the same sense when referring to swiftness (e.g. while running a long-distance race.

Quickies
Did you know ...
- the original purpose for a tablecloth was for wiping the diner's fingers and hands after eating?
- the word *chowder* derives from the French-Canadian settler's word *chaudière*, a catch-all cooking pot for stews and soups made from whatever was at hand?
- in Chinese, the assortment of dumplings, steamed dishes, and tarts known as *dim sum* literally means "to touch your heart"?
- *won ton* in Chinese means "swallowing a cloud," referring to the floating dumplings in the popular soup?
- *potato* comes from the Haitian aboriginal word *batata* through the Spanish *patata*, for "sweet potato"?

sports in general

Why is a sporting event called a "tournament"?

A tournament is a series of games played by contestants to decide a winner, and the process takes its name from twelfth-century martial arts contests between knights on horseback. The Anglo-Norman knights called these medieval jousting or tilting events *torneier* or *torneiement*, which literally means "turn around." The word became *tournament* or *tourney* in English, but still means that contestants must compete in a series of events to decide the winner.

What is the origin of the Ivy League?

The term *Ivy League* has nothing to do with the ivy-covered walls of the prestigious schools to which it refers. Several Eastern U.S. schools — Harvard, Yale, Princeton, and Columbia — became known collectively as the "Interscholastic IV League." The "IV" was the Roman numeral for four and was pronounced "eye-vee." After the Second World War, the league expanded to include Brown, Cornell, Dartmouth, and the University of Pennsylvania. Although there were then eight schools included in the league, the name didn't change; instead, "IV" was spelled the way it had long been pronounced, and so it became the "Ivy League."

Who was the first cheerleader?

Cheerleaders have become a major attraction at football and basketball games thanks to the enthusiasm of University of Minnesota student Johnny Campbell, who stood during a football game in November 1898 and started leading the crowd in "rah, rah, rah" cheers. Since then the culture of cheerleading has often become larger than the game. Today cheerleaders don't just wave pompoms and lead cheers. They also perform difficult individual and synchronized gymnastic exercises. Although the first cheerleader was a man, the vast majority since have been women. President George W. Bush (1946–) was a college cheerleader.

Why is a football field called a "gridiron"?

The word *football* first described a game involving two teams and an inflated animal bladder in 1486. The game evolved several times before North Americans introduced new rules, such as three chances to advance the ball five, then ten, yards, which led to the white lines being painted on the field. From the stands, these lines gave the field the appearance of broiled meat from the metal grating of a griddle or gridiron, and so that's what they called it.

What is the "taxi squad" on a football team?

A "taxi squad" is made up of those professional football players who are under contract but not dressed for a game. They are four extra players beyond the roster limit who are only eligible to play on short notice as a substitute for an injured player if the team is shorthanded. The name "taxi squad" originated with the National Football League's Cleveland Browns, who at one time, because the team couldn't put all its players on the forty-man roster, found these extra players work as part-time taxi drivers.

Why does the winner of the Indianapolis 500 drink milk in victory lane?

After winning the Indianapolis 500 in 1936, Louis Meyer was photographed drinking his favourite beverage, buttermilk. An executive from what is now the American Dairy Association saw the picture in the paper and, realizing it was a good example for children, ensured that from that point on every winner of the Indy 500 would receive a bottle of milk to drink.

How did a trophy become a symbol of victory?

After a victory on a battlefield, the ancient Greeks would build a monument dedicated to a chosen god, which they called a "trophy." These trophies were made of limbs stripped from the dead enemy soldiers and then hung on a tree or pillar, a ritual that is kept alive by modern "trophy hunters," who celebrate their victory over an unarmed animal by hanging its head on the wall. Be grateful for the Stanley Cup.

Why is an exercising weight called a "dumbbell"?

A dumbbell is a silent bell devised to strengthen the men who rang very large church bells. At Canterbury in the Middle Ages, it took twenty-four men to ring one bell. To build up strength (and develop their skills) novices used a silent or "dumb" bell: a heavy weight suspended by a rope from a pulley on a scaffold. People wanting to build up their physiques soon copied with dumbbells of their own.

Why are the victors in a competition called "champions"?

A boxing champion is, of course, the best in his class, but the word has a more honourable history than its use in sports. Derived from the Latin word *campus*, which refers to an open field where battles were fought, the word *champion* passed into French before being adopted into English in the thirteenth century. Its meaning was "one who fights on behalf of another" or "one who defends a person or a cause."

Why are both the manager of an athletic team and a large passenger vehicle called a "coach"?

The word *coach* comes from the Hungarian village of Kocs (pronounced "kotch"), made famous for its large, horse-drawn carriages in the sixteenth century. In Britain, the word became *coach*, and by the nineteenth century took on the second meaning of a sports trainer or private tutor. The implication is that, through his experience and knowledge, the coach, like a bus or a train car, carries the younger trainees to their destinations.

What is the origin of the sporting term *round robin*?

A round robin tournament is one in which everyone is treated equally. Each player must face every other player. This democratic process originated in the British Navy in the sixteenth century as a way of petitioning against grievances without being charged with mutiny. The names on the petition were all signed in a circle so that the captain couldn't tell who was the first to sign and thus who initiated the complaint. The sailors named this document a "round robin."

Why is the outcome of a game known as the "score"?

Scores are tallied to decide the winner of a game. *Tally* is from *talea*, the Latin for "stick." *Scoring* is the act of cutting notches or nicks onto that stick. A stick was sometimes split down the middle so a creditor and debtor could keep an honest tally by notching transactions at the same time. In sport, the side with the most scores or notches cut into a tally stick was the winner.

Why is an athletic supporter called a "jock strap"?

It is difficult to imagine men competing in today's high-contact sports without that essential piece of equipment informally referred to as a "jock." Officially known as an athletic supporter, the device was introduced in 1874 to protect bicycle riders from hurting themselves on the crossbar after slipping off the pedals while riding cobblestone streets.

Why are legal issues, basketball games, and tennis tournaments all settled on a "court"?

Like *courtesy*, the word *court* evolved from the Latin words *cum*, meaning "together," and *hortus*, from which we derive *horticulture* — so a court was an enclosed garden where young boys of noble birth learned proper social conduct. In both the judicial and sporting sense a court is a specified area within which you are expected to practise courtesy while respecting authority.

Why are basketball players called "cagers"?

When Canadian James Naismith introduced basketball, the game was played with a soccer ball and the baskets were peach buckets nailed to the balcony at each end of the gym. The early games were rough and crude before Naismith introduced his thirteen rules in 1892 — so rough that the Trenton basketball team, playing in the first YMCA League, built a fence around the court to keep the ball in play. This fence was like a cage, and so the players were called cagers.

What is the origin of the mascot?

A mascot brings good luck, and the name comes from *masco*, Latin for "witch." Primitive peoples believed that every tribe descended from a separate species of animal, which they recognized as their ancestors from what they hoped were their own characteristics of bravery and ferocity. It's the same reason most sporting teams name themselves after something they respect, hoping to attain the qualities of the Tigers, Indians, or even Mighty Ducks.

How did the stadium phenomenon called "the wave" get started?

"The wave," when crowds at sporting events rise up and down in a continuous pattern, gained its popularity among college crowds during the 1970s and '80s after it was first seen in North America during live telecasts from the 1968 Mexico Olympics. Known in Europe as "the Mexican wave," the move was practised en masse and on television by fans at the 1986 World Cup of Soccer.

How did tennis get its name?

In the eleventh century, French monks started playing a game by batting a crude handball around the monastery. It was a kind of handball with a rope strung across a courtyard. The game progressed and became popular with royalty before catching on in England in the thirteenth century. When returning a ball over the net, the French players shouted, "*Tenez*," meaning "Here it comes" or "Take it."

How did tennis get the terms *seeded* and *love*?

Tennis was popularized by the French nobility, and because a zero looked like an egg, that's what they called it. *Egg* in French is *l'oeuf*, which became *love* in English. The seeding or placing of the best players within favourable tournament positions required other players to graciously cede — yield or give up — the spots. In time, the word mutated to the spelling of its homonym, *seed*, and so players were said to be *seeded*.

Why isn't it over till the fat lady sings?

In the 1970s, Washington sports columnist Dan Cook wrote, "The opera isn't over till the fat lady sings." Later, basketball coach Dick Motta, referring to the Bulls' slim playoff chances, misquoted Cook when he said, "It isn't over till the fat lady sings," and it stuck. The inspiration might have been the old American proverb, "Church ain't out till the fat lady sings," but regardless, it's now accepted in sports as meaning that where there's life, there's hope.

> **Quickies**
> *Did you know ...*
> • the All England Croquet Club at Wimbledon added tennis to its menu of activities in 1875?
> • the grass on the tennis courts at Wimbledon is cut to exactly eight millimetres in height?
> • in a two-and-a-half-hour match, the tennis ball is in play for about twenty minutes?

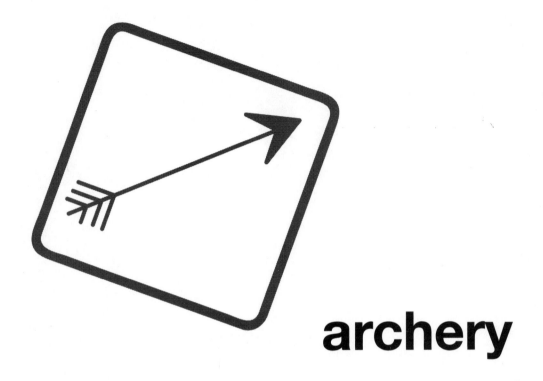

archery

Why is a non-relevant statement during a
debate or argument said to be "beside the point"?

The expression "beside the point" is from ancient archery and literally means your shot is wide of the target. Its figurative meaning, that your argument is irrelevant, entered the language about 1352, as did "You've missed the mark." Both suggest that regardless of your intentions, your invalid statement is outside the subject under discussion.

Where did we get the expression "second string"?

In sports jargon, the "second string" is the second-best group of players on a given team. The term has also found its way into business, where it is used in much the same way. In fact, it comes from medieval archers, who always carried an extra string in case the one on their bow broke. Therefore the second string had to be as good as the first, as did the third and fourth strings.

Why is someone ridiculed by humour said to be the "butt of a joke"?

A cleverly crafted joke can sometimes be used cruelly, and the victim of this kind of barb is often referred to as the "butt" of that joke. The expression is quite old and comes from seventeenth-century archery, where the area used to place a target for shooting practice was surrounded by a protective mound of dirt known as a "butt." Today, the area used for military target practice using bullets is still called a butt.

Why is a sudden surprise called a "bolt from the blue"?

The word *bolt* has many uses, but all suggest surprising quickness and all originated as a reference to an arrow from a crossbow. The word *thunderbolt* for lightning first appeared in the sixteenth century, while *blue* as a description of a clear sky appeared about a hundred years later. Since nothing could be more surprising than lightning from a cloudless sky, a "bolt from the blue" entered the language as a description of a sudden and unexpected event.

What medieval profession would you have if you heard the "highly strung Mr. Stringer tell Mr. Archer point-blank to brace himself for a quarrel"?

If you heard Stringer tell Archer point-blank to brace himself for a quarrel, you were probably an archer. Surnames taken from archery include Stringer, Bower, Fletcher, Abbott (meaning "at the butts"), and of course Archer. Point-blank is the bull's eye on a French target. "Brace yourself" meant prepare to shoot, while a quarrel is an arrow shot from a crossbow.

Archery was taken so seriously that Henry I of England passed a law that dismissed any punishment for anyone who killed someone while practising.

Quickies

Did you know ...

- Japan is composed of 3,000 islands with a population of nearly 129 million people living within 377,873 square miles?
- that since the end of the seventh century, the Japanese have called their country either Nihon or Nippon? (Both are correct and mean "sun's origin.")
- it was the Chinese who first called Japan "the Land of the Rising Sun," which in middle Mandarin was *Japang*?
- the name *Japan* came to the West through sixteenth-century Portuguese traders who picked up the name from the Malaysians, who called the country Jepang (from the Chinese)? In 1577, the first written record of Japan in English used the spelling "Giapan."
- the word *tsunami* is Japanese in origin, coming from *tsu*, meaning "harbour," and *nami*, meaning "waves"?
- the average Japanese woman has a life expectancy of 85.2 years while men live an average of 78.3 years? It's the highest life expectancy in the world.
- that sumo wrestling is Japan's national sport and was introduced in the eighth century A.D. by Emperor Shomu (724–749), who held lavish tournaments for the best wrestlers in the country?
- that karate was developed in Okinawa because the Chinese conquerors of the island prohibited the possession of weapons by the natives?
- Japan is the only country in the world with an emperor? He is the direct descendant of the original empire's founder, Jimmu (660 B.C.), who was believed to be the offspring of the sun goddess.

geography

What are the Seven Seas?

"The Seven Seas" is a figurative reference to all the waters of the world. Rudyard Kipling popularized the phrase for modern times as the title of an 1896 volume of poems. He acknowledged that some would interpret the meaning as the seven oceans — the Arctic, the Antarctic, the North and South Pacific, the North and South Atlantic, and the Indian — but the expression circulated long before these oceans even had names. In the ancient world, the seven seas were the Mediterranean, the Red Sea, the Indian Ocean, the Persian Gulf, the China Sea, and the East and West African seas.

What's the difference between the United Kingdom and Great Britain?

The United Kingdom includes England, Scotland, Wales, and Northern Ireland; Southern Ireland is a separate nation. The nations on the large island as well as Northern Ireland share a common government and passport. Great Britain includes the main island of Scotland, Wales, and England and excludes all of Ireland, including the north. It's called Great Britain to distinguish it from Brittany or Little Britain — a province across the Channel in France.

Why do the countries Afghanistan, Kazakhstan, and others all end in "stan"?

The Middle Eastern suffix *stan* is an ancient Farsi word for "homeland." Kazakhstan is from the word *kazakh*, meaning "free," while Kyrgyzstan means "home of forty tribes." Pakistan is an exception. This modern republic took its name from the first letters of Punjab, Afghanistan, and Kashmir, with the suffix *istan* taken from the province of Balochistan. The name *Afghanistan* can be traced to the ninth-century Iranian Emperor Apakan.

What part did the Big Dipper play in naming the frozen north "the Arctic"?

As part of the constellation of Ursa Major, the Big Dipper can be seen the entire year throughout Europe and most of North America, and it becomes brighter as you travel north. The Romans followed the Greeks in naming the seven-star constellation containing the Big Dipper "the Bear," which in Latin is *ursa*. In Greek the word for bear is *arktos*, which gave us the name Arctic for the northern land beneath the Bear.

Why do we call a perfect world "Utopia"?

The word *Utopia* was created by the English philosopher Sir Thomas More in 1516 and was the title of his book that compared the state of life in Europe at the time with an imaginary ideal society. *Utopia* is from Greek meaning "nowhere." The thrust of More's message was that an ideal world, or Utopia, will never exist, and that our only choice is to improve the standards of our existing society.

Quickies

Did you know ...

- that the eastern coast of Canada is closer to London, England, than it is to Canada's own West Coast?
- that in England the farthest one can get from the sea is sixty-five miles, while in Greece it is eighty-five miles?
- that the summit of Mount Irazú in Costa Rica is the only place on Earth where one can see both the Atlantic Ocean and the Pacific Ocean?
- that at 64 million square miles the Pacific Ocean is twice as large as the Atlantic Ocean and covers a greater area than all the land mass on Earth combined?

crime and
punishment

Why do we say that someone caught in a dishonest or criminal act "got nailed?"

In the early days of criminal justice, punishment was often barbaric. Public hangings and floggings were commonplace, and for lesser crimes, the infliction of public humiliation and pain on the criminal was considered necessary to deter others from committing similar crimes. One such deterrent was to nail the convicted person's ears to the hangman's scaffold, where he or she would spend the day as a public spectacle. They had been "nailed."

Why were executions held at sunrise?

In prehistoric times, executions of condemned prisoners were carried out as sacrificial ceremonies to the rising sun. In the Middle Ages, because executions were public, they continued to be held early in the day so as not to attract huge crowds. It wasn't until well into the twentieth century that more enlightened societies brought capital punishment indoors, not because executions were shocking, but because they were too popular.

What is the origin of the phrase "I'll be hanged if I do and hanged if I don't"?

When America was fighting for its independence, the British poet Thelwall was arrested after enraging King George with his liberal, seditious support for the colonies. In prison he wrote to his lawyer, "I shall be hanged of I don't plead my own case," to which his lawyer replied, "You'll be hanged if you do!" His lawyer got him off, and the phrase became a slogan that contributed to the demise of the royal cause in America.

Why when embarking on a difficult project does a group say they must "all hang together"?

The meaning of "all hanging together" is that our only hope is to combine our resources because we are already doomed as individuals. It's a quote from John Hancock, who was the first to step forward and sign the American Declaration of Independence. He said to those gathered, "We must all hang together; else we shall all hang separately," and the hanging he was referring to was death on the gallows for treason.

Why is an informer called a "stool pigeon"?

A "stool pigeon" is someone who betrays a group or cause to which he or she belongs. In their efforts to attract passenger pigeons, hunters would tie or nail a single pigeon to a stool and wait for a flock to be drawn to the cries of the desperate bird. Then, as they approached, the birds would be shot by the thousands. This practice continued until the species became totally extinct. The poor bird that unwillingly played the traitor was called a stool pigeon.

Why are prison informers referred to as "finks"?

A *fink*, whether in prison or not, is a derogatory reference to someone who seeks favour from the authorities for information that they have learned in confidence. It's said that a fink is someone who sings to the police or the boss like a canary, which all becomes logical when you realize that *fink* is the Yiddish word for "finch." Finches, or finks, are a family of songbirds, of which the canary is one of the most vocal.

Why do we refer to an important issue as "the burning question" of the day?

During a time when the church and the state were equal in government, anyone failing to follow the state religion was burned at the stake. Those who demanded the separation of church and state were considered heretics, and thousands who were caught discussing the issue were burned at the stake.

Because of this, whenever there was a secret debate on religious freedom, the subject was referred to as "the burning question."

What does it mean to be decimated?

Around 1663, the word *decimate* began to mean being destroyed through a catastrophe or severe loss, but the word originated as a disciplinary practice of the Roman army. Soldiers convicted of cowardice or mutiny were gathered into units of ten. Lots were drawn, and the loser was decimated (clubbed and stoned to death) by the remaining nine. Morale increased significantly after a Roman decimation.

After a decimation, the remaining nine convicted soldiers were given rations of barley instead of wheat and forced to sleep outside of the army encampment.

Although decimation inspired discipline and resolve, it was used sparingly because it significantly reduced troop strength.

If someone's running from punishment, why do we say he's "on the lam"?

Being "on the lam" means to be on the run and became popular in the American underworld near the end of the nineteenth century. *Lam* is from the Viking word *lamja,* meaning "to make lame," and was used in England during the sixteenth century to refer to a sound beating. The words *lame* and *lambaste* are related. If someone hit the road because staying would result in severe punishment, they were "on the lam," or on the list for a beating (or worse).

Baste is from a Nordic word meaning "thrash" or "flog," so *lambaste* is an even more severe beating.

If someone fails to perform under pressure, why do we say he "choked"?

To choke is to restrict airflow, whether to human lungs or the carburetor of a car. In ancient times, the guilt or innocence of an accused robber was established by making him swallow a piece of barley bread over which a Mass had been said. He had to do this while repeating words from that Mass. If he swallowed without choking, he was innocent, but if he choked he was pronounced guilty.

This gave us the expression "choking under pressure."

Legend has it that the Earl of Godwin died while choking on a piece of bread during this legal process.

Why when there is no doubt of someone's guilt do we say they were caught "red-handed"?

Redhand goes back to the fifteenth century Scottish people and became "red-handed" within judicial circles in Britain during the eighteenth century. It means that someone has been caught in the act of committing a crime or that there is an irrefutable body of evidence to establish the criminal's guilt. Its original reference was to murder, and the red on the hands of the accused was the blood of his victim.

If someone's caught red-handed why do we say, "The jig is up"?

If "the jig is up," then the dance is over. It was first used as "the jig is over" by lawmen in the eighteenth century when interrupting or solving a crime in progress. They took the word *jig* from the French *gigue* or Middle French *giguer*, which meant any lively dance in triple time. So whether it was a dance or a criminal caper, whenever it was over "the jig was up."

The French *gigue* came from the German word *geige*, meaning "violin."

Why is abduction called "kidnapping"?

The word *kidnap* was first recorded in 1666 and referred to the criminal practice of enticing children or apprentices to come away and be sold to sea captains who took them to British colonies to be sold as slaves, labourers, or indentured servants. *Kid* was an underworld reference to a child, while *nap*, a variation of *nab*, means "to seize" or "to steal." Today, *kidnap* means to abduct either a child or an adult.

A kid is a young goat, and that is the origin of the word's slang use for a child.

"Kidding around" is acting childish.

Why is extortion money called "blackmail"?

If there is blackmail, then there must be whitemail. *Mail* was a Scottish word for rent or tax, and during the reign of James I, taxes were paid in silver, which, because of its colour, was called "white mail." During the sixteenth and seventeenth centuries, bandits along the Scottish border demanded protection money from the farmers. Because black signified evil, this cruel extortion was called a black tax, or "blackmail."

Why is misleading evidence called a "red herring"?

A "red herring" is a false clue leading detectives off the track during a criminal investigation. The term comes from a practice once used to train police dogs. When herring is smoked it becomes red, and when the young dogs were being trained to follow a scent, the trainers tossed smoked fish around to test their ability to follow a trail. Escaping prisoners learned of the practice and often took red herring along to distract the dogs sent after them.

Why is a criminal record called a "rap sheet"?

Rap surfaced as a word imitating sound in the fourteenth century. Among other things, it perfectly describes the noise made by someone knocking, or rapping, at the door. In the criminal sense it's the rap of a judge's gavel sounding the end of a trial that gave us such phrases as "a bad rap" and "a bum rap." A rap sheet is a record of criminal charges wherein the suspect couldn't prove his innocence before the rap of the gavel.

How many people are in prison?

There are over 9 million people imprisoned worldwide. As of 2002, the United States led developed countries with 724 out of every 100,000 of its citizens in prison (most for drug offenses). New Zealand was a surprising second with a prison population of 169 prisoners per 100,000, followed by Great Britain and Northern Ireland at 124, Canada at 102, Germany at 98, Italy at 92, France at 80, Sweden at 64, Denmark at 61, and Iceland at 29.

There are no statistics for North Korea, but of all the other countries in the world, only Rwanda leads the United States as having the largest prison population per capita with more than 100,000 of around 8 million in custody.

Both China and Russia had prison populations of over 2 and 3 million respectively in the year 2002.

"No man who has not sat in prison knows what the state is like." — Leo Tolstoy

Why is a prison sometimes called "the clink"?

There was a rigid English prison built within a London borough in the district of Southwark known as "the Liberty of Clink." This prison was outside the jurisdiction of the City of London and was not a nice place to serve a sentence.

Why is a prison sometimes called "the hoosegow"?

Today we call a prison a house of correction, but around 1911 in the western United States, they were sometimes called hoosegows, which is an American mispronunciation of the Mexican word *juzgao*, meaning a "court of judgment."

Why is a prison sometimes referred to as "the brig"?

Brig is an eighteenth-century abbreviation of *brigantine*, a type of prison ship.

Why is a prison sometimes called a "calaboose"?

Calaboose entered American English through Louisiana French as *calabouse*, which is from the Spanish word *calabozo*, meaning "dungeon."

Why do we say a convicted prisoner has been "sent up the river"?

Being sent up the river means to be sentenced to Sing Sing Prison, thirty miles up the Hudson River from New York City. First called Mount Pleasant Prison, the name Sing Sing Prison comes from the original name of the village of Ossinig, where the penitentiary was built.

Why is a prison sometimes referred to as "the slammer"?

The verb *slam*, meaning to "shut with force," is Nordic in origin. It entered English around 1672 as meaning "a severe blow." In 1952, prisons began being referred to as "the slammer" by inmates who heard the heavy doors slamming behind them.

Why is a prison sometimes called "the stir"?

"Stir crazy" comes from long confinement, such as being in prison. *Stir* is an English slang reference to Start Newgate, a prison built in London in 1757.

Who invented the electric chair?

The electric chair was invented by a dentist. In 1881, Dr. Albert Southwick witnessed an elderly drunkard accidentally touch the terminals of an electric generator in Buffalo, New York. Amazed at how quickly the man was killed, the dentist began to sell the idea of replacing the hangman by using electrocution as a means of capital punishment. Thomas Edison became interested and conducted experiments by luring large numbers of cats and dogs onto a metal plate wired to a 1,000-volt AC generator.

On June 4, 1888, the New York State Legislature passed a law that officially introduced electrocution as that state's means of execution.

In December 1888, the state authorized further tests involving the electrocution of two calves and a horse.

In May 1889, a man named William Kemmler was sentenced to death for having killed his lover Matilda Ziegler with an axe. On August 6, 1890, at Auburn State Prison, Kemmler became the first person ever to be executed by electrocution. After being strapped into a chair, he was first jolted by a seventeen-second alternating current, but because he continued to struggle, a second jolt was administered lasting more than a minute, causing smoke to rise from his writhing body. The *New York Times* reported it as "an awful spectacle, far worse than hanging," but the state commissioner on humane executions saw it differently. He declared the execution to be "the grandest success of the age."

Why when something is stopped cold do we say somebody "put the kibosh" on it?

To "put the kibosh" on something is an Irish expression meaning to put an end to it. The word *kibosh* is Gaelic and means "cap of death." It was, in fact, the black skullcap donned by a judge before he sentenced a prisoner to death. In modern usage it means, as it did to the condemned, "Your path of destruction has ended."

Odds & Oddities

- The odds of being the victim of a serious crime in one's lifetime are 20 to 1.
- The odds of being murdered are 18,000 to 1, with the chance of being the victim of a sharp or blunt instrument being six times greater than being the victim of a gun (for which the odds are 325 to 1).
- The chance of dying from an assault of any kind is 1 in 16,421.
- The odds of getting away with murder are 2 to 1.

games and
gambling

What is the earliest known board game?

Archaeologists recently found a five-thousand-year-old twenty-slot hand-carved ebony backgammon board in southeastern Iraq. It was found along with sixty playing pieces, including the dice. Modern backgammon uses only thirty pieces. The ebony isn't native to the region and must have been imported from India, but the playing pieces were made from locally quarried stone, suggesting that the game might have been invented in the region.

Why do we use the word *checkmate* to end a game of chess?

The game of chess, played by two players, each trying to capture the other's king with a sixteen-piece army of horses, foot soldiers, chariots, and elephants, surfaced in India in around 500 B.C. The game was adopted first by the Persians and then by the Arabs, who introduced it to Europe during their conquest of Spain. The Persian word for king is *shah*. *Checkmate* is from the Arabic *shah mat*, which literally means "the king is dead."

Why when someone losing begins to win do we say he's "turned the tables"?

"To turn the tables" is a chess term dating from 1634 that describes a sudden recovery by losing player. The switch in position of the each side's pieces makes it look as though the losing player had physically turned the table on their opponent to take over the winning side of the board.

Incidentally, it's impossible to successively double the number of coins on each square of a chessboard. By the time you've finished you would need 18 quintillion coins, more than all that have ever been minted.

Why is a dicey situation considered a "hazard"?

A potentially dangerous situation was first called a hazard by the Western European Crusaders after returning from the Holy Land, where they encountered and were fleeced by unscrupulous local gamblers using loaded or doctored dice. "Hazard" is how they pronounced *al zahr*, which is the Arabic word for dice. In time *hazardous*, like *dicey*, became a reference to anything associated with risk.

Why is a lottery winning called a "jackpot"?

A *jackpot* is any large amount of money won through gambling. The word comes from a game of draw poker in which only a player who is dealt a pair of jacks or better can open. Several hands are usually dealt before this happens, and with each deal the players must add to the ante, which can grow to a considerable amount of money — the "jack pot." When two jacks are finally dealt and a player opens the betting, the winner will take the jackpot.

Why is communal gambling called a "lottery"?

It takes a lot of people to play a lottery or there won't be enough money to make the prize worthwhile. The word *lottery* refers to a very ancient practice from a time when people cast marked pebbles into a pot and then selected a winner through a draw. The word *lot* comes from *lottery*; to "throw in your lot" with others meant you had joined them in the gamble. "A lot," meaning a large quantity, took its meaning from the many balls or entrants in the lottery pool.

What are the odds of winning on a Lotto 6/49 ticket?

The odds of winning on a Lotto 6/49 are 1 in 13,983,816, because that's how many different groups of six numbers can possibly be drawn. This means the odds of winning are about the same as flipping a coin and landing on heads twenty-four times in succession. The odds of winning second place are 1 in 2,330,635. A recent Gallup Poll showed that 57 percent of North Americans have bought a lottery ticket in the last twelve months. The odds against hitting the jackpot on a slot machine are 889 to 1. If you add together all the numbers on a roulette wheel (1 to 36), the total is the mystical number 666, often associated with the Devil.

If a coin is tossed and lands tails ten times in a row, what are the odds that it will be heads on the eleventh try?

After a coin has been tossed and landed tails ten times in a row, many amateur gamblers would be inclined to bet that the law of averages would favour the coin landing heads on the eleventh try. The problem is, the law of averages doesn't exist. The coin's probability of landing heads is still fifty-fifty — the same as on each previous toss.

Why is the mystical board game called a "Ouija board"?

The Ouija board has been around since the fourth century, but the first patent was obtained by a German professor of music in 1854. Parker Brothers purchased the rights in 1966 and published the Ouija board game in 1967. The game begins by asking if any spirits are present, and the desired answer is in the name: *Ouija* is a compound of *oui*, which is "yes" in French, and *ja*, which is "yes" in German, so *Ouija* means "yes, yes."

Why is a disappointing purchase or investment called a "lemon"?

In 1910, the rotating slot machine appeared as a device for dispensing chewing gum and gave us the symbols still used on slot machines today. The spinning flavours were cherry, orange, and plum. Each wheel had a bar reading "1910 Fruit Gum," and three of those in a row paid off in a jackpot of gum. But, also like today, if any row came up a lemon there was no payout at all, which gave us the disappointed expression "It's a lemon."

Why is a swindle called a "double-cross"?

If you cross someone, you're cheating him. A double-cross means you are cheating both your employer and the one you've been hired to deceive. In the 1800s, Thackeray described a fixed horse race in *Vanity Fair* where the jockey who was prearranged to lose was instead allowed to win, costing the gamblers a fortune. Because the fixer had crossed or cheated both parties for a huge profit, the win was called a "double-cross."

How did "betting your shirt" come mean to gambling everything you own?

In 1823, the bitterness that led to the Civil War surfaced during a match race between the Northern horse American Eclipse and a Southern colt named Sir Henry. The grudge match inspired fortunes to be wagered, including that of Southern congressman John Randolph, who put up $10,000 and his entire wardrobe, which gave a newspaper the observation that he was "betting his shirt" on the race. (Incidentally, the race was won by the Northern horse American Eclipse.)

Where did the expression "according to Hoyle" come from?

An Englishman named Edmond Hoyle wrote a rulebook for the card game whist, the ancestor of bridge, in 1742. Hoyle's rules were used to settle arguments during that one game until Robert Foster published *Foster's Hoyle* in 1897, which included the rules for many other card games. Since then, "according to Hoyle" has meant according to the rules of any game, including those played in business and personal relationships.

How is "the full monty" related to "three-card monte"?

"The full monty," popularized as a movie title, is a British expression meaning "the whole thing." It came from illegal gambling, where the huge pot of a high stakes game was called the *monty*, from the Spanish word for mountain, which is *monte*. To win the monty meant you had won a mountain of money. Three-card monte, an illegal con game, has the same Spanish origin and refers to the same thing.

Why is the word *trump* used in card games, and what else in the deck, other than the cards, adds up to fifty-two?

A trump card or suit has been designated a higher rank than usual for the purposes of the game being played and will triumph over others of normally equal value. *Trump* is a distortion of the word *triumph*. If you add up the number of letters in the names of the cards, the total is fifty-two, the same as the number of cards in the deck (acetwothreefourfivesixseveneightninetenjackqueenking).

Why is a particular game of gambling with cards called "poker"?

A card game called poque was introduced to America by French gamblers in New Orleans. Both the name and the game came from the German word *pochspiel*, which literally means "boast game," while the derivative *pochen* means "to knock." This knock on the table is still part of the many forms of poker and indicates that a player is passing on a bet. In a Southern drawl, *poque* was pronounced "pok-uh," which, when spread to the rest of the country, became "poker."

Why do we say that a poker player, or anyone putting up a false front, is "bluffing"?

The word *bluff* is from the Dutch word *bluffen*, meaning "to deceive," and entered English as a nautical reference to the imposing front of a warship. For the same reason, the term *bluff* was applied to a bold coastline that rose straight and high out of the water. By the 1830s, bluffing had taken on the meaning of anything less intimidating than it appears and had entered the game of poker as a reference to the art of deception.

Why is a shifty person called a "four flusher"?

In poker, five cards from the same suit is called a flush and is very valuable. The highest possible poker hand is a royal flush, or five cards from ten to ace all from the same suit. However, four cards from the same suit, or a four flush, is nearly worthless. If a person continues to play with such a hand they are bluffing, or hiding the truth, which gave us the expression "four flusher" for someone not to be trusted or believed.

Why is a dishonest poker player called a "card shark"?

Scoundrels who avoid work or duty are said to shirk their responsibilities. The word *shirk* is from the German word *shurke*, meaning "a rogue" or "a villain who preys on others." *Shark* is an English variant of *shirk* and was given as the slang name for the predatory fish during the sixteenth century. The first cheaters or criminals to be called sharks were pickpockets. Soon it applied to other dishonest low-life predators who practised fraud and trickery, such as loan sharks and card sharks.

How did flipping a coin become a decision-maker?

The Lydians minted the first coins in 10 B.C., but it wasn't until nine hundred years later that the coin toss became a decision-maker. Julius Caesar's head appeared on one side of every Roman coin of his time, and such was the reverence for the emperor that in his absence often-serious litigation was decided by the flip of a coin. If Caesar's head landed upright, it meant that through the guidance of the gods, he agreed in absentia with the decision in question.

What are the chances of winning one thousand dollars at a casino game of craps?

If a gambler bets one dollar at a time at a craps table, the odds of winning a thousand dollars before losing a thousand dollars are one in 2 trillion (that's a two with twelve zeros!). If everyone on Earth played this way, betting a dollar at a time until they won or lost one thousand dollars, and then did it over again three hundred times, only one person would ever win, and then only once in all three hundred times.

Why do we judge someone by how they act when "the chips are down"?

Chips are used as a substitute for money in gambling. When things aren't going well a player's pile of chips dwindles until he loses everything or makes a recovery. How he acts under this pressure, "when the chips are down," is an indication of his character. That's how secure, relatively high-yielding stocks came to be called blue chips, because in poker, blue chips are more valuable than white or red ones.

How many five-card hands are possible in a deck of fifty-two, and what is a "dead man's hand"?

There are 2,598,960 five-card hand possibilities in a fifty-two-card deck, which makes the odds of drawing a flush 500 to 1. But in poker there is always fate. Wild Bill Hickok looked like a winner until he was shot in the back while holding two pairs, aces and eights, which is still known as "the dead man's hand."

If its symbol is in the shape of a black clover, why do we call the suit of cards "clubs"?

Playing cards are as old as history, but the suits we use today were introduced to Britain by soldiers returning from the wars of Italy and Spain in the fourteenth century. The Italian and Spanish cards included a suit picturing real clubs, which the French later changed to a trefoil leaf and the English to a clover — but because they had learned the game from the Spanish and Italians, English players continued calling them "clubs."

Card symbols are called "pips."

Card suits in Spain and Italy are coins, cups, swords, and cudgels (clubs).

In Germany they are hearts, leaves, bells, and acorns.

In Switzerland they are shields, roses, bells, and acorns.

What are the names from history of the jacks and queens in a deck of cards?

In a deck of cards the jacks are Hector, prince of Troy; La Hire, comrade-in-arms of Joan of Arc; Ogier, a knight of Charlemagne; and Judas Maccabaeus, who led the Jewish rebellion against the Syrians. The queens are Pallas, a warrior goddess; Rachel, Biblical mother of Joseph; Judith, from the book of Judith; and Argine, which is an anagram for *regina*, the Latin for "queen."

Parisian card names by suit:
Spades: (queen) Pallas, (jack) Ogier
Hearts: (queen) Judith, (jack) La Hire
Diamonds: (queen) Rachel, (jack) Hector
Clubs: (queen) Argine, (jack) Judas.

The kings in a deck of playing cards represent which real leaders from history?

The four kings in a deck of cards were designed in fifteenth-century France, and they represent great leaders from history, while the suits signify the cultures they led. Spades honour the Biblical Middle East, and the king is David. Clubs are for Greece, with the king being Alexander the Great. Julius Caesar represents the pre-Christian Roman Empire as the king of diamonds. Finally, hearts recall the Holy Roman Empire, and the king is Charlemagne.

Why are there jokers in a deck of cards?

The joker was introduced to a deck of cards by American sailors and was added to euchre as the best bower in around 1870. Euchre is an Alsatian card game, and was spelled "juker," with the *J* pronounced "you." In English it was spelled as it sounded: "euchre." Eventually, the sailors' translation hardened the *J*, and "you-ker" became "joo-ker" before marrying with "poker," where it became "joker."

The joker isn't included in the Canadian or British forms of euchre.

The word *bower* in "best bower" is related to *boor*, or "fool," which lends itself well to the joker.

Jokers are sometimes a wild card in poker.

The coloured joker outranks the black and white one.

The court jester on the joker card was added in the 1880s, and the backs of the cards were used for advertising.

Why do we say, "Make no bones about it" when stating an absolute fact?

"Make no bones about it" means nothing has been left to chance. The "bones" of the expression refer to gambling dice, which for thousands of years were made of animal bone. The oldest known dice were found in Iraq and date from 3000 B.C. Today, to make no bones about their honesty, the dice used in Las Vegas crap games are precisely calibrated and are manufactured to a tolerance of 0.0002 inches (less than one-seventeenth the width of a human hair).

How many ways can you win on a ninety-number bingo card?

In 1919, Edwin Lowe saw people playing Bean-O at a carnival in Florida, where they put beans on numbered cards for small prizes. He developed this into a game of chance that became a craze. During its development, a friend who shouted "Bingo!" after winning gave Lowe's game its name. On any given ninety-number bingo card, there are approximately 44 million ways to make B-I-N-G-O. According to suppliers, purple is by far the favourite ink colour in dabbers used by bingo players.

Why does "pony up" mean "show us your money"?

Gamblers understand that "to pony up" means to put your money into the ante to start a poker game or to make good on your losses. *Pone* (pronounced like *pony*) is from the Latin verb *ponere*, meaning "to seize," and its current use came from a legal writ of common law instructing a bailiff to seize a defendant's goods or obtain security to ensure his appearance at trial. This writ of pone is more commonly known as bail.

How did the letters in Scrabble get assigned their quantities and numerical values?

In 1931, an unemployed American architect named Alfred Butts invented the game we now call Scrabble. Turned down by every manufacturer he approached, he sold homemade sets out of his garage until 1946, when a company bought the rights and began mass production. Butts determined the scoring value and quantity of each letter by counting the number of times it was used on a single page of one particular edition of the *New York Times*.

Odds & Oddities
- The odds of being killed by a dog are 1 in 700,000.
- The odds of being killed by a tornado are 1 in 2,000,000.
- The odds of being in a fatal elevator fall are 1 in 77,000.
- The odds of freezing to death are 1 in 10,000. (Five hundred North Americans freeze to death every year).

the law

Why do we say, "Justice is blind"?

The Egyptian pharaohs, concerned that courtroom theatrics might influence the administration of justice, established the practice of holding trials in darkened chambers with absolutely no light. That way, the accused, the lawyers, and the judge couldn't see each other, and the judge wouldn't be moved by anything but the facts. It's this principle that inspired *Lady Justice*, the well-known statue of a woman in a blindfold holding the scales of justice that is often found outside contemporary courtrooms.

How did an English police force become known as Scotland Yard?

In the tenth century, in an effort to stop hostilities between their two countries, the English gave a Scottish king land in London with the provision that he build a castle on it and live there for a few months every year. Seven centuries later, with the two nations united under one king, the land returned to English ownership. In 1829, the London police took up residence on the land, which by then was known as Scotland Yard.

Why is a monetary deposit for freedom from prison called "bail"?

A bailiff is a sheriff's deputy, a subordinate magistrate with jurisdiction over a strictly defined area. He or she has responsibility over the custody and administration of prisoners. To the early English, *bailiff* meant "village" and derived from *bail*, which described the palisade or wall around a community or castle. *Bailey* came to mean any wall enclosing an outer court, and because the Central Criminal Court in London stood within the ancient bailey of the city wall, it took the name Old Bailey. Monetary bail for restricted freedom is simply a reference to the bailiff's office.

Bail, the root for *bailiff*, originally meant a "horizontal piece of wood affixed to two stakes," as in the case of the wicket in the game of cricket.

Why is private property called our "bailiwick," and how does it concern the sheriff?

Bailiwick is an old English legal term and is a compound of *baile*, which is now *bailiff*, and *wic*, meaning "a farm" or "a dwelling." From the mid-fifteenth century it's meant "under a bailiff's jurisdiction" — which leads us to the sheriff. During monarchial rule, each English shire had a reeve who acted as chief magistrate for the district. When the title "shire reeve" crossed the Atlantic it became "sheriff."

Why do we say that someone who's been through hard times has been "through the mill"?

The expression "through the mill" has nothing to do with a grist or paper mill. It came from legal circles, and in the commercial world it means to have been through bankruptcy. The phrase comes from the original English court, where petitions for discharge of debt due to insolvency were first heard. This special court was called the Mill. To have been through the mill now means to have gone through any hard time, including bankruptcy.

Why do we say that someone lost is going from "pillar to post"?

Going from "pillar to post" means moving from one bad situation to another. The expression comes from the Puritans of New England, who punished those who strayed from their strict moral code by taking them to the pillory where, in public view, their hands and feet were tied until they repented. If they refused to repent, they were taken to a whipping post and flogged until they acknowledged their sins. Thus, they had gone from pillar to post.

Why are pedestrians who break the law called "jaywalkers"?

When cars were introduced, crossing city streets became a lot more hazardous than when horse-drawn carriages were the only traffic. New safety laws were introduced, and anyone ignoring them was considered a country bumpkin.

In the early part of the twentieth century, unsophisticated rural people were often referred to as "jays," as in just another bird from the country, and so their ignorance about how to properly cross a street became known as jaywalking.

Why do we say that someone who avoids a punishment or obligation got off "scot-free"?

The *scot* in "scot-free" has nothing to do with Scottish people; as a matter of fact, the archaic word *scot* was borrowed from the Norse and meant a contribution of tax or treasure. Used in its present sense, *scot* first appeared in English in the thirteenth century, and its use with *free* became common in the sixteenth century. To be scot-free meant then, as it does now, "to be free from payment or obligation as well as punishment."

Why do we call a way out of a legal obligation a "loophole"?

Loops were originally holes in the thick stone walls of a medieval fortress. Some of these holes were small and used for observation. Others were slits that widened on the inside, enabling an archer to safely shoot out arrows during a siege. Finally, these walls had larger, hidden loops or openings through which it was possible to escape during a losing battle. These escape "loopholes" gave us the modern meaning.

If "possession is nine-tenths of the law," what are the points it outweighs?

The expression "possession is nine-tenths of the law" is from the eighteenth century and means that in the pursuit of justice possession in a dispute over property outweighs these nine other essential elements of a good court case: a lot of money, a lot of patience, a good cause, a good lawyer, good counsel, good witnesses, a good jury, a good judge, and good luck.

How did a broken straw come to stipulate the end of a contract?

Stipulate is from *stipula*, the Latin word meaning "straw," and refers to the specification of an essential part or condition of an agreement. When a landowner in feudal England wanted to remove a serf from his property, he would present the unfortunate tenant with a broken straw symbolizing the termination of their contract. During this time, men of questionable character would loiter around the courthouse offering to testify for money. They stipulated this by wearing a piece of straw in their shoes and were called "straw men."

Why are police vans called "paddy wagons"?

A *paddy wagon* sounds like a logical reference to the great number of Irish policemen in uniform during the late nineteenth century, but not so. "Paddy" is a slur against the common Irish name Patrick, and because the Irish were considered the lowest in the social order, whenever it was politically expedient to appear to crack down on crime, all of the Paddies were profiled and rounded up in police wagons.

What is a "grand jury"?

A grand jury is convened to determine if the prosecution has a case against a criminal suspect. Although still used in the United States, the grand jury has been dropped by Canada and Great Britain because they believe that it subverts the presumption of innocence and due process.

Two-thirds of all the lawyers in the world live in the United States. Los Angeles has more judges than all of France, while in Washington, D.C., there is one lawyer for every twenty-five men, women, and children.

What is the rule of thumb?

In 1976, a National Organization of Women report incorrectly linked the expression "rule of thumb" with a 1782 public statement by an English judge that in his opinion, a man should have the right to beat his wife as long as the stick used was no thicker than his thumb. In fact, the real "rule of thumb" is a reference to building or baking something through the knowledge of experience rather than precise science, with the thumb being an instrument for a rough and improvised measurement.

Why is a meaningless conclusion to an argument called "moot"?

If, after an argument, it is concluded that the point made is irrelevant, it's called "a moot point." *Moot* is an Old English word that means "an assembly of the people for making judicial or political decisions." That's how the word took on the meaning of a discussion or a debate. By the sixteenth century, *moot* had developed the specific meaning within the legal profession of a hypothetical discussion on a legal point as an intellectual exercise. Just as arguments at an original moot or town meeting were of little consequence, the conclusion of an academic exercise among lawyers carries no weight in the real world and so it, too, is irrelevant or moot.

Why is land called "real estate"?

Real estate is a piece of land that includes the air above it, the ground below it, and any buildings or structures on it. The term was first used in England in 1666. In 1670 the word *realty* surfaced to mean the same thing. *Real* means "actual" or "genuine," and *estate*, of course, means "property." Real estate became a legal term to identify a royal grant of estate land from the king of England.

In England a real-estate broker or realtor is called a land agent.

What is trial by combat?

Today, the phrase "trial by combat" is generally used as a reference to lessons learned through experience, such as a soldier who has seen action, but the term was, in fact, from a legitimate legal process also known as judicial combat. In medieval Christian cultures it was agreed that God decided the outcome of trials, a belief that rooted such proceedings in the legal theory of ordeals: torture tests that God would see you through if you were innocent.

Trial by combat was practised by the nobility and by military courts under the guise of chivalry, while commoners were tried by ordeal. The court determined a just outcome by sentencing the plaintiff and defendant to a trial by combat, often to the death, with the survivor or victor to be chosen by God. Trial by combat, or judicial combat, was usually the settlement of one man's word against another's. Most of these duels were fought over a question of honour and were most frequently performed in France up until the late sixteenth century.

Why is a meeting within a judge's chambers said to be "in camera"?

Camera is the Latin word for "room" and was used to describe a vaulted or upper chamber before it became an apparatus for taking photographs in the nineteenth century. "In camera" means "in the secure privacy of the judge's chambers." The photographic device began as a *camera obscura*, or "dark chamber," which was an invention used to project images externally before it became a *camera lucida*, or "light chamber," used to produce images within the instrument. In 1840, with the advent of modern photography, it was shortened to *camera*.

Why do we say a graduating lawyer has "passed the bar"?

In the sixteenth century, to control rowdiness, a wooden bar was built across courtrooms to separate the judge, lawyers, and other principal players from the riff-raff seated in the public area. That bar also underlies the English word *barrister*, the lawyer who argues the case in court. When someone has "passed the bar" or has been "called to the bar," it means he or she is now allowed into the closed-off area.

Why do we say someone who's been fooled has had "the wool pulled over his eyes"?

In British courts, both judges and attorneys wear wool wigs, a custom that originated in the eighteenth century. The judge's wig is larger than the lawyer's, so he's often called the "bigwig." When a crafty lawyer wins at trial against all odds, it's as though the lawyer had blinded the judge with his own wig. It's said he just had "the wool pulled over his eyes."

Why is support paid by one former spouse to another called "alimony"?

The court often orders the chief provider of a divorcing couple to pay an allowance to the other. This sum of money is called alimony because it literally keeps the recipient alive. In Latin *alimony* means "nourishment" or "sustenance."

The term *palimony* was coined in 1979 to apply to the separation of film star Lee Marvin (1924–1987) from a long-time live-in lover. Palimony applies the same rules to an unmarried couple who have co-existed equally and contributed to the couple's success.

Why is the letter *X* used to signify the legally unknown?

A contract in draft form will often use the letter *X* within areas were monetary conclusions are still being negotiated. The reason *X* is used in this and other manners of ambiguity comes from the original similar use of the Arabic word *shei*, meaning "something," which was interpreted by the Greeks as *xei*, which in time became abbreviated to the *X* we use today.

Why is a private detective called a "private eye"?

In 1850, the Pinkerton Detective Agency opened in Chicago with the slogan "We never sleep," and its symbol was a large, wide-open eye. Pinkerton was very effective, and criminals began calling the feared operation "the eye." Raymond Chandler and other fiction writers of the 1930s and 1940s simply embellished the underworld expression by introducing "private eye" as a description for any private investigator.

> **Quickies**
> *Did you know ...*
> • that the cigarette lighter was invented before the match?
> • that Lucky Strike cigarettes were given that name to promote sales to gold miners during the 1856 California gold rush?

measurements
and time

Why do we call midday "the noon hour"?

The meaning of "noon hour" has shifted several times throughout history, and at one time, when Christians prayed twice a day, it meant both midday and midnight. In the original Old English the noon hour was the hour for prayers, which at the time was the ninth hour of daylight, or three o'clock in the afternoon. The singular prayer time changed to midday, or twelve o'clock, during the Middle Ages in Britain, and so twelve o'clock became known as the noon hour.

Why do we call the end of the day "evening," and why is it divided into "twilight" and "dusk"?

Twilight is defined by the ancient word *twi*, which means "half" or "between," so twilight is the time between light and darkness. *Dusk* is the final stage of twilight and is from the lost English word *dox*, which meant "dark" or "darker." *Evening* comes from the ancient word *aefen*, meaning "late," and came to mean the general time between sunset and when you went to sleep.

How long is "in the meantime"?

"In the meantime" is often used as a general reference to the undefined time between two events, but its precise interpretation is "in the middle." The Latin origin of *mean* in this case is *medianus*, which is the same root as the word *median*, the centre strip between lanes on a highway.

How long is a moment and what is the precise time of a jiffy?

When we use *moment* or *jiffy*, as in "I'll be back in a moment" or "She'll be with you in a jiffy," we usually mean an undefined but brief period of time — but in fact, both have a precise length. Although lost through time, a moment was originally an English reference for ninety seconds, while a jiffy is from science and is one one-hundredth of a second, the time it takes light in a vacuum to travel one centimetre.

When we arrive at the last minute, why do we say we got there just in "the nick of time"?

A *nick* refers to a cut or notch made on a piece of wood. During medieval times, long before punch-in time clocks or other methods of modern tabulation, attendance, especially at schools and church services, was registered with a nick on a personalized stick of wood. If someone failed to show up on time, no nick was recorded, for which there would be suitable punishment.

Why do Orthodox and Catholic churches celebrate holy days on different dates?

By the mid-sixteenth century the Julian calendar was out of whack with the lunar calendar by eleven full days. In 1582, Pope Gregory XIII made an eleven-day adjustment so that October 4 was followed by October 15. A system of leap years was designed to keep the calendar in line. Catholics adopted the Gregorian calendar, while the Orthodox Church continued using the ancient Julian calendar for celebrations of Christmas and Easter.

Eastern Orthodox churches continue to use the Julian calendar today. It is currently thirteen days later than the Gregorian calendar.

Since 1923, the Romanian Orthodox and Greek Orthodox churches have adopted the Gregorian calendar. However, they continue to use the Julian calendar for Christmas and Easter calculations.

The gap between the two calendars continues to grow. Most Greek Orthodox churches currently celebrate Christmas on January 7 and New Year's Day on January 14 (according to the Gregorian calendar). This gap generally places Easter celebrations on the same Sunday in the Roman Catholic and Eastern Orthodox churches only once every three to four years. During non-leap years, Orthodox Easter is delayed by one, four, or five weeks.

Why is every fourth year called a "leap year"?

A leap year has 366 days, with an extra day added to February. Every year divisible by four is a leap year except those completing a century, which must be divisible by four hundred. It's called a leap year because normally the date that falls on a Monday this year will fall on Tuesday next year and then Wednesday the year after that. In the fourth year it will "leap" over Thursday and fall on Friday.

Why are the abbreviations of pound and ounce *lb*. and *oz*.?

The *lb*. abbreviation for *pound* comes from ancient Rome and is lifted from the Latin *libra pondo*, or "pound of weight." The *oz*. for *ounce* came from medieval Italy and is from *onza*, meaning a twelfth part, because at the time the English ounce was one-twelfth of the Roman pound (330 grams). Although an ounce is now one-sixteenth of a pound, it's still abbreviated as *oz*.

Why does *long* mean length, distance, and an emotion?

Longing for someone evolved from *long*, as in length, around A.D. 1000. Around A.D. 1300, *long* began to define a period of time because it seemed forever for someone to travel a great distance when a donkey cart was rapid transit. In this day of jet travel, yearning or longing for someone who is far away isn't the same, because you can always call long distance.

Why is the last minute before a deadline called "the eleventh hour"?

The reference is to the eleventh hour on the original clock devised by the Babylonians for use with their sundial. The period from dawn to sundown — when a sundial was usable — was divided into twelve hours, so the eleventh hour came just before sunset. In other words, if you did something at the eleventh hour, it was just before you ran out of daylight. You'll find this notion used metaphorically in Matthew 20:1-16, in which we learn that even a sinner can find salvation at the last minute, even someone who procrastinates and doesn't do what he has to do until, well, the eleventh hour.

How did the seven days of the week get their names?

Although originating in Roman mythology, many of our names for days of the week came from the Vikings.

"Sunday" is a tribute to the sun.

"Monday" is a tribute to the moon.

"Tuesday" is from the Germanic war god Tiu.

"Wednesday" takes its name from the god Woden.

"Thursday" is from the thunder god Thor.

"Friday" is from the Norse love goddess Frigg.

"Saturday" is named after the Roman god Saturn.

How do they calculate shoe sizes?

Roman shoemakers had discovered that the length of three barleycorns equaled one inch, so they used one kernel, or a third of an inch, as a measurement for shoe size. In 1324, King Edward of England decreed that three barleycorns was indeed one inch. In the seventeenth century, children's shoe sizes were deemed to be less than, and adult sizes more than, thirteen barleycorns. (Size zero was a baby's size, and the shoes went up in one-barleycorn increments to a children's thirteen, after which adult's sizes started again at one.) That calculation is still used to determine shoe sizes to this day.

Why is a manual counting board called an "abacus"?

The abacus is an ancient counting device with movable counters strung on rods and is used to solve arithmetic problems. Computers and calculators have made the apparatus obsolete. The word *abacus* has Semitic roots and came to English through the Greek word *abax*, meaning "dust" or "sand." Before the board with the beads, the ancients sprinkled a flat surface with fine sand for drawing geometric diagrams and solving mathematical problems. In 1387, written Middle English began referring to the sand-board calculator used by the Arabs by its Latin form *abacus*.

Why is a calendar book of predictions and facts called an "almanac"?

An almanac is an annual publication forecasting weather and providing other miscellaneous information relative to a calendar year. The earliest almanacs were largely preoccupied with astronomical and astrological information as well as dates for feasts and festivals. The seventeenth century saw almanacs begin to broaden their scope to include stories, poems, remedies, statistics, and jokes. Well-known almanacs include the *Farmer's Almanac*, which started publication in 1793, and *The World Almanac and Book of Facts*. *Poor Richard's Almanac*, produced by Benjamin Franklin (1706–1790), is a fixture in English literature.

The word *almanac* came into English from Arabic through Spain in the fourteenth century as *al-manakh*, meaning "calendar."

How far is a league as mentioned in *The Lord of The Rings*?

Folk tales refer to a league as a specific distance. There were seven-league boots, and Jules Verne sent Captain Nemo twenty thousand leagues under the sea. A league is an ancient measurement; in medieval England it was simply the distance a person or a horse could walk in one hour, which is about three miles (five kilometres), the same distance as defined by the Romans. The league is no longer an official unit of measurement in any nation.

Why is a country mile considered a greater distance than the average mile?

To "miss by a country mile" means you weren't even as close as if you'd only missed by a mile. A country mile is an exaggeration of the 1,760 yards in the standardized English mile. Rural roads in Britain twist and turn through the countryside, so although the distance to be travelled is a mile, the real distance travelled on a winding road will be considerably greater than "as the crow flies," or in a straight line.

Why are yards and metres different in length?

In the twelfth century, Henry I of England decreed that a yard would be the distance from his nose to the thumb of his outstretched arm. As crude as this seems, Henry was only off by one-hundredth of an inch from today's version. The metre was introduced by the French after the French Revolution and was intended to be exactly one-ten-millionth the distance between the North Pole and the equator, which was incorrectly calculated as 39.37 inches.

Why do we call a large timepiece a "clock"?

Like *cloche* in French, *clock* literally means "bell." When the large mechanical clock was invented in the fourteenth century it didn't tell time with a face and hands, but rather by sounding bells on the hour and eventually the quarter- and half-hour. This time device was named a *clock* because it told time by sounding bells. *O'clock*, as in "twelve o'clock" or "five o'clock," is an abbreviation for "of the clock" or "of the bells."

Why do the hands of a clock move to the right?

Early mechanical timepieces didn't have hands. They signalled time with bells. Then one hand was introduced, indicating the hour only, until eventually sophisticated mechanics introduced the more precise minute and then second hands. Because clocks were invented in the northern hemisphere, the hands followed the same direction as the shadows on a sundial. If they'd been invented in the southern hemisphere, "clockwise" would be in the opposite direction.

Why are there sixty seconds in a minute and sixty minutes in an hour?

Around 2400 B.C., the ancient Sumarians, who used six as their mathematical base, divided a circle into 360 degrees, with each degree subdivided into another 60 parts, and so on. The Romans called these units *minute prima*, or "first small part," and *secunda minuta*, or "second small part." This system was perfect for round clock faces, and that's why we use minutes and seconds as divisions of time.

What is the world's largest number?

In order to calculate massive quantities, American Edward Kasner coined the googol, which is a one followed by one hundred zeros. But the googoplex is now the largest number and is a one followed by a billion zeros, which allows us to calculate that the number of electrons passing through a forty-watt light bulb in a minute roughly equals the number of drops of water flowing over Niagara Falls in a century.

How long is a "rod"?

The rod is still used as a unit of measurement for portaging in recreational canoeing, possibly because a rod is about the same length as a canoe. A rod was established to be the combined total length of the left feet of the first sixteen men to leave church on Sunday. The distance was standardized in 1607 as 5 yards, or 16.5 feet. An acre is 40 rods by 4 rods, or the area a man and an ox could work in one day.

A rod is the same length as a perch and a pole.

Why are precious stones such as diamonds weighed in carats?

The word *carat* comes from the carob bean, which grows on the *cerantonia siliqua* tree. Each bean is so remarkably near the same size and weight that the ancients used it as a universal measurement for precious stones. There are approximately 142 carob beans, or carats, to the ounce. Each carat is divided into one hundred points, individually weighing about the same as three bread crumbs. A carat used for the measurement of gems is 200 milligrams.

Quickies

Did you know ...
- there are 86,400 seconds in a day?
- the only time Celsius and Fahrenheit temperatures have equal readings is at -40°?
- at 16° Celsius the Fahrenheit equivalent temperature is inverted to 61°?
- a BTU (British Thermal Unit) is the amount of heat required to raise one pound of water one degree Fahrenheit?
- a calorie is the amount of heat required to raise one gram of water one degree Celsius?
- a teaspoon holds 120 drops of water?
- a mile on land is 5,280 feet long? A nautical mile is 6,080 feet.

the early
african-american
experience

Why when someone is betrayed do we say they were "sold down the river"?

After 1808 it was illegal for Deep Southerners to import slaves, and so they were brought down the Mississippi River from the North to the slave markets of Natchez and New Orleans. This gave the northerners a way of selling off their difficult or troublesome slaves to the harsher plantation owners on the southern Mississippi, and it meant that those selected or betrayed would be torn from their homes and families to be "sold down the river."

Why is a carrying bag called a "tote bag"?

During the seventeenth century, American slaves did most of the heavy lifting in the American South. Most of these slaves were from West Africa and still spoke their native Bantu languages. *Tota* is the Bantu word for "lifting" or "carrying." From these slaves and then through the plantation owners *tota* entered English as *tote*. The term *tote bag* was derived from *tote* and was popularized around 1900.

Why do we call sad music "the blues"?

The blues were around long before African-Americans put them to music. The expression originates in the belief of early English settlers that "blue devils," or mean spirits, had followed them to their new land. These devils were thought to be the cause of sadness, and so a bout of depression was called "the blues." Because no one could have been sadder than the black slaves, their raw expression of the mood in a unique and brilliant musical form became known as "the blues."

Why do we say that someone indecisive is "on the fence"?

During the Revolutionary War, a prominent New Jersey jurist, Judge Imlay, hadn't yet committed to either the Revolutionaries or the Loyalists, so when Washington encountered one of Imlay's slaves he asked him which way the judge was leaning. Washington was so amused by the response that he retold it enough times for it to become part of our language. He said, "Until my master knows which is the strongest group, he's staying on the fence."

Why is a commercial record player called a "jukebox"?

Jukeboxes first appeared in restaurants and bars in the late 1930s. *Juke* is an African word meaning "to make wicked mischief" and came directly from American slaves, who described the illegal brothels or bootlegger shacks where they could occasionally escape their cruel lives with a jar of moonshine as "juke-joints." *Juke* had an exotic and forbidden appeal, which inspired the name *jukebox*.

What is the legal origin of the grandfather clause?

The term *grandfather clause* means something is exempt if in practice before a new law forbids it, and comes from a legal trick used by the Southern states to keep former slaves from voting. A law was introduced requiring the passing of a literacy test before anyone, black or white, could vote. The only exemptions were people whose grandfathers had voted prior to the new law. This gave all whites the right to vote, and virtually all blacks were disqualified.

Why is do we say someone who is successful is "bringing home the bacon"?

This thousand-year-old expression came from a common British competition of trying to catch a greased pig at a country fair. But the first time it was recorded and entered into modern use in North America was in 1910, when, after her son won a championship fight, Jack Johnson's mother told the press, "My boy said he'd bring home the bacon."

What does it mean to have your "mojo" working?

Mojo is a word from the Creole culture of the coastal regions of South Carolina and Georgia and probably arrived in some form with the slaves from Africa. It means "magic," and although it's had minor sub-cultural use as a jazz reference to drugs and sex, a mojo is a good luck charm enhanced through voodoo with the ability to cast a positive spell. If you've got your mojo working, then everything's going your way.

Why do we say, "That takes the cake" when something's done exceptionally well?

African-Americans of the Old South highlighted their social season with a dancing contest called a cakewalk. The contestants often practised for months and included couples of all ages. The prize was a huge cake which was set in the centre of the hall and around which the dancers exhibited their skills. A panel of judges would watch the innovative dancers until a winner was chosen, who would then "take the cake."

Why are racist laws called "Jim Crow"?

The term "Jim Crow" as a reference to the cruel racial segregation laws in the United States from 1876 to 1967 came from a song performed by a white comedic minstrel performer named Thomas "Daddy" Rice. The song was officially titled "Jump Jim Crow" and was first performed in blackface as a mockery of African-Americans in 1828. When it was published in the 1830s by E. Riley, the song became a huge international hit. The song and dance routine was supposedly inspired by the stage act of a crippled black performer from Cincinnati named Jim Cuff, who used the stage name Jim Crow.

By the early 1900s, the term *Jim Crow* was commonly used to define racist laws and practices that deprived African-Americans (and others) of their civil rights, especially those that segregated schools and public places such as buses and trains with separate facilities for whites and blacks.

Why do we call a powerful earth-moving tractor a "bulldozer"?

"Bulldozer" is a metaphor that originated in the Deep South during Reconstruction. A "bull-dose" was a dose of the bullwhip and was used by American terrorist groups to inhibit freed black slaves from using their new mandate to vote. In 1925, when a machine appeared that could change everything in its path through sheer force, it took the name *bulldozer* from the bullwhip and changed the meaning of the word.

What is the origin of the word *maroon*?

Maroon is a dark reddish colour or a chestnut flavour. As a verb, the word means "to be put ashore on a deserted island" or "to abandon someone in isolation." However, the obscure use of *maroon* as a reference to slaves who escaped or were set free in the seventeenth century is lesser known. These runaway slaves lived in the mountains of the West Indies. At times they fought guerrilla wars against the Spanish, French, and British colonists. Jamaican maroons were among the first slaves to be proclaimed free by the British in 1715. Some were brought to Canada, where they settled in Preston near Dartmouth, Nova Scotia, but the resettlement didn't go well, so most were relocated to Sierra Leone in West Africa, near where their ancestors had originally been captured.

Maroon, as it is used in reference to runaway slaves, is a corruption of the Spanish word *cimmarón*, which means "wild, untamed." Over time it came to signify lost in the wilderness and gained its association with desert islands from stories such as the novel *Robinson Crusoe* by the English writer Daniel Defoe (1660–1731).

Quickies

Did you know ...

- that "bad-mouth" came to English through African-American slaves and means to utter a curse or cast a spell on someone?
- about one year of your life will be spent looking for lost items?
- the average North American spends 148 hours a year waiting in lines?
- the average North American makes 7 telephone calls a day or 2,571.8 phone calls per year, which means you will spend about 2 years of your life on the telephone?
- because the average North American spends about twenty-seven hours a week watching television, by the time you're eighty you will have spent about four thousand days or about eleven years in front of the TV set?

origins of
everyday words

Why is desperately wanting something called "jonesing"?

Jonesing is a relatively new word that has surfaced from within the hip hop and rap cultures of modern youth. It means to lust, crave, or desperately desire something — and for good reason. Around 1965, the word *jonesing* emerged as a slang reference to craving heroin, or "crank," and was commonly used by the grunge and punk rockers during the pre-rap era. *Jonesing* is taken from Jones Alley in Manhattan, where hopeless addicts went through hideous withdrawal while desperately waiting for a dealer. For the same reason, *jonesing* sometimes means "to vomit."

Why do some men call a special buddy a "sidekick"?

The slang word *sidekick* describing a close male associate comes from the criminal world and first appeared in about 1905. The word referred to the criminal accomplice of a pickpocket. From the mid-nineteenth century, the slang term for men's pants had been *kicks*, and his pockets were on the side of his kicks. The term arose because one man would trip or bump the mark while the other, his "sidekick," would reach into and withdraw cash from the unlucky victim's pocket.

When we want someone to move faster why do we say "Hurry up" instead of just "Hurry?"

The expression *hurry up* caught on during a time when most eating establishments had a dining room on the main floor and a kitchen in the basement. "To hurry," of course, means to increase your pace, so "hurry up" became a specific order shouted by the headwaiter to speed the food up from the basement kitchen and into the dining room, where the phrase was heard so often by the patrons that it entered our language.

Why is a disaster called a "fiasco"?

The word *fiasco* is Italian for an ordinary flask or bottle and comes from the opera, where audiences would greet a false note or a bad performance with the cry "*Ola fiasco*." The logic was that they had come to hear perfection but were getting a second-rate performance, and so just as a glass blower's flawed attempt at a beautiful piece of art was discarded or assigned to be a common flask, the opera was second rate.

How did the word *okay* come to mean "all right"?

The word *okay* (or *O.K.*) is American and surfaced for the first time in the *Boston Morning Post* on March 23, 1839. It was a comedic use of "All Correct" and was deliberately misspelled as "Oll Korrect," which when abbreviated becomes the letters *O.K.* The abbreviation caught on around Boston and New York and became a slogan for President Martin Van Buren's campaign for re-election.

Why do we use the word *neat*, as in "that was a neat idea"?

The word *neat*, although dated, is often used to describe something pleasing. *Neat* is also used to order a shot of alcohol straight from the bottle without any mix or ice, and it's within this context that the word became popular. The original meaning of *neat* was to describe anything clean or undiluted, without any impurities. This gave us the extension of meaning tidy, as in a teenager keeping a neat room, which is a neat idea.

How did street riff-raff get to be called "hooligans"?

In 1898, a London newspaper wrote a series of articles about a gang of street toughs known as "Hooley's Gang" or, as they called themselves, "Hooligans." Strangely, the name also came up in San Francisco and New York about the same time, but because no one named Hooley was ever found it's presumed to be an Irish reference for "rowdy."

Riff-raff means "common" and is from the Anglo-Saxon words *rief*, meaning "rags," and *raff*, meaning "sweepings."

Where did the word *tomboy* originate?

A "tomboy" has meant a bold, aggressive girl since about 1579, but before that, a "Tom" was a boisterous, rude boy. If you think of the nighttime habits of a tomcat you might understand that a tomboy, a girl who liked the company of men, was used as late as the 1930s as a reference to a prostitute. This use of the word *tom* is from the Anglo-Saxon word *tumbere*, meaning "to dance and tumble around."

Why are planks of wood called "lumber"?

Lumber as a noun means timber sawed or split into rough boards or planks. The word is derived from Italian immigrants from northern Italy's Lombardy region, who, after settling in England in 1598, became moneylenders and pawnbrokers in a London neighbourhood that included Lombard Street, named after their homeland. Since these Italian pawnbrokers had all sorts of odds and ends lying around the shop and yard, including barrel staves and ship timbers, that kind of clutter became know as "lombard" or a "lombard yard," which became "lumber" in the local dialect. The word then was applied to any wood storage area.

The word *lumberjack* was coined in Canada in 1831 and referred to the hard-working, heavy-drinking migratory loggers of the time.

Why is a negative perception of someone called a "stigma"?

People held in low esteem are stigmatized for their actions by some outward sign or symbol of weakness. Although *stigma* is a Greek word meaning "puncture," we get the word from the Romans, who called the scar branded on a slave's forehead a stigma. In Hawthorne's *The Scarlet Letter*, the letter *A* stigmatized Hester Prynne and made a public example of her adultery.

Why are cigars called "stogies"?

Tobacco was picked up from the natives of the West Indies and introduced to Europe by the Spanish in the sixteenth century. The English word *cigar* is from the Spanish *cigarro*, which they took from *cigarrales*, a Cuban word meaning "a place of leisure." *Stogie* is an abbreviation of Conestoga, and because the drivers of that wagon company (based in tobacco country) always had a roll-your-own cigar stuck in their mouths, observers called them stogies.

What is the origin of the phrase "tabloid journalism"?

On March 4, 1884, a British drug company registered the word *tabloid* for a very small tablet it was marketing. About the same time, large broadsheet newspapers were challenged by small-format journals, and because *tabloid* had come to mean anything small, that's what the new papers were called. These tabloids often resorted to gossip instead of hard news, which gave sloppy reporting the name "tabloid journalism."

Why is a small newspaper called a "gazette"?

In 59 B.C. Julius Caesar introduced the first handwritten daily newspapers, which were posted in prominent locations around Rome. However, it wasn't until long after Gutenberg's printing press was invented that news became an industry. During the mid-sixteenth century, citizens of Venice paid to hear public readings of the news, and the price was a small copper Italian coin called a *gazetta*, which gave us the word *gazette* for a newspaper.

Why are both the contents of a novel and the level of a building referred to as a "story"?

The Latin word *historia* entered English as *history*, meaning an account of significant events. By the sixteenth century the abbreviated *story* took the meaning of an imaginative narrative. In the Middle Ages, by using sculpture and stained glassed windows, architects told themes from history on the fronts of large buildings, each being the height of one of the building's floors. Each floor told a story.

Why is something small called "dinky"?

Dinky is one of those words that just sounds right when it's used to describe something insignificant. It began as a Scottish dialect word to describe anything small and dainty and ended up being used to describe a shabby little rundown locomotive used for shunting larger engines in a railway yard. Today *dinky* can mean anything of little consequence.

Dinky Toys are indeed small, but the trademark company (Meccano Dinky Toys) is anything but inconsequential. Starting as die-cast miniature model cars and trucks, Dinky Toys first appeared in 1934 and are successfully sold around the world.

Why is an alley with only one exit or entrance called a "blind alley"?

Have you ever heard the Biblical quotation about how a rich man's chances of getting to heaven are about the same as a camel passing through the eye of a needle? An "eye" is an ancient reference to an opening in a wall or a gate, because you could see through it. If there is an obstruction (or in the case of the alley, a wall), then there is no eye to see or escape through — it is a blind alley.

Why is someone who is always late called a "slowpoke"?

A slowpoke is someone who fusses around, and this preoccupation with nosiness or detail makes them habitually late. *Poke* is from the old German word *poken* and means "to jab" or "to thrust with a stick or other device," so a slowpoke wastes time by dawdling or poking into meaningless matters, making him or her less than punctual. A punch is sometimes called a poke because it's the thrust of a clenched fist.

Why do we call an enthusiastic amateur a "buff"?

A buff (i.e., a film or sports buff), is someone with a keen interest in a subject that is not related to his or her profession. The term was coined by New York firefighters, who were often hindered by crowds who gathered at fires either to help or stand around and criticize. At the time, around 1900, most winter coats worn by the spectators were made of buffalo hide, and from those the firemen came up with the derogatory term *buffs* to describe those pesky amateur critics.

Why are rental accommodations called "digs"?

Digs comes from Australian gold prospectors who used the word *diggings* to describe their mining claims, which usually included makeshift lodgings. In 1893 *digs* first appeared as a slang term for rooms and small apartments in boarding houses that were strictly supervised by landladies who usually forbade visits by the opposite sex. Students have since adopted the word to describe the humble places they temporarily call home.

Why do we call someone who does things differently a "maverick"?

In the nineteenth century, Samuel A. Maverick was a stubborn Texas rancher who, because he said it was cruel, refused to brand his cattle even though it was the only way to identify who owned free-range livestock. Instead he would round up all the unbranded cattle he could find, even those not from his own herd. At first any stray unbranded cow was called a "maverick," but the word has grown to mean anyone who doesn't play by the rules.

Why are women temporarily separated from their husbands called "grass widows"?

The expression *grass widow* originated hundreds of years ago in Europe where summers were unbearably hot. Because grass was scarce in the lowlands, husbands would send their wives and children, along with their resting workhorses, up into the cooler grassy uplands while they stayed in the heat to till the land. It was said that both the wives and horses had been "sent to grass," which gave us the expression *grass widows*.

Why do we say someone charming has "personality"?

In the Greek and Roman theatres, actors wore masks to indicate the different characters they were playing. The Latin word for mask, *persona*, came to mean a personality other than that of the actor. Today, *persona*, or *personality*, still refers to the mask a person wears to hide his or her true character while playing a role for the outside world.

Why do Mexicans call Americans "gringos"?

Some say that during the Mexican-American war at the end of the nineteenth century, locals heard the invaders singing "Green Grow the Lilacs" and simply picked up *gringo* from "green grow." Others say that because the American uniforms were green, the expression came from a rallying cry: "Green, go!" But, in fact, *gringo* is a Spanish word on its own and is a slang insult for anyone who is fair-skinned and looks foreign.

Why do Americans call Canadians "Canucks"?

The word *canuck* first appeared in 1835 as a derogatory American reference to French Canadians working in the lumber camps of Maine. Today it means any Canadian and is no longer an insult unless used by non-Canadians to describe our French brothers. It's most likely an alteration of the French word for "canoeman," *canaque*, with the "uk" exaggerated from a very common ending to Native American nouns like Tuktoyuktuk.

But the word could also be from Canada/Kanata (the name derived from a First Nations word meaning "a collection of huts"), abbreviated with "uk" as a suffix.

Over a million French Canadians migrated to New England during the second half of the nineteenth century. Jack Kerouac's family was among them.

Johnny Canuck, the cartoon character, dates from 1869 and was used for propaganda during the Second World War.

Why are Americans called "Yankees"?

It's said that *Yankee* comes from an English pirate reference to the Dutch, who were known for their diet of cheese, which in their own language is *kaas*. The Christian name *Jan* tied to the word *kaas*, or *Jan-kaas* (pronounced "yan-kas"), was a derogatory English reference to the Dutch who settled New York. However, it's more likely that *Yankees* evolved from *yengees,* an early Native American pronunciation of *Anglais,* the French word for the English who had settled the northeast.

Why is the word *mayday* used as an aviation distress call?

The distress call *mayday* comes from the French, who were leading pioneers in flight. In 1911 there were 433 licensed aviators in France, compared to just 171 in Britain and even fewer in the United States. Flying was a risky business, and it wasn't until parachutes and radios were introduced that the French call "*M'aidez*," or "help me," became Anglicized to the modern international distress call, "Mayday!"

Why is a large, controlled fire called a "bonfire"?

On June 24, or St. John's Day, early Britons lit chains of huge fires to support the diminishing sun. These fires were fed with the clean bones of dead farm animals and were called "bone fires," which evolved into *bonfires*. There were bone fires and wood fires, and a mixture of both wood and bones was called a "St. John's fire," a name given, naturally, to the fires that burned heretics at the stake.

Why after a foolish error do we call someone a "laughingstock"?

In early English, a *stock* was a tree trunk, and by the fourteenth century it figuratively meant the family tree or the consequences of breeding. For example someone might be from "farming stock" or "good stock," while an animal's breeding line was traced through "livestock." If someone calls you a laughingstock, they are insulting your family tree as being one filled with fools, from which you are the current crop.

Why is noisy chaos referred to as "bedlam"?

The word *bedlam* is a medieval slang pronunciation of "Bethlehem," and its use to describe a mad uproar dates back to a London hospital for the insane. St. Mary in Bethlehem was incorporated in 1547 as the Royal Foundation for Lunatics. Because people could hear but only imagine the chaos inside, they began referring to any noisy, out-of-control situation as like that in Bedlam — Bethlehem hospital.

Why do we call a bad dream a "nightmare"?

There are different degrees of frightening dreams, but the most terrifying cause sensations of suffocation and paralysis. Literature best describes the sleeper's sensation in the stories of Dracula, but there was also a common female demon known as "the night hag." *Mare* is an Old English term for *demon* and comes from the same root as *murder*; therefore the demon, or mare, who visits at night was called a "nightmare."

Why does *criss-cross* mean "back and forth"?

Schoolchildren in the sixteenth century worked lessons on a thin wooden board that hung from their belts. On it were printed the alphabet, the numbers, and the Lord's Prayer. Because it was preceded by a Maltese cross, the alphabet was called the Christ-cross-row. Students reciting from the board always began with the prayer, "Christ's cross be my speed." Two centuries later, Christ's cross had become "criss-cross."

Why are the secondary consequences of a greater event called the "aftermath"?

The chain of events set in motion by a major occurrence is often called an "aftermath." *Math* is from an old English word meaning "to mow." The second, smaller crop of hay that sometimes springs up after a field has been mowed is called the *aftermath*, or "after mowing," and although it is next to useless, it is a problem that has to be dealt with for the good of the fields.

Why is a concise commercial promotion called a "blurb"?

The word *blurb,* meaning an inspired recommendation, comes from an evening in 1907 during an annual trade dinner of New York publishers where it was customary to distribute copies of new books with special promotional jackets. For his book, humourist Gelett Burgess caused a sensation with a cover drawing of a very attractive and buxom young woman whom he named "Miss Belinda Blurb." From then on, any flamboyant endorsement would be known as a *blurb.*

Quickies

Did you know ...
- the sound of thunder is caused by air rushing into the vacuum created by a bolt of lightning?
- thunderstorms can approach as fast as 50 miles per hour?
- thunder travels at around 1,120 feet per second, or approximately 1 mile every 5 seconds (760 miles per hour), depending on the temperature and air density? This is why when you see lightning, if you count the seconds until you hear the corresponding thunder, the lightning bolt will have been one mile away for every five seconds you count.
- at any given moment there are there are approximately two thousand thunderstorms happening on Earth?

trivia

Why do we call gossip or unimportant information "trivia"?

The Romans were well-known for their road building, and from their Latin noun *trivium*, meaning "a place where three roads meet," there derived a word for insignificant information. At a three-road intersection, traffic would slow and congest, offering a great chance for light gossip and meaningless conversation. So from *tri*, meaning "three," and *via*, meaning "roadway," the Romans gave us *trivia*, a word for useless information.

Why do so many Scottish and Irish surnames begin with "Mac" as in MacDonald, and "O" as in O'Connor?

One of the ancient Celtic traditions of Scotland and Ireland was (in much the same manner as for American slaves) that all the serfs who worked his land used the name of the clan chieftain. In Gaelic, the prefix *Mac* means "son," while *O* means "grandson" or "descendant of." Both were used to keep track of the true bloodline. MacDonald means "the son of Donald," while O'Connor means "the grandson [or descendant] of Connor."

Is there a difference between a penknife and a jackknife?

The original difference between a jackknife and a penknife was size. Both had blades that folded into the handle for safety. The small penknife came first and was carried in a pocket in a sheath and was used for making or repairing quill pens. *Pen* is derived from *penna*, the Latin word meaning "feather." The jackknife was simply a large, all-purpose penknife, so called because it was a handy tool for sailors, who, at the time, were called "Jacks."

Why are inappropriate actions called "taboo"?

If something is unacceptable, it's considered "taboo." When Captain James Cook visited the Friendly Islands in 1777, he noted in his diary that the Polynesians used the word *taboo* to signify that a thing was forbidden. Cook and his men carried the word to the rest of the English-speaking world, not realizing that it also means "go away," which is what the Islanders were telling him when he landed.

Why do doors generally open inward on houses and outward on public buildings?

Doors generally open outward on public buildings as a precaution against fire. If dozens of people have to rush for the exit, they won't have to fight to pull the door inward against the crush. The exceptions are those institutions fearing robbery, which have doors opening inward to delay the getaway and, like the doors of your home, to keep the hinges on the inside so that burglars can't simply remove the door.

What dates define Generation X, Generation Y, and the Echo Boomers?

For those people born after the post–Second World War baby boomers, advertisers have created labels to define their targets. Those born between 1964 and 1983 are known as Generation X. Echo boomers, or the children of the baby boomers, were born between the late 1970s and the early 1990s. Generation Y's members are the children of Generation X and were born after 1983.

The confusion lies in the use of the word *generation* by advertisers and the media. For marketing purposes, an echo boomer can also be part of both Generations X and Y. Historically, a generation of humans was defined as the average interval of time between the birth of parents and their offspring — in other words, about twenty-five years.

We all know what a "YUPPIE" is,
but what are a "TAFFIE," a "DINK," and a "DROPPIE"?

YUPPIES are Young Urban Professional People. The U.S. Census Bureau has created many other acronyms to identify other social groups. TAFFIES are Technologically Advanced Families who are wired to the Internet. DINK stands for Dual Income No Kids, while DROPPIES is from the first letters of Disillusioned, Relatively Ordinary Professionals Preferring Independent Employment Situations.

Why is a couched insult called a "backhanded compliment"?

A compliment intended as an insult is termed a "backhanded compliment" and is directly tied to the ancient belief that the left side of the body was under the influence of the Devil. A backhanded slap would generally come from the right hand of the majority of people. It is similar to the backhand stroke of tennis players who must reach across their bodies to deliver blows from the left (or evil) side. Anything delivered from the left, including a compliment, was considered sinister or devious.

The word *sinister* comes from *sinestra*, Latin for *left*. Seven percent of the world's population is left-handed. Among the forty-three American presidents, the percentage of lefties is higher (12 percent). Bill Clinton (1946–), George H.W. Bush (1924–), Ronald Reagan (1911–2004), Gerald Ford (1913–), and Harry Truman (1884–1972) are or were left-handed. James Garfield (1831–1881) and Thomas Jefferson (1743–1826) were reportedly ambidextrous.

Where did the motorcycle gang Hells Angels get their name?

The outlaw motorcycle gang known as Hells Angels grew from a small group of post–Second World War servicemen who longed for the danger, excitement, and comradeship they had experienced in the wartime military. In Fontana, California, on May 17, 1948, two small biker gangs joined to form the first Hells Angels Motorcycle Club. The initial membership was twenty-five. Fuelled by 1950s movies, media hype, and their own sense of rebellion and outrageous behaviour, the Hells Angels have gone off track and grown into an international underworld organization.

The motorcycle gang took its name from a famous American B-17F bomber whose heroic crew of six named themselves and their Flying Fortress the Hell's Angels. The aircrew, in turn, was inspired by the title of the 1930 Howard Hughes film that introduced and starred the legendary Jean Harlow. The bomber crew known as Hell's Angels became famous when after flying forty-eight missions its members toured the United States, pointing out the combat scars and patches that covered their "fort." While flying a bombing run, the famous B-17's Captain Baldwin first suggested over the interphone that his men name the plane and themselves after the Hughes film. One of Baldwin's crew, remarking on the mission being flown, replied, "Why not? This is the closest to hell that angels will ever get!"

What's the difference between a "spider's web" and a "cobweb"?

All spiders create their webs through a liquid secretion that hardens in the air. These webs are nearly invisible, especially to the insects they trap. In modern language, the spider's web becomes a cobweb only after it collects dust and becomes visible, so the webs are different in name only. The word *cob* came from writings as early as the thirteenth century and had evolved from *coppe*, an early word meaning "spider."

What is a "Catch-22"?

A Catch-22 is an impossible situation. In Joseph Heller's 1961 novel *Catch-22*, the protagonist tries every means possible to avoid flying dangerous missions in order to survive the war. The problem was Catch-22, a regulation that specified that if a man was afraid to fly then he was sane and had to, but if he flew he was crazy and didn't have to. Either way, he had to fly.

question and feature list

Everyday Expressions

Place Names and Nicknames

Animals

The Human Condition

Lovers and Loving

Flowers

Transportation and Automobiles

Sailing on the High Seas

The Dope on Horse Racing

Holidays and Special Occasions

Religion and Beyond

All About Numbers

Royalty and Heraldry

Business and the Marketplace

Medical Complications

Games and Gambling

The Early African-American Experience